THE YEAR
OF LIVING
LIKE JESUS

Also by Ed Dobson

Prayers and Promises When Facing a Life-Threatening Illness

Starting a Seeker-Sensitive Service

THE YEAR

OF LIVING

LIKE JESUS

My Journey of Discovering
What Jesus Would *Really* Do

ED DOBSON

Foreword by A. J. Jacobs, author of *The Year of Living Biblically*

 ZONDERVAN®

ZONDERVAN.com/
AUTHOR**TRACKER**
follow your favorite authors

ZONDERVAN

The Year of Living like Jesus
Copyright © 2009 by Edward G. Dobson

Requests for information should be addressed to:
Zondervan, *Grand Rapids, Michigan* 49530

Library of Congress Cataloging-in-Publication Data

Dobson, Ed.
        The year of living like Jesus : my journey of discovering what Jesus would really
    do / Ed Dobson.
            p.   cm.
        Includes bibliographical references.
        ISBN 978-0-310-24777-7
        1. Dobson, Ed. 2. Christian biography. 3. Christian life. 4. Jesus Christ — Example.
    I. Title.
    BR1725.D59A3   2009
    280'.4092 — dc22   2009018577

Interior design by Beth Shagene

Printed in the United States of America

09 10 11 12 13 14 15 • 23 22 21 20 19 18 17 16 15 14 13 12 11 10 9 8 7 6 5 4 3 2 1

Contents

Foreword by A. J. Jacobs

In some ways, Ed Dobson and I couldn't be more different. He's Christian and I'm Jewish. He grew up in a religious home and went to the strict Bob Jones University. I grew up without a speck of religion and attended the ultra-secular Brown University. He spent most of his professional life as a pastor at a large church in Michigan. I've spent most of my professional life writing about ungodly topics as a journalist in New York City (the modern-day Gomorrah).

We come from totally contrasting perspectives. We are, to use a biblical metaphor, as different as Jacob and Esau.

And yet—to stretch the metaphor—in some ways I feel like I'm Ed Dobson's spiritual brother. And not just because we both had huge beards.

We both decided to undertake religious journeys that changed our lives forever. I spent a year following the Bible as closely as possible. I explored both the New and Old Testaments, but my journey was weighted toward the Hebrew Scriptures, mostly because I'm Jewish.

Ed was inspired by my book *The Year of Living Biblically* (a fact that makes me commit the sin of pride) and decided to spend a year living as much like Jesus as possible. His was a more Christ-centered journey.

Both Ed and I are strong believers in the phrase "to understand someone, try to walk a mile in their shoes." Or their sandals, I suppose. To understand Jesus better, Ed tried to eat like Jesus, talk like Jesus, think like Jesus, and hang out with sinners like Jesus.

You might have heard the phrase "pray with your feet." I adore that phrase. Because a large part of spiritual living involves getting up off your butt and *doing*. No doubt, deep thought can change your behavior. But it's also a two-way street: Deep behavior can change your thoughts. Often our transformation starts on the outside and works its way inward—and I think you'll see that in Ed's story. (Sorry about the butt comment, Ed.)

I loved reading Ed's book, not just because it's wise and surprising, filled with humility and open-mindedness. I loved it too because I recognized so many of my own struggles in his journey. In fact, I think anyone who has been on a spiritual trek of any kind will relate to Ed's.

We can all relate to his struggle against the small sins. Should he keep his iPod turned on as the plane is taking off, despite the airline rules against electronic equipment? Really, what's the harm in leaving it on? No, Ed decides, Jesus would not deceive.

And we can admire how far he went outside his comfort zone. A nondrinker, Ed decides to go to a bar, drink Miller Lite, and talk to the barflies about God. Jesus, after all, spent time with drinkers.

I was moved by how difficult it was for Ed at times. How do you love your enemy? It's hard enough to tolerate an enemy. Even to ignore him. But to love him? How many of us have really tried? And I was blown away by Ed's willingness to follow his heart and take unpopular positions. I won't ruin it for you, but he did something very controversial because he believed in his heart that it best conformed to the teachings of Jesus. And remember: Jesus took some pretty unpopular positions himself.

As a Jew, I loved reading about Ed's take on Jesus' Jewish roots. We often forget how Jewish Jesus really was. As Ed points out, he grew up in a Jewish town. He ate like a Jew and prayed like a Jew. He probably wore a version of the fringes worn by Orthodox Jews today. I think Ed would say he became a better Christian by learning about—and experiencing a version of—Jesus' Jewish roots. Just as I believe I became a better Jew by learning about

Jesus' teachings and evangelical Christianity. The two religions are intertwined at the deepest level.

Regardless of whether you agree with Ed's decisions or conclusions, I think you'll be fascinated by his journey. And you'll admire his commitment.

In my book, I talk about the Jewish legend of Nachshon. He was an ancient Israelite who was with Moses when Moses arrived at the Red Sea. Moses lifted his rod and waited for the sea to part. But actually, nothing happened. So a Hebrew named Nachshon just waded into the water. He waded up to his ankles, knees, shoulders, and then—right before the water got to his nose—the sea parted. As one rabbi told me, "Sometimes miracles occur only when you jump in."

Ed jumped in.

A. J. Jacobs
New York Times bestselling author
of *The Year of Living Biblically*
and *The Know-It-All*

Introduction

I don't like the word *Christian*. I know it's a biblical term, but in other parts of the world people assume that if you're from America, you must be a Christian. So I don't like the word because many associate it with America, capitalism, and democracy.

I don't like the word *evangelical*. In the United States, it has come to mean anti-gay, anti-abortion, and believing that you're right all the time. It's associated with a political movement known mostly for what it's against, not what it's for. So I don't like the word *evangelical*.

And I don't like the word *Baptist*. Even though I was ordained by the Baptist church and worked at a Baptist college for fourteen years, I'm not fond of the word because there are so many varieties of "Baptist"—and they often don't get along with each other.

When people press me to identify myself, I simply say, "I'm a follower of Jesus."

So what if we were to push past all the labels and get back to that idea—just being a follower of Jesus? What would that look like? Is it even possible? What if we were to get beyond Catholic and Protestant, evangelical and liberal, Baptist and Presbyterian, Christian and non-Christian, and just get back to being a follower of Jesus?

I never intended to spend a year living like Jesus. While driving down the road one day—can't remember where I was going—I flipped on National Public Radio. A man named A. J. Jacobs, whom I'd never heard of, was being interviewed for a book he'd just written called *The Year of Living Biblically*. I only caught a few minutes of the interview, but Jacobs was one of the funniest people I'd ever heard.

When I got home, I logged on to Amazon.com and bought the

11

book. I even ordered it to be shipped overnight—which cost me nearly as much as the book itself. After it arrived, I read it within several days.

The book is about Jacobs, a nonreligious Jew, who decides to take the Bible literally and obey its commands. He wrote the Ten Commandments on the doorposts of his apartment. He grew his hair and beard long. He collected small stones to stone adulterers with. He refused to sit on seats that women having their period had sat on. He wore a robe. He carried a staff.

Once, when he came home to his apartment during his wife's menstrual cycle, he started to sit down on the chair and his wife informed him that she had sat there. So he moved to another chair, and his wife informed him that she had sat there as well. In fact, she had sat on every seat in the apartment so he couldn't sit down on any of them.

I was hoping that by the end of the book Jacobs would somehow "find God" as he sought to obey the various commands in the Bible. He didn't. Although, it's clear from the book that he took a major step toward God—and God promises that if we take a major step toward him, he will take a major step toward us. So maybe he did find God.

But as I read the book, I was deeply convicted by the fact that someone had taken the Bible seriously enough to attempt to live it out. Toward the end of my reading, I began to think about doing something similar. As a Gentile and a follower of Jesus, what if I were to take the teachings of Jesus seriously? What if I were to try to live like Jesus lived? What if I tried to do some of the things Jesus did?

Maybe just for a year.

There's a story in the Bible about Jesus and his disciple Peter. After Jesus finishes preaching to a crowd, he tells his disciples to get into their boat and go to the other side of the Sea of Galilee (which is actually a lake, not a sea). Jesus, however, goes up on a mountain and begins to pray. Meanwhile, his disciples are in the middle of the lake when a storm blows in. Just as they think the wind and the waves are about to sink their boat, Jesus comes to them—by walking on the water.

They think it must be a ghost, but Jesus says, "Take courage! It is I. Don't be afraid." Then Peter says, "Lord, if it's you, tell me to come to you on the water." Jesus tells him to come and he does—he walks on water.

> Then Peter got down out of the boat, walked on the water and came toward Jesus.
>
> **Matthew 14:29**

Eventually, Peter begins to sink, but at least he did something that no other disciple ever tried. Why did Peter even get out of the boat? What possessed him to attempt to walk on water?

One of the desires of a disciple (*talmid* in Hebrew) is the desire to be just like the rabbi. The disciple wants to walk like the rabbi, talk like the rabbi, live like the rabbi, move like the rabbi, respond like the rabbi. So when Peter sees Jesus walking on the water, his own consuming desire is to be just like Jesus. He figures that if Jesus can do it, he can do it as well.

So he gets out of the boat.

I want to be like Jesus. I too want to walk like Jesus, talk like him, live like him, move like him, respond like him.

One night, as an eleven-year-old in Northern Ireland, I was upstairs in my bedroom at 46 Martini Ave. It was a Sunday. I got down on my knees by my bed and asked Jesus to take over my life. My father, a pastor, spoke often at church about asking Jesus to take over your life. He never forced it on me, but he told his congregation frequently that every human had to either accept Jesus or turn their back on him. He would often say—and, in

13

fact, Jesus himself said it—that Jesus was the way to God and came into this world to reconcile us to God.

Why I made that commitment on that night and not another night, I have no idea. I'd experienced no traumatic event, but I remember the night clearly. The next morning when I got out my bicycle to go to school, I felt that for the first time I really wanted to read the Bible and pray. Before, it had been an obligation.

As I rode to school, I felt like the bicycle was floating on air.

The person of Jesus has always been central to my thinking and living. And now, for perhaps the first time in my life, I'm not constrained to follow Jesus the way a church or religious organization tells me to. I'm free to do exactly what Jesus did.

Of course, I'm a bit nervous. At this point I don't know where this journey will take me. Jacobs, a nonreligious Jew, spent the whole year trying to obey the Bible as literally as he could, and at the end of the year he didn't seem to find God.

I begin the year having already found God. Now I hope and pray that by the end of the year I don't lose God.

January

Day one. We flew to Florida today. On the way to the airport, we were sitting at a stoplight. When it turned green, the person in front of me just sat there, so I honked the horn. Not a very Jesus thing to do. It seems to me that Jesus was kind and patient with others. He never seemed to be in a hurry. Not me!

After boarding the first flight, I took my seat in the last row beside the bathroom and settled in to listening to the book of Matthew on my iPod. I've decided to work my way through the Gospels every week this year—and for a specific reason. For several years my oldest son studied in Israel, and one day one of the rabbis who taught at the school said to him, "If you're a Christian and aren't reading through the Gospels every week, then you're not a very good Christian. How can you claim to take Jesus' teachings seriously when you spend so little time actually reading them?"

That has troubled me for years. So my plan now is to read through the Gospels every week during my year of living like Jesus.

Also, since I tend to speed-read, I decided that I would listen to the Gospels rather than reading them. This would force me to pay attention. So I put several versions on my iPod. Knowing that listening to the Gospels would be very demanding and time consuming, I said good-bye to Pink Floyd, U2, Dropkick Murphys, Rolling Stones, Green Day, and Keith Getty.

What's the point of listening to the Gospels over and over? So I can better understand their teachings—and the better I understand their teachings, perhaps, the more it will help me to obey them. Jesus himself said, "Not everyone who says to me, 'Lord, Lord,' will enter the kingdom of heaven, but only he who does the will of my Father who is in heaven" (Matthew 7:21). I have a consuming desire to do the will of the Father, and I do not want to substitute theological positions or denominational loyalties for that will.

The sole flight attendant on the plane was sitting up front by the pilots. Since I knew it was illegal to use electronic devices during takeoff, I struggled with the decision to shut off my iPod. After all, the flight attendant couldn't see me. Still, as much as I wanted to keep listening, I decided to turn it off. I was surprised by how much of a struggle it was. Part of me felt that listening to the Bible was far more important than obeying some human rules of airline safety. But listening would be deceptive, and deception is not living Jesus-ly.

Day two. Listened to the gospel of Mark today. Did not have any special revelations. I enjoyed hearing the whole narrative of the life, death, and resurrection of Jesus, but I'm beginning to realize —on the second day nonetheless—that this is a major undertaking. I've spent most of today either reading the Bible, listening to the Bible, writing about the Bible, or studying the Bible. I'm glad I don't have a full-time job. (My part-time job right now is leading Bible studies and small groups at a gated community in southern Florida. Not a bad gig.) I can't even imagine how someone would do this if they were working full-time.

We've been invited to some friends' home tonight for shrimp. They are from Kansas but spend winters here at the community in southern Florida. I know I can't eat shrimp tonight because I've decided to eat only certain types of food prepared in certain ways, just as Jesus did. So I'm struggling with what to do.

I remember the instructions of Paul, who was Jewish but was

also instrumental in bringing the gospel to the Gentiles. He said to eat whatever is set before you and don't ask questions. I also remember Peter, who was very anti-Gentile, who had a vision of a large sheet on which were all kinds of kosher and unkosher animals. (In Leviticus 11 and Deuteronomy 14 we find instructions concerning the kinds of food that can be eaten—and what kinds cannot. The food that is allowed is called *kosher*, and all the rest is *unkosher*.) God told Peter to get up and eat both the kosher and unkosher meats. God says, "Rise, Peter, kill and eat." Peter responds that he has never eaten anything unclean, or unkosher. God says, "Do not call anything impure that God has made clean."

In light of this, why does the whole issue of eating shrimp bother me so much?

How do you go about eating like Jesus?

Today I came across a book called *The What Would Jesus Eat Cookbook*. All my problems are solved, I thought. I'll simply study this cookbook and eat like Jesus. What could possibly be in it? Perhaps it has information about eating olives and using olive oil. Perhaps the top ten ways to use goat's milk. Perhaps a series of recipes for lamb. Perhaps the top five breads—leavened or unleavened —or a detailed description of animals, birds, and fish that are clean as opposed to unclean. The introduction states,

> If you truly want to follow Jesus in every area of your life, you cannot ignore your eating habits. It is an area in which you can follow him daily and reap great rewards for doing so. Following Jesus in your diet requires a commitment to change, a commitment to be all that God created you to be, and a commitment to yield your desires to God's instruction. God, in turn, will honor your heartfelt commitment by giving you more energy, better health, and a greater sense of well-being.[1]

Now that speaks to me! I want to follow Jesus in every area of my life, and now I have the answer—the Jesus cookbook.

The author continues in a section called "Making the Change to a Mediterranean Health Style." He gives ten recommendations for switching to a Mediterranean diet, and the rest of the cookbook deals with recipes from a Mediterranean perspective. I actually like the recipes and am looking forward to cooking some of them, but what in the world do they have to do with Jesus and how he ate? The author's logic seems to be as follows:

1. Jesus was from the Middle East.
2. The Middle East is on the eastern part of the Mediterranean.
3. Therefore Jesus ate a Mediterranean diet.

So what did Jesus really eat?

Jesus was a Jew, not a Christian. His followers founded Christianity, but Jesus was authentically Jewish. He lived within the constraints of the Torah (what we now think of as the books of the Law in the Old Testament). So what does that mean for me? It means I should try to eat authentically Jewish for a year.

Some in the Christian community believe that by eating kosher, observing the Sabbath, and observing Jewish feasts and festivals, they are in a superior position. In other words, doing all those things will make them more spiritual.

But I am not trying to be more spiritual, nor am I even trying to be Jewish. I'm Irish! I've only committed to live in a more Jewish way as a means of better understanding the teachings of Jesus in their Jewish context. When the year is over, I fully intend to go back to being a Gentile.

My struggle is simply this: shrimp is unkosher.

The evening turned out to be wonderful—and I didn't have to eat the shrimp! Hallelujah! As an appetizer they had hogfish, which was cooked in olive oil with special seasonings. Before eating it, though, I asked, "Is hogfish a bottom-feeder?" because bottom-feeding fish are not kosher.

"No, it's called hogfish because its face is flat and looks like a pig's," someone told me.

So I ate the hogfish. And a lot of it! Ordinarily I don't spend much time thinking about food. I just eat! Some people (mostly Christians) believe that the Jewish laws restricting certain foods are primarily for health reasons; in other words, God was trying to keep the people of Israel from getting sick. But that is not what the rabbis say. They believe that the point of avoiding foods prohibited in the Bible is not to make you healthy—but to make you *holy*.

In a loud voice she exclaimed: "Blessed are you among women, and blessed is the child you will bear!"

Luke 1:42

Day three. Listened to thirteen chapters from Luke and also read about praying the rosary. One of the prayers is: "Hail, Mary, full of grace, the Lord is with thee; blessed art thou among women and blessed is the fruit of thy womb, Jesus. Holy Mary, mother of God, pray for us sinners, now and at the hour of our death. Amen."

Having grown up as an evangelical Protestant, this kind of prayer is foreign to me. In fact, I've always believed it to be unbiblical to call Mary the "mother of God." She was the mother of Jesus, of course, but she was certainly not the mother of God. If she were the Mother of God, I feel it would imply that she's greater than God.

So I've always been bothered by that kind of prayer.

Trying to be like Jesus and obeying his teachings, I am quickly finding, is a full-time job. Even listening to the Bible on the iPod takes a lot longer than actually reading the Bible. Still, it's good because it forces me to slow down and really listen to what's being said.

I found out today that a group of believers in Boston is trying to live out every command in the book of Leviticus for the entire month of January. It's a good idea, but doing something for a month is not the same as doing it for a year. Maybe I should have committed to only a month!

But I didn't. So here we go.

Day four. Things did not go well at lunch today. Lorna made a salad. After the meal I told her how good it tasted, to which she replied, "Well, I was kind of wondering. You didn't say a word during the entire meal. Your dad was like that, and I'm hoping you won't be like him."

The reason I was so quiet, however, was that I was so focused on what I had just been listening to, from the gospels of Luke and John, that my mind was racing a mile a minute. I'll have to be careful in the future so that I don't get so consumed with thinking about following Jesus that I forget to love the people around me.

Jesus was really into people. I need to be as well.

Tonight *Shabbat* begins. That's the twenty-four-hour period each week when Jews do not work. At 6:00 p.m. we went to the service at the gated community, where about thirty people had gathered for the monthly Shabbat service. It was a wonderful experience. As we went through the prayer book for Shabbat—in English, not Hebrew—I was struck by how many times it talks about doing justice.

I was also struck by the connectedness Jews have to past generations. After we drank a glass of kosher wine, I looked into the faces of those Jewish people and realized they were the actual racial descendents of Jesus and the apostles.

Day five. Today the iPod died. So I read the rest of the gospel of John from the Bible. I was disappointed that I couldn't listen to it, because hearing the text makes me feel so caught up in the drama of the story.

Maybe the iPod broke down because it's Shabbat, a day on which you're not supposed to listen to the radio, television, or, presumably, an iPod. On Shabbat you rest. On the other days of the week you can work and create, but on Shabbat you don't. Just as God did when creating the world, we are supposed to work for six days and rest on the seventh.

Almost everyone here at the community drives a golf cart. Since I wanted to go to the beach today, which is less than two miles away, I decided I'd drive the cart—but only leisurely, since it was Shabbat. Normally I drive the cart as fast as possible, pressing the accelerator to the floor. But not on Shabbat.

The first thing I discovered was that it's really hard to drive a golf cart that slowly. Second, it's frustrating for the people behind me. They were like, "You idiot! It's the *other* pedal." Several carts got frustrated and pulled out to pass me. As they passed, they looked at me like I was crazy.

"I'm just trying to be like Jesus," I muttered under my breath.

Day Six. My iPod is working again. It died and came back to life. Since Jesus raised the dead, and rose from the dead himself, my iPod's coming back to life is a very Jesus thing for it to do.

Every Sunday morning at the gated community I teach a Bible study. About seventy or eighty people attend, and the class is very interactive, filled with give-and-take. Today I told them about my project to live like Jesus for a year and explained that this is why I'm letting my beard grow out (Leviticus instructs men not to cut their beards). Talking about this publicly, I think, will actually encourage me to continue my experiment.

One visitor, a man named Reuben, grew up Jewish, though he now belongs to a Unitarian Church. He's a Buddhist and gay. He's one of the most delightful, funniest, and most genuine people I've ever met. (And I'm grateful, for purposes of living like Jesus for a year, that Jesus never mentioned the subject of homosexuality in any of his teachings.) Reuben loved the class this morning and contributed to the discussion. He told me afterward that one thing he appreciated was my willingness to answer questions by saying, "I don't know." His partner is a Unitarian minister, and Reuben has always had the impression that ministers are supposed to know all the answers. So when I said, "I don't know," Reuben was moved.

When I first became pastor at Calvary Church in Grand Rapids, Michigan, one of the long-time members wanted me to perform her daughter's wedding. In talking through it, however, I discovered that the future son-in-law had been divorced. Even though I believed that a biblical basis for divorce exists, I didn't even ask about the cause of his divorce. I'd already made up my mind and declined to marry them. How could I marry someone who'd been divorced? I was an absolutist, and I caused great offense to the family involved.

Years later, I apologized to them. The truth is that I should have married them, but when I started in ministry I thought I had all the answers. As I enter more deeply into the lives of real people, however, I realize how few answers I really have. In life's most difficult circumstances, the best I can do is to be present to represent Jesus and the community that we call the church. I am there to love, pray, and encourage. I'm not there to answer all the questions.

Day seven. It's hard to believe that I began this journey only a week ago. In some respects I've been doing it a whole lot longer. It has been all-consuming, and there's still so much I don't know. For instance, the "kingdom of God" is one of Jesus' central teachings, and yet I'm not sure I even understand what that means. A kingdom, I realize, involves a king and his subjects, but beyond that, I'm not sure I understand Jesus' take on the matter. I'm familiar with the "dispensational" take on the kingdom, a theological perspective that believes Jesus came to offer the kingdom to the Jewish nation. Then, when the Jewish nation rejected Jesus, he ended up dying on the cross to establish the church, and, therefore, the passages in the Gospels that refer to the kingdom aren't relevant for us today.

To me that seems like a ridiculous interpretation.

Today I prepared a Bible study on the life of Joseph, which I'll teach next Sunday. The text says that when Joseph was in Egypt and was summoned before Pharaoh, he shaved his face and changed his clothes. So how does that apply to me? This week I'm supposed to pray for the blessing of the fleet at the Community Yacht Club, and I'm also supposed to perform a wedding. With my ragged beard, I'm beginning to look like a homeless person — so, like Joseph, should I shave in order to look more acceptable at the Yacht Club and at the wedding? Even though Joseph was bound by the spiritual laws to grow a beard, he understood that the Egyptians did not wear beards, and he did not want to offend Pharaoh. Should I be concerned about offending others as well? Maybe I ought to consider the context in which I live and, like Joseph, adjust to that context. But if I do, I'll be "adjusting" all year long.

This living like Jesus is getting more complicated every day.

Day eleven. Today I don't feel like reading or praying. After ten intense days, I'm tired of it. But I do listen to thirteen chapters from the gospel of Matthew anyway.

Give to the one who asks you, and do not turn away from the one who wants to borrow from you.

Matthew 5:42

Day thirteen. My wife and I drove to Key West. I decided to take a day off from reading. As we walked past a restaurant on Duvall Street, a man, who'd obviously been drinking, called from the steps: "Hey, could you spare some change so I can get something to eat?"

I've heard that line a lot, and I know a number of responses. First, you can simply ignore such people. After all, he will most likely use whatever money you give him to buy more alcohol, and, therefore, you'd be enabling his habit. Second, you can offer to take him to a restaurant to buy him something to eat. In most cases the person will not go because he mainly wants the money to buy alcohol. Third, you can point him to an organization that provides meals for the homeless. Many such organizations exist in most cities.

What did my wife and I do? We walked past the man without

24

doing anything, as we have done with so many other people over the years. After all, it's not our fault that he is where he is.

But after we'd walked on a little farther, he called after us, "Can you help a Vietnam vet?" My youngest son is a veteran, and I deeply respect those who have served their country in that way. So I stopped, walked back to him, and gave him a dollar. At that moment I remembered the words of Jesus: "Give to the one who asks you, and do not turn away from the one who wants to borrow from you." It's as simple as that—give to the one who asks. He asked. I had an obligation to give.

As I walked on down the street, a wonderful peace came over me because I felt I'd actually obeyed one of Jesus' teachings. I knew he'd probably use it to buy more alcohol and that I probably hadn't made the wisest choice. And I also knew that a dollar wasn't really going to help him. But I had no other choice. He asked and I was obligated.

Still, what caused me to give him the money was not really my responsibility to follow Jesus, but the fact that he was a veteran. So after my initial euphoria, I realized I had done the Jesus thing for the wrong reasons.

Day sixteen. I prayed the "blessing of the fleet" at the Yacht Club luncheon today. I selected Psalm 107, which I read from a Jewish translation of the Hebrew Scriptures—the *Tanakh*.

> They reeled and staggered like drunken men;
>   they were at their wits' end.
> Then they cried out to the LORD in their trouble,
>   and he brought them out of their distress.
> He stilled the storm to a whisper;
>   the waves of the sea were hushed.
> They were glad when it grew calm,

and he guided them to their desired haven.

Psalm 107:27–30

After the program, a Jewish man came up to me. He was excited. "I love that you quoted from the Jewish translation of the Hebrew Scriptures. Thank you so much."

And by the way, no one mentioned the beard. I still haven't shaved.

Do not cook a young goat in its mother's milk.

Exodus 23:19

Day twenty. Today I flew back home to Grand Rapids. At the Atlanta airport I decided to get something to eat at Wendy's (knowing, of course, that almost nothing at Wendy's is kosher). The woman behind the counter asked, "Can I help you?"

"I'll have chili, a baked potato, and water, please," I said.

"Do you want cheese with your chili?"

Immediately I realized that having cheese with chili would be a violation of kosher—no meat with milk.

The specific command occurs three times in the Torah, twice in Exodus, and once in Deuteronomy. It seems to me an unusual and somewhat bizarre command; who in the world would cook a young goat in its mother's milk? According to the rabbis, it refers to the mixing of meat and milk together. "Later on, by rabbinic law, this prohibition was extended to eating meat and milk dishes at the same meal. Later on still, the law was introduced that dairy dishes should not be eaten after meat until a certain period of time had elapsed. The time for waiting has varied according to local custom."[2] But why? The rabbis give a variety of reasons, but my favorite is this: "Another suggestion that has been offered is that meat represents death (the animal is killed before the meat is eaten) whereas milk represents life. Life and death must be kept separate; death must not be allowed to encroach upon life."[3]

"Uh, no, thank you," I said.

I felt good about the situation because I'd actually followed the Torah.

After finding a table, I sat down and opened the butter and the sour cream. I spread them evenly across the baked potato, and then I poured some of the chili on top of the baked potato. I said a blessing in Hebrew and began eating. As I took my first bite, however, I began to laugh. There I was, thinking highly of myself for not mixing cheese and chili, but at the same time I put sour cream and butter on the baked potato along with the chili. I was still violating the laws of kosher.

Don't ever think you have your act together, I told myself, because you don't. You're still a Gentile!

Do not cut the hair at the sides of your head or clip off the edges of your beard.

Leviticus 19:27

Day twenty-one. It's late January. Today I met with Rabbi David at the synagogue. He's got a short beard, is about my height, and we've been friends a long time. Actually, my eldest son and I once took Rabbi David's official Jewish conversion course every Monday night for nine months. Several of us Christians took the course to better understand the Jewish faith.

"I've made a one-year commitment to live like Jesus," I said. "I want to live like he lived, act like he acted, and obey his teaching. I'm reading through the Gospels every week."

"If you really want to live like Jesus," he said, "then the Gospels shouldn't be your primary source. Your primary source should be the *Mishnah* in the Talmud." The Mishnah, I knew, is a collection of Jewish traditions that are appended to the Hebrew Bible.

I knew he was right. I needed to understand Jesus in a more cultural, historical, and traditionally Jewish context. For one thing, we're certain that Jesus had a beard, and as a religious Jew, he would not have cut the sides of his hair or clipped the edges off his beard.

So I asked Rabbi David: "Why does the Torah say that we're not supposed to cut the hair at the sides of our head or clip off the edges of our beard?"

Rabbi David immediately opened his Hebrew Bible and took out a series of commentaries—all of which were in either Hebrew or Aramaic.

"One perspective," he said, "is that it was a prohibition within the context of pagan death rituals. The pagans would cut themselves for the dead. They would shave the sides of their heads and pluck out their beards. That was simply the pagan custom when someone died. So the prohibition is actually against pagan rituals and customs. By Jesus' time," he added, "men grew out their beards and didn't cut them at all."

The rabbi himself had a neatly trimmed beard, so I wondered if he perhaps was in violation of this specific command. "I hope this is not an offensive question," I said, "but what about you?"

He laughed. "Not at all," he said, "it's a good question. I think that it's a prohibition against using a razor on one's beard, but not against using scissors. I trim my beard with an electric razor that uses a scissors action to cut, but I have never allowed a razor blade to touch it."

After our talk he took me down to the library in the synagogue and showed me several commentaries. "These books might be helpful in your journey," he said. "You're welcome to come and use the library anytime."

There's a fascinating story about beards in the Hebrew Bible. During the reign of King David, after the king of the Ammonites died, David sent a delegation to express the nation's sympathy to his son Hanun. The new king assumed that David was sending his men to spy on the country so that he could wage war against them. So he took David's men, shaved off half of each man's beard, cut their garments down the middle in back, and sent them home. "When David was told about this, he sent messengers to meet the men, for they were greatly humiliated. The king said, 'Stay at Jericho till your beards have grown, and then come back" (2 Samuel 10:5). They were "greatly humiliated," of course, because they were missing half their beards.

Day twenty-four. Tonight began another Shabbat, so I went to Temple Emanuel in Grand Rapids for the services — they are a Reform synagogue and have Friday evening Shabbat services. There were about sixty people there, but only seven or eight were Jewish. The rest were from two youth groups from two Christian churches in the area. I felt kind of funny. I went to a synagogue and found it mostly filled with Christians. Who'd have thought?

But the service got my mind going in another direction. What kind of clothes did Jesus wear?

Several of the Jews at the synagogue were wearing *tallit*, prayer shawls. Some were also wearing *tzitzit*, a sort of ceremonial tassel traditionally worn by Jewish men. Since I'm trying to live like Jesus for a year, shouldn't I wear a tallit and tzitzit too? And beyond that, how should I dress?

I've lived most of my adult life with restrictions on how I should dress. I went to college at Bob Jones University — a conservative, fundamentalist Christian school in South Carolina that had a strict

29

dress code. Male students' hair was required to be off the collar and off the ears—which is really short! Sometimes after chapel, administrators would wait for us so they could check our hair. Male students were also required to wear dress slacks, a shirt, and a tie. Female students were required to wear dresses to class and the dresses had to be below the knee.

Of course I was a bit of a rebel. I wore the required shirt and tie, but I also wore "hippie" pants—bellbottoms with big and small stripes of every imaginable color. They hung low on the hips and had buttons down the front. I was called into the dean of men's office because several people had complained. When the dean told me that my pants were not conducive to someone studying to become a minister, I told him I was in full conformity to the dress code.

So I continued to wear my hippie pants.

After graduating, I took a job at Jerry Falwell's Liberty University (called Lynchburg Baptist College at that time), where the dress code was similar to the one at Bob Jones: dress slacks, shirt, and tie.

As an administrator and faculty member, I was required to wear a suit and tie, which I did faithfully. Well, sort of. I also wore Mickey Mouse socks—my quiet form of rebellion.

When I arrived in Grand Rapids as senior pastor at Calvary Church, I wore a suit and tie nearly every day. It was expected. But I also wore Doc Martens shoes or boots with the suit. For years Doc Martens were my form of rebellion. They were worn by people who were countercultural, although I wore them before they were "in," while they were "in," and after they were "in." And I wore them with pride.

So how should I dress if I want to live like Jesus?

One of my favorite pastimes is watching religious television, and I confess that I don't do it for spiritual edification—I watch it for pure entertainment. It is a conglomeration of the bizarre, the weird, and the unbelievable. And sometimes good things get mixed in as well.

Perhaps the people on religious television can answer my question about how a follower of Jesus should dress. Here's what I discovered.

Robert Schuller. His program, called *The Hour of Power*, is, as far as I know, the longest-running religious television program on the air. Reverend Schuller dresses in a doctoral robe. It's similar to my own doctoral robe from the University of Virginia. The problem with that is that doctoral robes are extremely heavy and hot! Not a good idea, I thought.

Benny Hinn. One of the most popular people on religious television. He holds massive meetings in large arenas and is known for his "healing powers." At some point in each program he invites people forward who are in wheelchairs, sick, and dying. Then he heals them. He regularly wears a white French-cuffed shirt that buttons high on his neck and has no collar. Over the shirt he wears a coat that buttons up the front—similar to the kind people in India wear. On the front of the coat is a funny looking symbol. During some of his crusades he dresses in an all-white suit—with shoes to match. Since I'm not a faith healer, I have no power to heal people of their sicknesses. Otherwise I'd have healed myself of ALS, the terminal disease I've lived with for the past nine years. So I don't think Benny Hinn would make a good role model.

Rod Parsley. He is a wild man. He paces back and forth and preaches with more energy than I could muster in twenty sermons. He yells. He sweats. He's loud. And from time to time the Hammond organ chimes in to complement his preaching. It reminds me of the black church I attend and occasionally preach at in Grand Rapids. Parsley regularly wears a dark T-shirt underneath an open-collared dark shirt. Over the shirt he wears a coat. But I don't yell and sweat. And the last time I preached in the black church and the music began to play, I looked at the organist and said, "Brother, if you keep playing that organ, it'll really confuse me."

Bishop T. D. Jakes. Now this is one of the most remarkably dressed people on religious television. He's also one of my favorite preachers. Not only is he entertaining, he has wonderful insights on the Bible. And man, can he dress! He wears some of the most beautiful suits I've ever seen. I was in an all-day meeting with him several years ago, talking about the issue of racism in the church. He's a wonderful, engaging man, the real thing. If I were to choose one person to emulate, it would be Bishop Jakes. My problem is that even though I have custom-made suits, none of them quite measure up to Bishop Jakes'.

Catholic, Episcopal, and Lutheran priests. Though there are not a lot of priests on television (other than the official Catholic channel), they all seem to dress alike: dark suits with a clerical collar. The collar is meant to remind them that they are "slaves of Christ." I've always admired people who wore clerical collars. They're cool. Maybe that's because I grew up in a movement that was quite anti-high church. The pastors in my movement never would have worn a clerical collar—and they were proud of the fact. Even though I never bought the party line, the anti-high church feelings in the movement sank deeper into my soul than I ever realized. The idea of emulating the dress of a Catholic or Episcopal priest is a bit beyond my comfort zone.

So who should I follow?

The answer is, I think, none of them. Nor should I even try to dress as Jesus dressed—in a floor-length robe and sandals. Given the snow and cold of Michigan winters, this would be a problem. In the twenty-first century, dressing like Jesus would be bizarre. (Actually, I'm beginning to think this whole "following-Jesus" journey is a bit bizarre.) If I lived in the Middle East, perhaps it wouldn't seem so odd. But here in America, it seems that the only people who dress in long robes every day are cult leaders.

> Do not plant two kinds of seed in your vineyard; if you do, not only the crops you plant but also the fruit of the vineyard will be defiled.
> Do not plow with an ox and a donkey yoked together.
> Do not wear clothes with wool and linen woven together.

Deuteronomy 22:9–11

These laws deal with things that shouldn't be mixed.

Don't plant two kinds of seeds in your vineyard. I'm not entirely sure about this law, but perhaps it's best for the farmer to focus on one seed in the vineyard and not two.

Do not plow with an ox and a donkey. This one I understand; an ox is immensely strong and the donkey is not. If you plow with both of them together, you will most certainly plow in circles since the strength of the ox will overcome the strength of the donkey.

Do not wear clothes with wool and linen. I have no earthly clue why this particular command was given. I need to talk with Rabbi David and get an explanation. Perhaps there's no reason for this law and it's simply a test of whether we will obey it.

Which raises an important question about what Jesus wore. Did he really conform to this particular law from the Torah, not to mix wool and linen? Most likely he did, and therefore I must do it too. While it appears that Jesus obeyed the commands of the Torah, there are also stories in the Gospels that suggest he did not obey *all* of the traditions of the elders. Frequently, for instance, he violated Sabbath traditions, and during the Passover feast, when Jews remember the exodus from Egypt, he inaugurated a whole new idea — what we call the Lord's Supper.

The LORD said to Moses, "Speak to the Israelites and say to them: Throughout the generations to come you are to make tassels on the corners of your garments, with a blue cord on each tassel. You will have these tassels to look at and so you will remember all the commands of the LORD, that you may obey them and not prostitute yourselves by going after the lusts of your own hearts and eyes. Then you will remember to obey all my commands and will be consecrated to your God."

Numbers 15:37–40

This brings me back to the tassels I saw at the synagogue. The Hebrew word for these tassels is *tzitzit,* and according to the book of Deuteronomy, they are to be worn on the four corners of your cloak. In the ancient world, and during the time of Jesus, people wore garments that were four cornered. Since Jesus was a religious Jew, he wore tzitzit on the corners of his robe. The reason for this command was to wear something visible to remind Jews of their obligation to obey God's laws. Notice the verbs that are used in the text—*remember, obey, do not prostitute,* and *remember* (once again).

In the world in which we live, four-cornered garments are rare. In fact, I don't think I even own a four-cornered garment. Orthodox Jews often wear a four-cornered garment underneath their regular clothes. Attached to the corners are the tzitzit. You can see the tzitzit hanging down from their waist. A few religious Jews also have a blue cord in their tzitzit. Several years ago I attended a lecture sponsored by some of the Orthodox Jews in our community, and the lecturer was an Israeli who, among other things, used a rare shellfish for the blue dye in the tzitzit. He had several of the tassels for sale after the lecture, and I bought one.

So should I wear a four-cornered garment with tzitzit? I don't think so. I'm afraid that if I wore them it would be offensive to deeply religious Jews. After all, I am not Jewish; I'm an "uncircumcised Philistine." Then again, Jesus offended the religious establishment in his day. So maybe I shouldn't care what other people think.

But I do.

So what do I do? As I read and reread this command, the emphasis is that you are to do something that is visible to remind you of your obligation to obey all the commands of God. So I need to do something visible to remind me of my responsibility to keep all of God's commands.

> I also want women to dress modestly, with decency and propriety, not with braided hair or gold or pearls or expensive clothes, but with good deeds, appropriate for women who profess to worship God.
>
> **1 Timothy 2:9–10**

Since this command is for women, I exclude myself from it. But why couldn't it apply to men as well? The principles are sound: modesty, decency, propriety, no expensive clothes. It seems that all of these ideas are suitable for both men and women. Jews in the time of Jesus were extremely modest when compared to Greek culture, which glorified the human body. In Greco-Roman culture, the gymnasium was filled with naked athletes. The Olympic Games were performed in the nude. The Jews were the complete opposite. They were modest. So when Paul writes to young Timothy, he instructs him to teach the women to dress with modesty and decency.

So I will try to dress modestly, which is a challenge since I'm in Florida most of the winter, and we go to the beach a lot.

Now I have some guidelines: modesty, decency, and, perhaps, tassels. But making the actual choice of clothes is difficult. I could

35

wear dark pants and a white shirt—like some Orthodox Jews do today. I could dress in dark colors like the Amish. I could dress in white (like A. J. Jacobs). I could dress in jeans and a T-shirt. So even the simple matter of what to wear is still a complicated issue.

Day thirty-one. Today we flew back to Florida. On the way I finished listening to the gospel of John—which means I've read through the Gospels five times this month. I don't know if I'm proud of myself or just relieved that I've finally finished a whole month trying to live like Jesus. Maybe a little bit more pride than relief.

I began the month by honking at people who were too slow when the light turned green, and I've ended the month being proud of myself.

Not very Jesus-like!

February

> By the seventh day God had finished the work he had been doing;
> so on the seventh day he rested from all his work. And God blessed
> the seventh day and made it holy, because on it he rested from all
> the work of creating that he had done.
>
> **Genesis 2:2–3**

Day one. The quotation above follows the creation narrative
found in the early chapters of Genesis. For six days God was involved in the work of creation, but on the seventh day he rested.
And he made the seventh day "holy." Most people think of the
word *holy* in theological terms. God is holy. The sanctuary of the
church is holy. The altar is holy. When we use the word *holy* in
this context, we are essentially saying that it is sacred. But in the
creation account, the word *holy* doesn't carry the idea of sacred-
ness. It simply means "different." For six days God was involved
in the work of creation but the seventh day was different. On the
seventh day, he rested. He did no work. He did not create. So the
seventh day was different than all the others.

This is the fundamental idea of Shabbat. It is a day that is different than all others. For six days we are involved in work and
creation, but on the seventh day we do something different—we
do no work and we do not create.

Later in the story of the Jewish people, God gives the Ten Commandments on Mount Sinai. The fourth commandment is about
Shabbat.

> Remember the Sabbath day by keeping it holy. Six days
> you shall labor and do all your work, but the seventh is
> a Sabbath to the LORD your God. On it you shall not do

any work, neither you, nor your son or daughter, nor your manservant or maidservant, nor your animals, nor the alien within your gates.

Exodus 20:8–10

A number of years ago a judge in Alabama refused to take the Ten Commandments off the wall in his courtroom. This led to a huge legal battle. Eventually he stepped down (or was fired, I'm not sure). Many conservative Christians were deeply upset that the judge was asked to remove the Ten Commandments. After all, America was founded on Judeo-Christian principles, and these principles include the Ten Commandments.

At that time, I was asked to come back to Liberty University to attend a conference on the subject with Dr. Falwell. On the platform was a huge replica of the Ten Commandments. As I sat there, I was uncomfortable. I was afraid that someone might take my picture in front of the Ten Commandments, and it would appear in newspapers all over the country.

I've never been an advocate of plastering the Ten Commandments in the public square. Why? Because every Christian I know who is in favor of posting the Commandments breaks at least one of them regularly—the commandment to keep the Sabbath. If we were really serious about the Ten Commandments, we would work six days and rest on the seventh. But apparently we are not very serious about them.

Day two. Today is Shabbat. The sun is shining, it's a warm and beautiful day. It's the kind of day that's ideally suited to going for a long drive with the top down. I'm tempted, but it's Shabbat. So I decide not to drive at all. My first good choice for Shabbat.

I talked to my oldest son on the phone. He lived in Jerusalem for almost three years and studied his last year at Hebrew University.

"Son, I've been reading about the need to wear tassels to remind me of the commandments of God. I'm not sure what to do."

"What do you mean, Dad?"

"I've seen a lot of Orthodox Jews with dark pants and a dark coat and the tassels hanging below the coat. I'm not sure I want to do that since I'm not Jewish, and I don't want to offend people in the Jewish community."

"Actually, those tassels are part of a T-shirt that they wear underneath their white shirt. You can either let the tassels hang out so others can see them or you can tuck them in your pants."

"I didn't realize that. Where do you get those T-shirts?"

"Just get on the Internet and look up *tallit katan*. There should be several companies that sell them."

After hanging up, I got on the Internet and found the company that sold them. I ordered two medium T-shirts and had them shipped as quickly as possible. I was really excited as I closed the computer. Then I realized:

I had talked on the phone.

I had used a computer.

I had bought two T-shirts.

And I did all of this on Shabbat!

I wonder what the representative at the T-shirt company thought (at least when he or she came into work the next day) — "Who in the world would order T-shirts on Shabbat? A Gentile!"

Apparently I'm not very serious about the Ten Commandments either.

Day five. Several years ago a Roman Catholic woman in our community came to see me at Calvary Church. Even though she attended Mass nearly every day, she watched me preach on television each week. My sermons were broadcast by a local station, and according to the ratings, some 80,000 people watched me around the state of Michigan.

"I have something I want to give you," she said. This was not the first time she'd come to see me, and every time she would give me Catholic booklets to read.

But this time she reached into her pocketbook and pulled out a rosary. "Several weeks ago I had a private audience with Pope John Paul II," she said. "I brought several rosaries with me and Pope John Paul II personally blessed each of them. So I'd like to give you one."

A rosary blessed by Pope John Paul II! Incredible. How in the world did she get a private audience with the pope? And why in the world would she give me one of the rosaries he personally blessed?

I think she's trying to convert me, I thought.

She continued, "And you'll notice that this rosary, made of wooden beads, has a simple cross—not a crucifix. I know that you're a Protestant and you might object to the crucifix. So I got your rosary with a simple cross." (A crucifix has a cross with Jesus on it. A simple cross is empty. Protestants traditionally favor the simple cross because they want to emphasize that Jesus was raised from the dead and the cross is now empty.)

At first I thought it was really kind of her to bring a rosary with a simple cross. Then I realized that her main objective was to get me to pray the rosary, and the simple cross rather than the crucifix would encourage me to do it.

Now I *knew* she was trying to convert me.

I thanked her and took the rosary home. But I didn't know what to do with it. Hang it on the mirror in my truck? But then, people driving past might think I'm a Catholic. So I hung it over the lamp on the dresser by my bed. And it stayed there for years.

Today as I got out of bed, I glanced at the rosary. Maybe I

should pray the rosary as part of my journey in following Jesus. As quickly as that thought came, another one followed: that's crazy. Praying to Mary? You've got to be kidding. We only pray to God. Not Mary, not the saints, not anybody! And besides, praying the rosary has absolutely nothing to do with living like Jesus.

Or does it?

> Any Israelite or any alien living among them who eats any blood—I will set my face against that person who eats blood and will cut him off from his people. For the life of a creature is in the blood, and I have given it to you to make atonement for yourselves on the altar; it is the blood that makes atonement for one's life. Therefore I say to the Israelites, "None of you may eat blood, nor may an alien living among you eat blood."
>
> **Leviticus 17:10–12**

Day six. I'm still struggling with my dietary restrictions. It's all the more frustrating because it's unlikely that Jesus struggled with restrictions on his diet. After all, he lived in a culture where everyone ate kosher. Even when he was with friends and partied with tax collectors and sinners, the food was kosher.

I went out to eat tonight with friends. I decided to order steak—well-done. I actually prefer my steaks medium rare, but the Torah prohibits the eating of meat that has even a trace of blood in it.

It is interesting that when Gentiles began to be included in the early church, a controversy arose over whether they needed to become Jews and obey the Torah. Some felt they should. Some felt they shouldn't. So the church elders gathered in Jerusalem to discuss the issue. After much discussion and debate, they came up with the following requirements: "You are to abstain from food sacrificed to idols, from blood, from the meat of strangled animals and from sexual immorality. You will do well to avoid these things" (Acts 15:29).

So the prohibition against blood was required for Gentile believers as well. Yet I have never heard a pastor, teacher, or preacher ever deal with this issue. Most commentators simply suggest that it is culturally based—in other words, an issue only for the early church that no longer applies to us today. Or does it? Certainly the last part of that passage from Acts deals with sexual immorality and *that* still applies today, doesn't it? So why not the part dealing with blood? Maybe after this year I will try to continue to follow the requirement of not eating blood.

To ensure that blood is removed from the meat, Jews follow a procedure called *melihah*: "The meat should first be soaked in water for half an hour. It is then salted (with salt neither too coarse nor too fine) over all the surface and left on the draining board for an hour. It is then rinsed free of salt and can be cooked."[1] Never have I heard anyone preach on this subject, nor have I ever heard anyone talk about making sure that most of the blood is taken out of the meat before it is cooked. I don't know why. I like my steaks medium rare—very pink! But this is a violation of the Torah.

Of course there are many other traditions associated with the dietary laws: certain plates and utensils for meat and certain plates and utensils for dairy. Essentially every Orthodox Jewish family has two sets of plates, and they would never eat in a restaurant unless it was kosher. So I'm already violating kosher because I'm using a plate on which meat and dairy may well have been previously served together.

I also love my steak with a baked potato—topped with butter and sour cream. But since I'm unable to eat meat and dairy at the same time, I asked for french fries instead of a baked potato. The people I'm with have ordered a variety of appetizers, including pizza—with lots of cheese! At this point I'm sorry that I ordered steak, because I love pizza. Why didn't I order fish? At least then

I could have eaten cheese with the fish. But no. I *had* to have a steak. And I am regretting it.

At the end of the meal the hosts ordered desserts, but I was unable to eat any of them because they all have milk or butter in them.

The lesson I've learned is that I need to think through an entire meal before I order anything. I was so hung up on having a steak that it ultimately ruined the rest of the meal. From now on I will try to weigh my options before I order.

Day ten. Today I drove to the nearest Catholic church to get some information about praying the rosary. It was a large complex of buildings so I parked next to the chapel and walked to the front. The chapel was locked. The larger church building was also locked. So I walked around the back toward the school building. As I was walking through the parking lot, a middle-aged man was making his way to his car.

"Excuse me, sir," I said, "could you tell me where I can find the priest?"

"In that building. Go to the office and you'll find him."

So I walked into the office area and asked, "May I please speak with the priest?"

"I'm sorry, he's not here right now," said the receptionist. "He just went to lunch. But if you check back in about an hour, you might be able to find him."

(Several days later I discovered that the man who met me in the parking lot was, in fact, the priest. I didn't recognize him because he was not wearing a clerical collar. When I found this out, I laughed. How many times have I done the same thing? Someone walking through the parking lot at the church asking me where to find the pastor. I would tell them to go to the office area and ask for him there.)

I came back about an hour later but the priest was still not in. The receptionist asked me if she could help me.

"I'd like to get some information about how to pray the rosary," I said.

"Oh, I can help you with that," she said. After fumbling through a whole stack of booklets in her desk drawer, she finally handed me two booklets on praying the rosary.

I was excited.

The rosary is composed of a large string of fifty-four beads—fifty small beads and four large ones. Attached is a short string composed of three small beads and two large beads with the crucifix at the bottom (in my case, a simple cross). The idea of using beads for prayers is an ancient idea, dating back to the desert fathers who used individual beads to count their prayers. Beginning with the crucifix, you make your way around the rosary and say specific prayers for the various beads. You begin by touching the crucifix. Then you cross yourself (touching your forehead, your lower chest, your left chest, and your right chest). As you cross yourself you say, "In the name of the Father, and of the Son, and of the Holy Spirit. Amen." Then, while you are still touching the crucifix, you say the Apostles' Creed:

> I believe in God, the Father Almighty, Creator of heaven and earth; and in Jesus Christ, his only Son, our Lord; who was conceived by the Holy Spirit, born of the Virgin Mary, suffered under Pontius Pilate, was crucified, died, and was buried. He descended into hell; the third day he rose again from the dead; he ascended into heaven, sits at the right hand of God, the Father Almighty; from thence he shall come to judge the living and the dead. I believe in the Holy Spirit, the holy catholic Church, the communion of saints, the forgive-

ness of sins, the resurrection of the body, and life ever-lasting. Amen.

You then move above the crucifix to the first large bead. On this bead you say the Lord's Prayer:

> Our Father, who art in heaven, hallowed be thy name; thy kingdom come; thy will be done on earth, as it is in heaven. Give us this day our daily bread; and forgive us our trespasses, as we forgive those who trespass against us, and lead us not into temptation, but deliver us from evil. Amen.

You then move up to the three small beads, where you say three Hail Marys:

> Hail Mary, full of grace. The Lord is with thee. Blessed art thou among women, and blessed is the fruit of thy womb, Jesus. Holy Mary, Mother of God, pray for us sinners, now and at the hour of our death. Amen.

You then move up to the large bead before the circle of many beads. On this bead you say the Glory Be:

> Glory be to the Father, and to the Son, and to the Holy Spirit. As it was in the beginning, is now, and ever shall be, world without end. Amen.

You then began to meditate on the first mystery (which I'll explain in a moment). After you meditate on the mystery, you say the Lord's Prayer again. Then you move through the next ten small beads by saying ten Hail Marys. At the end of those, you say another Glory Be. You then meditate on the second mystery followed by the Lord's Prayer. The cycle repeats itself until you've gone all the way around the circle, and then you conclude by saying Hail Holy Queen:

Hail! Holy Queen, Mother of Mercy! Our life, our sweetness, and our hope! To thee do we cry, poor banished children of Eve, to thee do we send up our sighs, mourning and weeping in this valley of tears. Turn, then, most gracious advocate, your eyes of mercy toward us; and after this our exile show unto us the blessed fruit of thy womb, Jesus. O clement, O loving, O sweet Virgin Mary. Pray for us, O holy Mother of God, that we may be made worthy of the promises of Christ.

There are four sets of mysteries: the joyful mysteries, the luminous mysteries, the sorrowful mysteries, and the glorious mysteries. The mysteries are basically meditations on Scripture passages that follow the life of Jesus: his birth, his life, the institution of the Lord's Supper, his death, and his resurrection and ascension to heaven. So the rosary basically forces one to meditate on the birth, life, death, and resurrection of Jesus. So even though it was not something that Jesus prayed, it is helpful in reflecting on the Gospel story. It forces one to repeatedly deal with the biblical text and with the life and teachings of Jesus.

Day eleven. I sat in a nearby coffee shop and prayed through the rosary. It was a strange, bizarre, and unusual experience. First of all, I was deeply moved by the passages of Scripture that described the sufferings of Jesus. As I prayed through the rosary, I read five different Scriptures that emphasize the sorrows of Jesus:

The first sorrowful mystery: the agony in the garden (Luke 22:39–46)

The second sorrowful mystery: the scourging at the pillar (Mark 15:6–15)

The third sorrowful mystery: the crowning with thorns (John 19:1–8)

The fourth sorrowful mystery: the carrying of the cross
(John 19:16–22)

The fifth sorrowful mystery: the crucifixion and death of
Jesus (John 19:25–30)

The Scripture texts in the booklet that I was using are from the
New American Bible—one of the official Catholic translations. I
found it helpful to read those passages in an unfamiliar translation.
Still, saying all those Hail Marys seemed to distract me from the
sorrowful mysteries surrounding the death of Jesus.

The man with two tunics should share with him who has none, and
the one who has food should do the same.

Luke 3:11

Day fourteen. Some of Jesus' teachings were never intended to
be taken literally. Years ago, at Liberty University, I was teaching about Jesus' Sermon on the Mount, where Jesus says, "If your
right eye causes you to sin, gouge it out and throw it away" (Matthew 5:29). After class a young male student came up to see me.
He was missing his right eye. He said, "That verse—I tried it! I
have a problem with lust, so I literally gouged out my right eye.
And I'm here to tell you, I am a left-eye luster."

I immediately looked down to see if he had cut off one of his
hands as well. To this day I can't believe I actually met this student. It's bizarre but true.

Although I don't intend to gouge out my eye or cut off my
hand, I do want to take the teachings of Jesus seriously. I intend
to try to live them out as best as I can. Now some theologians
will object to this idea of strictly obeying Jesus' teachings. They'll
suggest that I'm moving away from Grace (the kindness and favor
of God) and moving toward Law (gaining merit with God by

obeying commands). So you need to know up front that I don't care. I am trying to understand Jesus and his teachings without the long history of theologians and theological systems, knowing, of course, that the goal will probably be impossible.

John the Baptist was one wild and crazy guy. When he saw the religious leaders coming out to him, he said, "You brood of vipers! Who warned you to flee from the coming wrath? Produce fruit in keeping with repentance" (Luke 3:7–8). Not exactly politically correct. When the crowds heard his message of baptism and repentance, they asked John, "What should we do then?" to which John responded, "The man with two tunics should share with him who has none."

So how many suits and shirts do I have?

More than enough!

Years ago, one of the businessmen in our church called me. "I know you need some new suits," he said, "and for years I've been having my suits custom made. I've got more than enough, so right now I'm sending my tailor over to you to measure you for some new suits." I had never possessed a tailor-made suit. Most of mine were bought for around a hundred dollars. Cheap, cheap, cheap. But now a tailor was on his way to see me.

After measuring me, he opened up a huge briefcase and pulled out bundles of fabrics. "Look through these fabrics and choose one for your suit," he said. I couldn't make up my mind. Then he said, "Actually, you're going to get two suits." Then I had to make decisions about whether I wanted pleats in the pants, cuffs at the bottom, and a two- or three-button suit. Inside I was laughing. I'd never bought suits this way. Then I had to order shirts to go with the suits. The tailor asked, "You want your collars and cuffs to contrast with the main part of the shirt? You want regular buttons on the cuffs or French cuffs?" All sorts of choices.

Several weeks later the suits arrived. They were the nicest I'd ever owned. In the lining of the coat was a beautiful patch that said "Custom styled for Ed Dobson." I wanted to go around opening the front right of the coat so people could see the patch. Kind of like flashing!

Over the years the tailor kept coming back. I now have twelve suits and fifteen shirts that are custom made. Some of the suits have patches on both sides of the lining! Now that's impressive!

So should I give half of them away? Or should I give all of them away, except one?

After some thought, I decide to give half the suits and shirts away. So I go to my closet. Which ones should I give away? Do I give away the ones that I like the least? Do I give away the ones that I wear the least? Or is it more in keeping with the Scripture to give away my favorites? I stand there looking at all those beautiful suits and shirts, and the truth is, I can't bear to part with any of them. But I must. The more I stand there looking at them, the more attached to them I become.

Finally I decide that I don't have the guts to select the suits to give away. Maybe tomorrow. I know that part of my journey in following Jesus is to give away half of my suits and shirts. And I will. But just not today.

Blessed are you among women, and blessed is the child you will bear!

Luke 1:42

Day fifteen. Elizabeth was the mother of John the Baptist, the forerunner of Jesus the Messiah. While Elizabeth was pregnant with John, Mary was pregnant with Jesus. So Mary went to visit Elizabeth while they were both pregnant, and Elizabeth greeted her in a loud voice: "Blessed are you among women, and blessed is the child you will bear!"

As I prayed the rosary again today, the one phrase I repeated over and over again was the Hail Mary, which includes Elizabeth's words. For the first time I realized that when I pray the Hail Mary, I am actually praying the words of Scripture. Maybe the rosary isn't as bad as I thought.

Today, as I pray the rosary, I focus on the joyful mysteries.

> The first joyful mystery: the annunciation of our Lord (Luke 1:26–33, 38)
>
> The second joyful mystery: the visitation (Luke 1:39–45)
>
> The third joyful mystery: the nativity of Jesus (Luke 2:6–12)
>
> The fourth joyful mystery: the presentation in the Temple (Luke 2:25–32)
>
> The fifth joyful mystery: the finding in the Temple (Luke 2:41–50)

I don't want to jump to premature conclusions, but I'm beginning to think that the rosary might be a helpful way to pray. I especially like the meditations from Scripture. They deal with the story of Jesus' life—from birth to resurrection. Maybe the rosary was developed to help people reflect on the life of Jesus. Furthermore, praying the Scriptures is a very Jewish thing to do.

Day twenty. I pray the rosary again today. I say the Hail Mary fifty-three times, enough to realize that the second part of the Hail Mary troubles me: "Holy Mary, mother of God, pray for us sinners, now and at the hour of our death. Amen."

I actually like the idea of asking someone to pray for me at the hour of my death. I have a slow-progressing form of ALS—Lou Gehrig's disease—and only have a limited time here on earth. So the idea of someone praying for me as I approach the inevitable is quite comforting! But what about praying to Mary? I grew up believing that you pray only to God, in the name of Jesus and empowered by the Holy Spirit. You don't pray to the saints. And you certainly don't pray to Mary.

I was diagnosed with ALS nine years ago. Since then I've walked with several people with ALS who have died, and I've known many others who have died of cancer. One of my closest friends died of ALS a couple of years ago. As he approached the end of his journey, I said to him, "If you get there before I do, put in a few good words for me, okay?"

I've asked several other people who are dying to do the same thing. And they all agreed that they would put in a few good words for me. I know that each of these people ended up in heaven, where they are conscious and can talk.

Jesus once told the story of the rich man and Lazarus. They both died. The rich man went to a place of suffering and torment while Lazarus, a poor beggar, went to Abraham's bosom. The rich man sees Lazarus at a distance and says, "Father Abraham, have pity on me and send Lazarus to dip the tip of his finger in water and cool my tongue, because I am in agony in this fire." Of course, Abraham says that's impossible.

I learn from this story that when people get to heaven they are aware and can talk, so it makes sense to me to ask dying people to chat with the powers that be.

So if I'm okay with asking a dying person to put in a few good words for me, why wouldn't I ask someone who's already dead to put in a few good words for me? Is it such a huge theological leap? I don't know.

But I'm still troubled by the idea of praying to Mary. Maybe when I get a chance, I will ask one of the Catholic priests to help me better understand this.

Day twenty-five. I read through most of the gospel of John today. I was struck with the first miracle that Jesus performed—at the wedding in Cana. In Jesus' day, weddings were village-wide celebrations. The wedding feast would last for several days; people would eat and drink and celebrate.

At this particular wedding feast they run out of wine, which would ordinarily be a permanent embarrassment to the family. For the rest of their lives they'd be known as "the family who didn't have enough wine for the wedding feast." So Mary comes to Jesus and says, "They have no more wine." Jesus responds, "Dear woman, why do you involve me? My time has not yet come." His mother tells the servants, "Do whatever he tells you." Then Jesus instructs the servants to fill some large stone jars with water. Then he turns the water into wine.

What strikes me about this story is not the miracle, but that Jesus tells his mother that his "time has not yet come." He seems to be saying that he's not yet ready to perform miracles, and yet he goes ahead and performs one! Why? It must simply be because his mother asked him. Mothers have a way of changing our minds.

So Mary is able to change Jesus' mind. Is that, perhaps, a reason to pray to her? Does she still have that kind of influence? Could she change Jesus' mind? As I pray the rosary today, I think of this story about the wedding feast in Cana, a story in which Jesus does something he wouldn't ordinarily—only because his mother asked him.

The LORD said to Moses, "Speak to the Israelites and say to them: 'Throughout the generations to come you are to make tassels on the corners of your garments, with a blue cord on each tassel. You will have these tassels to look at and so you will remember all the commands of the LORD, that you may obey them and not prostitute yourselves by going after the lusts of your own hearts and eyes. Then you will remember to obey all my commands and will be consecrated to your God. I am the LORD your God, who brought you out of Egypt to be your God. I am the LORD your God.'"

Numbers 15:37–41

Day twenty-nine. Today I received in the mail my tassel T-shirts. I immediately went into the living room and opened the box. I was excited. I held them up to my chest and realized that I should have ordered smalls, not mediums. The mediums were a tad too big.

But first I needed to find out what I'm supposed to say when I put on one of the T-shirts. I know I'm supposed to say one of the traditional blessings, but I'm not sure which one. Time to get back on the Internet.

The tassel on these garments is significant. It's made of four strands, with one of the strands being much longer than the others. The strands are then placed through a hole in the corner, and approximately two inches from the hole the first double knot is tied. Then the long strand is wound around the other strands seven times. Then another double knot, followed by the long strand wound around the other strands eight times, followed by a double knot, followed by eleven times around the other strands, followed by a double knot, followed by thirteen times around the other strands, followed by a double knot.

The tying of the knots and the number of coils is significant in trying to remember God and his commands. In biblical numerology, the numbers seven and eight add up to fifteen—which is equal to the letters *yod* and *heh* in Hebrew. These are the first two letters of the sacred, unpronounceable name for God. Eleven is the number of *vav* and *heh*. These are the last two letters of the sacred, unpronounceable name of God. The last thirteen coils

53

are the equivalent of the Hebrew word *ehad*, the word for "one." This is from the Shema, a prayer with which Jews begin and end every day, which is found in Deuteronomy 6: "Hear, O Israel, the Lord is our God, the Lord is one." In Hebrew numerology, the word *tzitzit* equals 600. On the tzitzit there are eight strands plus five knots, which equals thirteen. This adds up to 613 commands —the number of commands in the Torah.

I didn't listen to any of the Bible today or read from it. I'm tired of reading the Bible. Didn't think I'd ever say that, but it's true. So I'm giving myself a one-day break. It's my Shabbat from the Bible.

March

Day two. Today I put on my T-shirt with the tassels for the first time. Before that, however, I said the correct traditional prayer in Hebrew: "Blessed are you, Lord, our God, King of the universe, who has sanctified us with his commands and has commanded us to wrap ourselves with the fringes." Then I kissed one of the tassels and put on the shirt.

I thought that by putting on the shirt with the tassels I'd feel some sort of deep allegiance to God's commands. I thought it would be a spiritual experience. But it wasn't. And I was quite disappointed. The first thing I noticed was that it's difficult to tuck the tassels in your pants. The good news is that once you've got them tucked in, no one knows you're wearing them.

I attended the Messiah Missionary Baptist Church today but felt funny wearing Jewish tassels. I was wearing a coat and pants that had been given to me by a Jewish friend—Spencer. Years ago I used to meet with Spencer to discuss what it meant to be a follower of Jesus. He was a businessman in our community and, as a Jew, not a follower of Jesus.

At the end of one of our Christmas programs back then, I stood up and gave a brief presentation of what I thought it meant to follow Jesus. Then I led a public prayer and asked people who wanted to become followers of Jesus to silently pray the prayer after me.

Spencer was sitting up in the balcony. He later told me that when I started to pray the prayer, he prayed it along with me even though he had no intention of praying the prayer. For the next several years I met with him every other week to discuss the Bible. He read through the New Testament and every week came to me with a whole series of questions. When he got home, he would write out the questions and my answers in a notebook.

He was killed one day in a terrible automobile accident. I preached at his funeral, and a few weeks later, his wife gave me a copy of his notebook with the questions and answers.

Since Spencer and I were the same height and size, his wife also gave me most of his clothes—which were really nice! It was a dramatic improvement in my wardrobe. So the clothes I wore to the Messiah Missionary Baptist Church this morning were clothes that he had given me. So on both the outside and the inside I was wearing Jewish clothes, even though I felt really odd wearing the T-shirt with the tassels.

But then I noticed that one of the pastors on the platform was wearing a beautiful blue scarf with tassels on each corner. He was wearing a garment with four corners and in each corner was a tassel! He was living in obedience to the command in the Torah just as much as I was!

One of the major problems in wearing the T-shirt with the tassels occurs when you go to the bathroom. I undid my pants, pulled them down, sat on the toilet, and guess what? Two of the tassels plopped into the water. Disgusting. So I had to wring them out as well as I could and tuck them back in my pants. There's nothing like having wet tassels in your pants!

Next time I sit on the toilet, I'll make sure to hold the tassels.

This afternoon I listened to the entire gospel of Mark. So far I'm not writing down my thoughts or reactions to the Gospels, but eventually I want to begin doing that. But right now, I just want to listen to their story. I enjoy being able to hear the entire gospel of Mark in one sitting. I'm drawn into the story and feel like I'm actually listening to Jesus.

Day four. I went to see Rabbi David again, this time to talk about prayer. We meet in his office, which is very tiny and cluttered with books. He's into books. Books are what matter. He studied at Hebrew University even before he was a particularly religious person. His roommate, however, was a Christian who strictly observed the Sabbath. If a Christian could be serious about the Bible, Rabbi David had concluded, maybe he should be as well. So he became a rabbi.

Jesus often went out into solitary places to pray, but there is no record of exactly what words he said (other than his prayer in John 17). So I wanted to ask Rabbi David what he thought Jesus prayed, given his understanding of that time.

"Is it true that from a Jewish perspective prayer is much more communal than private?" I asked. "In other words, prayer was done more with a group of people than alone, right?"

"Not really," he said. I was surprised. "Prayer is equally effective privately and publicly. You are right, however, that Jewish tradition prefers public prayer."

"So how do you pray when you pray privately?" I asked.

"Basically I use two prayers. The *Shema* and the *Amida*. I pray them both in the morning and the evening. The Amida is a substitute for the Temple worship that ceased in AD 70."

"The Gospels say that Jesus often went into a solitary place to pray. So are those the prayers he prayed?" I asked.

"He probably recited the Shema and prayed the Amida, although not exactly as they are found in the modern siddur. The themes of the prayers are ancient, but the text was not fixed in the first century."

"Then what did he pray?" I asked

"He probably prayed more like the seventeenth-century Hasidic rabbis do today. Some had a practice of going out into the woods to be alone, to meditate and pray to God. Their prayers were much more free flowing. Jesus likely improvised his prayers according to the themes of the Shema and the Amida."

I confess, I was hoping for something more specific.

But Jesus was Jewish. He lived in the Jewish village, worked as a Jewish carpenter, attended synagogue, and read the Torah. He ate like a Jew, dressed like a Jew, and prayed like a Jew. So what were his prayers like? Well, we know he gave the disciples what we now call the Lord's Prayer.

Also, right before he was arrested, he prayed to his Father in heaven a prayer that is recorded in John 17. In that prayer he asked God to give him the glory he had before the world began, and he also prayed for his disciples as well as those of us who believe in him through the teaching of those disciples. Apart from these two texts, there is not much in the Gospels about Jesus' prayers.

So what did he pray? I thought that Rabbi David would help me understand how Jews prayed, but I still had questions. So I ordered a book called *To Pray as a Jew: A Guide to the Prayer Book and the Synagogue Service*, written by a rabbi.

The key to understanding Jewish prayer is the prayer book, called the *siddur*, which means "order." The basic idea of the siddur is to give the person who prays a sense of the order in which the elements of the prayer should come. There are four types of prayer:

> the prayer of petition
>
> the prayer of thanksgiving
>
> the prayer of praise to God
>
> the prayer of confession

> The Hebrew word for prayer ... does not mean to ask or to petition God. It is derived from a stem ... that is closest in meaning to the last of these four types of

prayer. It means to judge; therefore ... [to pray] ... could also be translated as to judge one's self. Here lies a clue to the real purpose for engaging in prayer. Whether we petition God to give us what we need, or thank him for whatever good was granted, or extol him for his awesome attributes, all prayer is intended to help make us better human beings.[1]

But what should we actually say when we pray? What words should we use when we petition God or thank him or extol him? This is one of the fundamental questions that Jewish people struggle with. How do we as finite human beings address an omnipotent God? What words are adequate? The answers to these questions are found in the siddur.

Jewish prayer is prayer that uses the idiom of the Hebrew Bible and reflects the Jewish soul. It is prayer that expresses the basic values of the Jewish people and affirms the central articles of the Jewish faith. It is prayer that reflects our historical experience and gives expression to our future aspirations. When the prayer of a Jewish person does not reflect one of these components, he may be praying, but it cannot be said that he is praying as a Jew.[2]

The vast majority of Jewish prayer, therefore, is praying the language of the Bible — word for word.

A number of years ago I spent five weeks walking through Israel with three friends. At the monastery in Latrun we observed the evening prayers of the French-speaking monks. They simply prayed from the Psalms. So for the next year I prayed five psalms in the morning, five at noon, and five in the evening, which meant that every ten days I read (actually prayed) through the entire book of Psalms. Most Christians read the Psalms for personal instruction and guidance, but from a Jewish point of view, they are *prayers*.

I found that praying the Psalms for an entire year was a moving experience. These ancient prayers are thousands of years old. I was praying words that people of faith have prayed over and over since they were written. I did not use the Psalms as a beginning point for my own prayers. I didn't interpret their meaning. I simply prayed them.

"Attending synagogue services and praying are often thought of as one and the same. It is assumed that the person who does one also does the other."[3] The synagogue service is primarily a prayer service, at the core of which is the Amida, one of the prayers that Rabbi David had mentioned to me. The Amida is from the Hebrew word meaning "standing." Whether it is the morning service, the afternoon service, or the evening service—all the services include the Amida. It is a series of eighteen blessings that are divided into three categories: words of praise, petitions, and thanksgiving. All of these prayers are done while standing.

Here are the first three of the eighteen blessings:

First Blessing: Fathers

Blessed art Thou, O Lord, our God, and God of our fathers,
God of Abraham, God of Isaac, and God of Jacob,
The great, mighty, and awesome God,
Supreme God, who extends lovingkindness and is Master of all,
Who remembers the gracious deeds of our forefathers,
And who will bring a Redeemer with love to their children's
*   children for His name's sake,*
King, Helper, Savior and Protector. Blessed art Thou, O Lord,
*   Protector of Abraham.*

Second Blessing: Powers

Thy might is eternal, O Lord,
Who revives the dead,
Powerful in saving,

Who makes the wind to blow and the rain to fall,
Who sustains the living with lovingkindness,
Who revives the dead with great mercy,
Who supports the falling, heals the sick, frees the captive,
And keeps faith with the dead;
Who is like Thee, Almighty, and who resembles Thee,
O King who can bring death and give life,
And can make salvation blossom forth.
And faithful art Thou to revive the dead.
Blessed art Thou, O Lord, who makes the dead live.

Third Blessing: The Holiness of God.

Thou art holy, and Thy name is holy,
And those who are holy shall praise Thee every day.
Blessed art Thou, O Lord, the holy God.

These prayers are central to the synagogue service and Jewish prayer. All of these prayers are based on the words of the Hebrew Scriptures. When you pray these prayers, you are literally praying the Bible.

In Northern Ireland, where I grew up, we were part of the non-conformist church movement, which meant that we were against all forms of liturgy. Invocations, benedictions, and even praying the Lord's Prayer were all foreign to our experience. We believed that prayer ought to be free-flowing—flowing along with the Holy Spirit who guided the prayers. We were taught that formal liturgical prayers were "vain repetitions" (Matthew 6:7 KJV). As I listened to these free-flowing prayers, of course, I soon realized that most people generally said the same thing over and over again. Even though we were against liturgical prayers, our free-flowing prayers ended up being pretty liturgical themselves.

Still, for me, praying ancient Jewish prayers was a new experience. I have prayed the Amida on numerous occasions in the synagogue and in private and have found a compelling power in actually praying in the words of Scripture. When I pray in the free-flowing manner, I often find myself distracted by my concern for what I'm about to say, always thinking ahead to the next request or thanksgiving.

But when I pray the words of Scripture, I relax and let the prayers speak for themselves.

Day five. This morning I drove to the Catholic Church for the 8:00 a.m. public praying of the rosary. I was looking forward to praying the rosary with a group of people. Last night I kept waking up thinking about it. Usually I don't wake up at night unless I'm preaching the next day and my sermon keeps going through my brain, but last night I was excited about the rosary.

The service took place in the chapel, which seats about a hundred people. The outside wall is composed completely of beautiful blue stained glass. Around the chapel are several paintings of the Virgin Mary and the baby Jesus, and behind the altar is a huge life-size statue of Jesus with his arms pointing toward the congregation, showing the nail prints in his hands. Of course, he didn't look Jewish. He actually looked Irish. Next to the statue of Jesus is a large crucifix on the wall. I arrived about ten minutes early and sat alone in the chapel until 8:00.

Finally three other people arrived. The receptionist who had originally given me the booklets about the rosary was there to lead the prayers. She had gray disheveled hair, was a bit plump and short. An elderly couple were there as well. They looked like they were from Eastern Europe and had thick accents when they prayed. The woman led the prayers from the front row; I sat in the back row, left side; and the Eastern European couple sat on the far right side of the church. Though chapel was not large, it seemed bizarre for all of us to be sitting so far apart.

Although I had prayed the rosary a number of times already, the way the group did it was different. The woman would lead: "Hail Mary, full of grace. The Lord is with thee. Blessed art thou among women, and blessed is the fruit of thy womb, Jesus." Then the rest of us would join in, "Holy Mary, Mother of God, pray for us sinners, now and at the hour of our death." So one person would lead and then we would all join in together. This was also the way they did the Lord's Prayer and the Glory Be.

When we came to the fifth and final meditation, the woman who was leading turned to me and said, "Would you like to lead?"

I wanted to say, "No, I'm not Catholic!" but I didn't. Instead, I said, "Sure!" Now I usually don't get nervous in a church setting, having preached hundreds upon hundreds of sermons to thousands of people. This morning, I was really nervous.

I immediately began with "Hail Mary, full of grace. Our Lord is with thee—"

She interrupted, "You begin with the Lord's Prayer ..."

Of course I knew that, but I'd forgotten. So I began with the Lord's Prayer.

As I led the ten Hail Marys I kept looking at the statue of Jesus—the one behind the altar with his arms stretched toward the congregation. Then something really strange happened. It was as if the statue became alive, as if I'd been shifted into a completely different dimension. Maybe I was concentrating too hard on getting the words right. Maybe it was the peculiar lighting in the chapel. Maybe it was the sun coming through the stained-glass windows. I don't know. All I know is that for a few brief moments the statue of Jesus seemed to be alive. For the first time in my journey of trying to live like Jesus, I felt as though Jesus himself was present and in the chapel—and in a Roman Catholic chapel of all places.

Not quite what I'd expected.

After praying the rosary, they celebrated Mass, but I didn't stay.

I only came to pray with the others—but did I really pray? I'd said the Lord's Prayer. I read words from the Scriptures. But was that prayer? What about all the repetitions of the Hail Marys? What good was that? Why was it necessary to repeat it over and over? Didn't God get it the first time?

I'm still not sure about praying the rosary. Maybe my Protestant friends are right and it really isn't praying. Still, there was that strange moment when Jesus seemed alive. So I intend to keep trying and see how it goes.

Judge for yourselves: Is it proper for a woman to pray to God with her head uncovered? Does not the very nature of things teach you that if a man has long hair, it is a disgrace to him, but that if a woman has long hair, it is her glory?

1 Corinthians 11:13–15

Day nine. Almost every painting I've ever seen of Jesus shows him with long hair, a beard, and a European face. But did Jesus really have long hair? Probably not. It was only the sides of his hair that the Torah wouldn't let him cut. Did he have a beard? Absolutely. Did he look like a European? Not at all.

Not everyone in biblical times grew their hair long. In the book of Ezekiel, there are specific instructions for the prince, the Levites, and the priests: "They must not shave their heads or let their hair grow long, but they are to keep the hair of their heads trimmed" (Ezekiel 44:20). It appears that they were to avoid the extremes—either shaving their head completely or letting their hair grow long.

Paul takes up the same idea in his letter to the church at Corinth. His instructions are part of a larger narrative dealing with propriety in Christian worship, and what he says has been controversial ever since. He begins by reminding everyone that

God is the "head" of Christ, Christ is the "head" of man, and man is the "head" of the woman. And so what does he mean by "head"? Some suggest that he is speaking of the idea of honor. The woman is to honor the man, the man is to honor Christ, and Christ is to honor God. Others interpret the word "head" to mean authority. According to these interpretations, the husband is the head of (has authority over) the wife. And Christ is the head of (has authority over) the husband. And God is the head of (has authority over) Christ.

Paul argues that when a man prays or teaches with his head covered, he "dishonors his head," but when a woman prays or teaches with her head uncovered, she "dishonors her head." According to the NIV footnote, "For a woman, taking off her head covering in public and exposing her hair was a sign of loose morals and sexual promiscuity. Paul says that she might as well have her hair cut or shaved off." During the first century, if a woman had her head shaved it was a sign of disgrace. Paul is also arguing that to pray or prophesy with your head uncovered was either a sign of sexual promiscuity or complete and total independence from her husband.

In the church in Northern Ireland where I grew up all of the women wore hats to church. It was considered a sign of submission to their husbands and was done in obedience to Paul's instructions in this passage. As I sat there watching the women coming into church I realized that we were in the midst of a "hat war" — each woman trying to outdo the others in terms of hats.

The church I served in Grand Rapids, of course, did not practice this. Some in the church believed that a woman's long hair was her covering, which made any sort of hat unnecessary. Others believed that Paul's instructions were culturally based—a specific teaching for a problem inherent to the church at Corinth. Consequently, admonitions about head coverings were not binding on believers in the twenty-first century.

Paul goes on to talk about the interdependence of men and women (husbands and wives) and raises a series of questions, such as: "Does not the very nature of things teach you that if a man has long hair, it is a disgrace to him, but that if a woman has long hair, it is her glory?" So how long is "long"? The Greek word, which is used only in this particular passage, means "to let one's hair grow long," but it doesn't specify how long. The only hint we get from the text is in comparing a man's hair to a woman's hair. A woman's hair should be long; a man's hair, by comparison, should not.

Since my wife's hair is curly and she has worn it short for years, my goal now is to make sure my hair is shorter than hers. Perhaps this whole question seems utterly ridiculous to you. "Wear your hair any way you want!" But in trying to live like Jesus, the best I can come up with is that I should wear my hair shorter than my wife's.

So even though I won't cut my beard, which is actually looking pretty good right now, I *will* cut my hair.

Day twelve. I prayed the rosary again today. During the Reformation, I learned, Martin Luther advocated the continued use of the rosary, but he refused to add the phrase "Holy Mary, Mother of God, pray for us sinners now and at the hour of our death. Amen." Maybe I should do the same. Maybe I should substitute that phrase with "Holy Jesus, Son of God, pray for us sinners, now and at the hour of our death. Amen." Maybe I should talk to a Catholic priest about my struggles. I will admit, however, that there is something powerful about the repetition. It helps me stay focused. And I really enjoy the meditations on the life of Jesus.

Day fourteen. Today I talked to Father Robert, a Catholic priest. He's an engaging and articulate man, one of those guys who looks impressive in a clerical collar. He runs the Acton Institute, a conservative think tank here in Grand Rapids. One of their basic beliefs is that creating wealth is the best way to help the poor.

In college, Father Robert had a born-again experience through an evangelical campus group. After college, he took part in the gay rights movement, the feminist movement, and the socialist movement. Through a series of circumstances he ended up coming back to God through the Catholic Church and then went on to study for the priesthood. So I figured he was a good person to talk to since he understands both evangelicals and Catholics.

"I have been praying the rosary," I said.

"That's wonderful," he said.

"Well, I'm not sure," I replied. "I really struggle with the idea of praying to Mary. I've always believed that you prayed to God, in the name of Jesus and empowered by the Holy Spirit. Sometimes I am okay with praying to Mary, but most of the time it troubles me."

"Maybe at this point in your journey you should focus on praying *with* Mary instead of *to* Mary. One of the mysteries that you meditate on is the coming of the Holy Spirit at Pentecost. We know that Mary was part of that prayer meeting, and when you pray to her it is much more like you are praying with her. After all, the purpose of Mary is to simply introduce you to Jesus. He is the one through whom our prayers are answered."

His advice seemed helpful. Now when I pray, "Holy Mary, Mother of God, pray for us sinners now and at the hour of our death. Amen," I will try to focus on praying *with* Mary, not *to* her. So I got down the rosary today and prayed. Praying *with* Mary didn't trouble me at all.

> I was a stranger and you invited me in.
>
> **Matthew 25:35**

Day eighteen. This quotation is from the parable that Jesus tells about sheep and goats. It's a story about judgment. The sheep enter eternal life, but the goats go away to eternal punishment. The sheep are those who fed the hungry, gave the thirsty something to drink, took in strangers, clothed the naked, looked after the sick, and visited people in prison. Of course, when the sheep ask, "When did we do all of these things?" the King replies, "I tell you the truth, whatever you did for one of the least of these brothers of mine, you did for me" (Matthew 25:40).

This is one of the most disturbing stories in all of the Gospels. What separates the sheep from the goats? It's not what they *believe*, but rather it's what they *do*! Sheep do the following:

> They feed the hungry.
>
> They give the thirsty something to drink.
>
> They take in strangers.
>
> They clothe the naked.
>
> They look after the sick.
>
> They visit people in prison.

I was a stranger and you invited me in. So how do I do that? How do I take in strangers? One of the ways I intend to do this is by picking up hitchhikers (strangers) and taking them wherever they want to go.

So today I'm driving down the road in the middle of a Michigan winter. It's cold. It's snowing. It's blowing and drifting. It's a mess! It's so bad that even the sidewalks in our neighborhood aren't shoveled. I turn the corner near our house, and there, walking down the middle of the road, is a large African American man, probably 6'7" and weighing close to three hundred pounds. He's all bundled up with a ski cap and sunglasses.

68

I stop the car and ask, "Dude, you need a ride?"

He gets in. Before I even speak, he says, "You're a little white guy. What are you doing picking up a big black guy like me? I look mean. I could hurt you."

At this point I'm not sure I should've picked him up. But it's too late. So what should I say? For a moment I thought of saying, "I'm trying to live like Jesus, and Jesus says you are to invite strangers in. So I'm just trying to obey Jesus' teaching."

Instead, I say, "It's cold, snowing, and windy. You just looked like you needed a ride. So I picked you up."

"Thanks. I really appreciate it. I been walking for about a mile and I'm nearly frozen."

"Where'd you like to go?" I ask. I'm really hoping that he doesn't say Detroit or Chicago, since I've already decided to take my stranger wherever he wants to go.

"Just a few blocks," he says.

I heave a sigh of relief.

After dropping him off, I head back to my house and turn onto the street where we live. Three young African American teenagers are walking down the middle of the street. So again I stop the car and ask, "You guys need a ride?" I can tell they're really hesitant about getting in—I'm not sure they trust "a little white guy." But it's cold. The snow is blowing and drifting. So they get in. All three sit in the backseat.

"Where'd you like to go?" I ask.

"About six blocks from here," one of them says.

After a few blocks they relax a little and another one says, "When you stopped your truck and rolled down the window, we thought you were going to cuss us out for walking down the middle of the street."

Again I'm tempted to tell them, "Jesus says we are to invite strangers in. So I'm just trying to obey his teaching."

But I don't say a word.

Do not forget to entertain strangers, for by so doing some
people have entertained angels without knowing it.

Hebrews 13:2

Could the big black guy and the three black teenagers have
been angels? Even though we all live in the same neighborhood,
I've never seen them again.

Years ago I went with three friends to Israel for five weeks.
We walked everywhere. The first night we stayed in Jaffa, which
is just south of Tel Aviv. The next morning we got up early, went
down to the Mediterranean, dipped our boots in the sea, and
began the long walk up to Jerusalem. We had decided to stay
overnight at Latrun. Three of us were pastors, and the fourth
friend taught photography at Harvard.

It was a long, brutal, and demanding day. We walked seventeen miles with full packs, and the heat was horrible—it was the
end of May. David, who taught at Harvard, had arranged for us to
stay at a Catholic monastery at Latrun. A friend of his in Boston
knew someone at the monastery and had arranged for us to stay
there.

When we finally arrived, none of the monks spoke English,
only French. A young Arab who was visiting spoke a little English
and also French, so we talked to the monks through him.

We soon discovered that the monk who knew our friend in
Boston was in Lebanon, and he had not told anybody that we
were coming. So we sat on the porch for several hours of negotia-
tions, back and forth.

Finally one of the pastors in our group told the young Arab,
"Look! We are three Protestant ministers and a photographer, and
we're supposed to stay here!" I trembled inside. I was going to say
that I was a Notre Dame football fan. I thought that maybe if I
showed some Catholic connection we could stay there. But no!
Our jig was up.

But eventually they let us stay. The monastery sits on top of a hill where you can see almost all the way to the Mediterranean. The gardens next to the monastery were stunning—the colors of the flowers. It is a quiet, peaceful place, almost like another world. We stayed in lovely rooms, ate dinner and breakfast, and the monks refused to take any money. At dinner that night was another American, a Catholic working in Lebanon who had come to the monastery for a week of rest and relaxation.

Several weeks later we were up in Nazareth when we bumped into the same American we'd met at the monastery. "I'm so glad to see you again," he said. "You made quite an impression with the monks at Latrun. They thought you were angels! They figured that if God was going to test their generosity, he would send them three Protestant ministers who claimed to have walked all the way from the Mediterranean Sea up to Latrun. So they took care of you and refused to take your money—because they thought you were angels."

I guess it doesn't really matter whether the four guys I picked up were angels or not. What matters is that I tried to follow the teaching of Jesus.

Day twenty. I've been looking up information about the rosary on the Internet. In the process, I came across the Orthodox prayer rope and the Anglican prayer beads. So I decided to stop by the Orthodox church and find out what the prayer rope is all about.

Father Dan is an Orthodox priest and my friend. He began his spiritual pilgrimage as a Roman Catholic priest assigned to a remote part of Africa. During his experience there he became very lonely, as well as concerned about the post-Vatican church, so eventually he resigned as a Catholic priest, got married, and then became an Orthodox priest.

Dan is personable, engaging, and loves to talk. I first met Father Dan when I went by the church one day, and as I walked in, he was walking out. He immediately recognized me as former pastor of Calvary Church and invited me to tour the building with him.

He explained to me that the primary focus of the Orthodox Church is on the incarnation of Jesus. As we walked around the church he pointed out the various icons and their significance. He talked so fast and was so excited about his Orthodox theology that it left me in a bit of a blur. Before I left, he took me to the bookstore and gave me a book entitled *The Way of the Pilgrim*, which is about a nameless pilgrim who wanders all over Europe repeating the Jesus Prayer: "Lord Jesus Christ, son of God, have mercy on me, a sinner." I also asked the priest if he would order me an Orthodox prayer rope, which he agreed to do.

Day twenty-one. I continue to wear the T-shirts with tassels. I have to admit that part of me thinks it's ridiculous. It's supposed to remind me of God's commands, but once I've tucked the tassels in my pants, I completely forget about them. They don't really remind me of much of anything. But since Jesus wore tassels on his garment, I need to do the same.

Today I came across this story about the tassels:

> A man hears of an exceptionally beautiful and expensive harlot in a far-off land. He sends the payment required to sleep with her, then journeys to meet the woman. When he sees the harlot, he is overwhelmed by her beauty, but when he starts to undress, the fringes fly up in the air and slap him across the face. Realizing [how much money] is going to a prostitute, the young man sits down on the floor.... The prostitute comes down

72

from her bed, sits down opposite him and queries him as to the fault he had seen in her that caused him to turn away. The young man assures her that he finds her beautiful, but explains to her about the *tzitzit*. Amazed and impressed by the power of this ritual to overcome sexual lusts, the prostitute follows the young man back to Jerusalem, where she converts to Judaism and marries him.[4]

So maybe there's more power in the tassels than I imagined.

Tonight was Shabbat, and Lorna and I decided to observe it more strictly, more in the true spirit of Shabbat. We lit the Shabbat candles and did the Hebrew blessing for the wine and bread. Yes, it was real wine! I decided that I would not pick up a pencil and write. I would not type on the computer. I would not listen to the iPod. I would not turn on the television. I would not turn the light on or off. I would not listen to the radio. I would not turn the stove on or off. I would not use the microwave. We would rest.

After we ate dinner we played a game. Now generally I hate games. But tonight Lorna and I played bingo. (I argue that since the Catholic Church allows bingo, I'm being true to my exploration of Catholic theology.) Of course, since you can't pick up a pencil to write, you can't keep score. So we played without caring who won.

Which felt weird to me because when I play a game I want to *win*.

But on Shabbat, winning is not the issue.

(Later, Rabbi David explained to me a method by which you can keep score. You take a piece of paper and put it in a book next to the number that represents your score. Picking up a book and pieces of paper is okay. Opening a book is okay. So you're not violating the Sabbath.)

After the game, I read the Bible, which is completely appropriate on Shabbat. I could not underline any of the phrases or take notes, however. This would have been a violation of Shabbat.

About nine o'clock in the evening, I needed to go to the bathroom. It was dark. So what do I do? Do I turn on the light and violate Shabbat or do I go to the bathroom in the dark?

On Shabbat, I go to the bathroom in the dark.

> When he heard that it was Jesus of Nazareth, he began to shout, "Jesus, Son of David, have mercy on me!"
> Many rebuked him and told him to be quiet, but he shouted all the more, "Son of David, have mercy on me!"
> **Mark 10:47–48**

Day twenty-four. Jesus passes through the city of Jericho on his way to Jerusalem. He has already told his disciples that when he gets there, he will be betrayed, arrested, and killed. Of course, this goes over the heads of the disciples. As he passes the city a blind man named Bartimaeus is sitting along the side of the road, begging for a living. He hears that Jesus is passing by so he cries out, "Jesus, son of David, have mercy on me!" Jesus stops and calls the blind man to him. "What do you want me to do for you?" The blind man answers, "Rabbi, I want to see." Jesus tells him to go, that his faith has healed him. He is instantly healed and he follows Jesus along the road.

I've always had trouble knowing what to pray in regard to my ALS. I have a degenerative, incurable, and terminal disease. It's only a matter of time. So how do I pray? On the one hand, some people tell me to pray in faith and if my faith is strong enough, then God will heal me. On the other hand, other people pray for healing but always temper their prayers with the statement "according to God's will." I've never been comfortable with either kind of prayer.

As I read the Gospels over and over it occurs to me that the blind man did not initially ask for healing. He simply says, "Jesus, son of David, have mercy on me!" He threw himself on the mercy of Jesus and ultimately on the mercy of God. I realize that this is something I can pray for myself and for others who are seriously ill. "Jesus, son of David, have mercy on me!"

It's interesting that the blind man describes Jesus as "the son of David." It's a messianic title for the Jews, but the blind man's use of this title may be much deeper than simply acknowledging that Jesus is the Messiah.

The first king of Israel was Saul. He had trouble from time to time with an evil spirit, but "whenever the spirit from God came upon Saul, David would take his harp and play. Then relief would come to Saul; he would feel better, and the evil spirit would leave him" (1 Samuel 16:23). In the ancient world in which Jesus lived, many people believed that sickness was the result of demonic influence. So when Saul was deeply troubled by the evil spirit, David played the harp, calmed his spirit, and Saul felt better. David demonstrated a power over evil spirits. So perhaps the blind man in declaring that Jesus is the son of David is calling upon the one who has power over demonic influences—including sickness and blindness.

One of my closest friends in ministry is Ed Hindson. We've written several books together, including The Jesus Study Bible. We taught together at Liberty University many years ago and have remained close friends ever since. We have walked together through some of the most difficult circumstances of life. He has been a constant encouragement to me, and I hope I've been a constant encouragement to him.

He called me a few weeks ago to tell me he was having open-heart surgery. "It's really no big deal," he said. "They'll do several bypasses, and a few weeks later I'll be back on my feet."

Shortly after the surgery I received word that Ed had contracted a staph infection in the hospital. His kidneys began to shut down, and the doctors immediately put him on a ventilator. He was close to death. His wife told me that they were going to anoint him with oil (a New Testament tradition), and she asked me if I'd be willing to be part of that event.

So I got on a plane for Lynchburg, Virginia. The entire way there I prayed the prayer of the blind man, but I changed the name: "Jesus, son of David, have mercy on Ed."

In Lynchburg, I went to the hospital, and as soon as I walked into the room, I realized that Ed was in worse shape than I had anticipated. He was dying.

"Hi, Ed," I said. "It's me, the other Ed."

He looked up, opened his eyes, and smiled. I think he recognized me.

A number of ministry friends gathered that afternoon for the anointing. I anointed him on the forehead with the sign of the cross. Then we prayed. We quoted promises from the Bible about healing. It only lasted about ten minutes. After the anointing, he raised his arms toward us. We thought that he was deeply moved by the anointing and wanted to say something. He kept moving his arms. Finally his son-in-law said, "I think he wants us to move away from the fan so he can feel the air."

So we moved. Ed felt the air and smiled.

In my car on the way to the hotel, I prayed for him again: "Jesus, son of David, have mercy on Ed." That evening, alone in my room, I prayed for him again.

My flight back to Grand Rapids had a layover in Atlanta, where the weather was so bad that my next flight was delayed. While waiting, I went to the bar and had a beer. Eventually, after midnight, my flight left for Grand Rapids, but about thirty minutes into the flight, the captain came on the intercom: "We're having some difficulties with the air-conditioning system, so we're going to turn around and go back to Atlanta."

All of a sudden everything got quiet. I am thinking, *the air-conditioning system? Who are you kidding?* We must have had serious problems with the plane or we wouldn't have been turning around. I think everyone else was thinking the same thing.

The woman next to me reached into her purse and took out a rosary. She began stroking the crucifix.

"That a rosary?" I asked.

"Yes, it is. I figured I better get that out since we're having problems on the flight."

"Good idea. But you know that one of the prayers is 'Holy Mary, Mother of God, pray for us sinners now and at the hour of our death.' You sure you want to pray that?"

"Oh sh—!" she said. "Maybe I ought to put it away."

"No, I think you ought to keep it in your hands," I said.

Gradually, over the next several months, Ed's health improved. He's back at Liberty University, teaching his classes. He's a living, breathing miracle.

April

Day two. Back in Florida. I continue to wrestle with the idea of prayer. I'm reading *The Way of the Pilgrim*, a wonderful book. The main character has set out to discover what it means to "pray without ceasing," so he visits various monasteries and talks to priests, but their advice doesn't help. Finally he discovers the "Jesus Prayer": "Lord Jesus Christ, son of God, have mercy on me, a sinner," and he sets off on a journey all over Russia praying this prayer. He describes himself this way: "By the grace of God I am a Christian, by my deeds a great sinner, and by my calling a homeless wanderer of humblest origin, roaming from place to place. My possessions consist of a knapsack with dry crusts of bread on my back and in my bosom the holy Bible. That is all!"[1]

Initially he began praying the Jesus Prayer six thousand times a day. Then his spiritual elder encouraged him to do it twelve thousand times a day. After the first day he wrote:

> At first I felt tired from reciting the prayer constantly; my tongue seemed numb and my throat was tight. There was both a pleasant sensation and a slight pain in the roof of my mouth. My left thumb, with which I counted the beads, was sore, and there was an inflammation in my wrist extending to the elbow which produced a pleasant sensation. All this seems to attract and compel me to greater accomplishment, and I spent five days faithfully reciting twelve thousand prayers today, experiencing both joy and longing for the prayer.[2]

As he travels he writes,

> When the cold air chills me, I begin saying the prayer with greater intensity and I warm up. When hunger

begins to overcome me, I begin saying the name of Jesus Christ more frequently.... When I become sick and feel rheumatic pain in my back and legs, I pay greater attention to the prayer and I do not feel the pain. When someone offends me, I remember how sweet the Jesus prayer is and the offense and anger disappear and I forget everything. I walked in a semiconscious state without worries, interests, and temptations.[3]

So I will add the Jesus Prayer to my daily routine. Once I get the prayer rope, I'll try to pray through it at least twice a day. That will mean saying the prayer two hundred times. That's not quite six thousand—or twelve thousand—but it's a beginning. Father Dan says that it's much better to pray the prayer rope only once or twice with meaning than to attempt to repeat it for the sake of repetition.

Day three. Read through most of the gospel of Matthew today and was struck by how often Jesus refers to the heart. He says that people honor God with their lips but their hearts are far from him. He says that out of the heart come evil thoughts, murder, adultery, sexual immorality, theft, false testimony, and slander (Matthew 15), and he also says that "every careless word will be judged," and by our words we will either be acquitted or condemned. This is serious stuff.

I finished *The Way of the Pilgrim*. I've been trying to say the prayer more often during the day. I don't know if it's just a mantra, but I find that it helps me keep my mind focused on God—and when I'm focused on God, the words I speak don't seem as careless or idle. I need to be more careful with my use of words, so I will ask God, through the Holy Spirit, to help me control my tongue so that I do not use careless words.

When you give a banquet, invite the poor, the crippled, the lame, the blind, and you will be blessed.

Luke 14:13

Day nine. On the flight back from Florida I finished listening to the Gospels. I realized, when I arrived in Grand Rapids, that I hadn't communicated well with Lorna. She thought I was getting in at 9:00 p.m. when I actually arrived at 5:00 p.m. So I called her to pick me up.

As I waited in the airport, I noticed, seated about fifteen feet away from me, a blind man. He was wearing dark glasses, and his clothes looked like he'd been wearing them for a while. He had a folded white cane. I wonder, does he live in Grand Rapids? If he does, then I should invite him to a banquet so I can obey the teaching of Jesus.

At that moment, he unfolded his cane, stood up, and said, "Can somebody help me, please?"

Immediately I jumped up. He told me that en route to Grand Rapids his flight had been canceled, so he was arriving later in Grand Rapids than he'd anticipated. He lived about twenty miles south of Grand Rapids, and the person who was supposed to pick him up hadn't arrived.

"I'd be happy to take you wherever you want to go," I said, but he declined, saying that the people who were supposed to pick him up would eventually come. But he asked me to take him to the information desk so his ride could be paged, just in case they were somewhere in the airport looking for him. I was more than glad to do it. It was a bit inconvenient for me to lead him around because I had to pull his suitcase as well, which was difficult for me because of my disease.

It was quite a Jesus moment: a guy with ALS leading a blind guy.

Day ten. Thursday, my first day back. I did not read from or listen to the Gospels—or even pray—today. Maybe I needed a break. I don't know. Still, I'm finding that the more I read and pray, the more I want to read and pray. The less I read and pray, the less I want to read and pray. It's peculiar.

Day eleven. Tonight we had a meal with the other two couples who live with us in community and some of their relatives. We lit two candles, broke the bread, drank the wine, and said the Jewish blessings for Shabbat. Then after the meal we sat around and talked and played a card game. The name of the game was BS (some call the game "I Doubt It!"). In the game you lay down your cards and try to lie and deceive others. We laughed about the fact that we were playing cards and deceiving each other on Shabbat. It was actually a very relaxing evening, and I'm beginning to enjoy Shabbat.

On Saturday morning, however, I had to videotape several teaching sessions for a television mission in India. So I really didn't observe a full Shabbat. In fact I have yet to observe an entire twenty-four-hour Shabbat.

Day twelve. I've been really busy. On Wednesday I flew back from Florida, and on Thursday, Friday, and Saturday I did more videotapes for the Indian television program. Several years ago a number of businessmen in our church got involved in helping a man in India who oversees about twenty thousand churches. Because he's extremely busy and broadcasts a daily religious program on television, he doesn't have time to study. So one of the men in our church took him some of my transcribed sermons. He began using them. Then he invited me to come to India, but my doctor vetoed the idea. So one of the businessmen came up with the idea that maybe he should come to the United States, and we could videotape something together. So we did. The programs we videotape are now on Indian television (we have taped about fifty programs).

This week it was not a wise thing to do, especially on Shabbat. After videotaping, I came home and slept for quite a while. I was exhausted.

The tax collector stood at a distance. He would not even look up to heaven, but beat his breast and said, "God, have mercy on me, a sinner."

Luke 18:13

Day fourteen. I received a prayer rope in the mail today from the Orthodox priest in Grand Rapids. I went on the Internet to discover meaningful ways to pray the Jesus Prayer. You are supposed to pray the prayer with your head bowed, and once you pray it through one time, you bow from the waist. When you get to the large beads, then you prostrate yourself on the ground. It was also recommended that you begin by having thirty minutes of total silence so that you can listen to God. I have to admit that I have really never taken time to be silent. Even though the Bible says, "Be still, and know that I am God."

The Orthodox prayer rope is made of wool and contains a hundred knots. It is divided into ten sections of ten knots each. After each section there is a bead. At the bottom of the prayer rope is a cross, and beneath the cross, a tassel. The purpose of the tassel is to catch our tears and wipe them away. As I pray the Jesus Prayer, I will breathe in on the first statement and breathe out on the second. I will pause between each prayer and do everything in an unhurried manner—which will be a challenge for me since I'm always in a hurry to get things done! In addition, I will bow at the waist after each prayer, reminding me of my submission to the Lord Jesus Christ. When I get to the large beads, I will prostrate myself on the ground. Again this is an act of submission to the Lord Jesus Christ.

Jesus tells a story about a Pharisee and a tax collector. In modern Christian circles, the Pharisees get a bad rap. For instance, whenever you play the hypocrite, you're accused of being a Pharisee. But in Jesus' day, the Pharisees were deeply respected. They had a serious commitment to living out all of the commands in the Torah. The word *Pharisee* means "a separatist"—they were separated to the Lord and to obedience to the Torah.

On the other hand, tax collectors were despised. They cooperated with the Roman government in collecting taxes, and they even charged extra tax as a way of paying their own salaries. Consequently, they became extremely rich by taking money from Jews. Tax collectors were therefore excluded from the religious community and became the most despised of all people in ancient Israel.

So, if you were listening to Jesus tell this story, you'd cheer when he mentioned the Pharisee, and you'd boo when he mentioned the tax collector. Both of them, says Jesus, go up to the Temple to pray—and at this point in the story you assume that God will hear the prayer of the Pharisee and not that of the tax collector.

But the opposite turns out to be true.

The Pharisee is grateful that he is not like other people— robbers, evildoers, adulterers. He avoids sin, fasts twice a week, and gives God a tenth of all he possesses—all wonderful qualities. As he sees the tax collector standing in the corner, the Pharisee is also grateful that he is *not* like the tax collector.

The tax collector, by contrast, simply beats his breast and says, "God, have mercy on me, a sinner." Jesus concludes the story by saying that the tax collector went home justified—but not the Pharisee. Then he adds, "For everyone who exalts himself will be humbled, and he who humbles himself will be exalted."

Several years ago I had the privilege of introducing Martin Luther King III at the annual black-history-month celebration in Grand Rapids. I arrived early. As I walked down the hall to the bathroom, a "brother" was walking toward me. He wore huge baggy pants, not quite pulled up all the way. He had long dreadlocks and walked slowly up the hall. I thought that maybe he was a drug dealer. When he got to me he stopped and said, "Dude, I watch you on TV every week. I love your sermons!"

Was I ever wrong! He was more than a "brother." He was a "brother in the Lord."

> *God, please forgive me for thinking I have the inside track on truth.*
> *God, please forgive me for thinking that I am better than others.*
> *God, please remind me that at best I am still a sinner.*

"Lord Jesus Christ, son of God, have mercy on me, a sinner." As you probably noticed, the Jesus Prayer comes directly from Jesus' story of the tax collector. As you say the prayer on the prayer rope, you are supposed to breathe in slowly as you repeat the words "Lord Jesus Christ, son of God." Then you breathe out slowly as you say "have mercy on me, a sinner." The idea is to get the rhythms of your body, your breathing, and your heart rate in rhythm with the act of praying.

When Jesus was with his disciples in the upper room the night before he was crucified, he told them, "Until now you have not asked for anything in my name. Ask and you will receive, and your joy will be complete" (John 16:24). Earlier in this conversation he had also told them, "You may ask me for anything in my name, and I will do it" (John 14:14). I had always understood these texts to mean that when you pray, you should always pray in the name of Jesus.

On many occasions I've been asked to pray at public or political events where many different kinds of religious and nonreligious people attend. At these events people prefer you *not* pray in the name of Jesus. After all, the name of Jesus is offensive to some. Still, I always pray in the name of Jesus. I feel that to do less would be tantamount to being ashamed of Jesus.

Is "in the name of Jesus" a magical incantation? Does it guarantee that God will answer our prayers? I don't think so. Then what does it mean to pray "in the name of Jesus"? It means that we are praying in the merits of Jesus. It means that we are praying in the power of Jesus. It is the recognition of our own helplessness when we pray. It is the recognition that for prayer to be effective we must pray in his name. It is a reminder that our dependence is not on churches or theologies, but on Jesus!

Day fifteen. I've been noticing the various prayers that occur in the Gospels. I still find it difficult to pray for healing from my ALS. As I reflected on some of the prayers, I came up with the following prayer.

A Prayer for ALS

Jesus, son of David, have mercy on me. [This was the prayer prayed by the blind man when he cried out for Jesus to heal him from his blindness.]

Lord I believe, help my unbelief. [This is the prayer of the father to whom Jesus said, "If you believe, it is possible to heal your daughter."]

Abba Father, everything is possible for you. Take this cup from me. Yet not what I will but what you will. [The prayer of Jesus in the garden.]

The above prayer gives me great encouragement. It's okay to ask Jesus to heal me. It's okay to have unbelief and ask him to help my unbelief. It's okay to ask that the cup be taken from me. But ultimately it's God's will that must be accomplished.

In addition to the prayer rope, the Orthodox Church also has bracelets that can be worn on the wrist that are made of wool and tied in knots. You can pray the Jesus Prayer by working your way around the bracelet. Maybe I can get a bracelet or two and use them to pray this prayer.

Day sixteen. I began today by setting aside fifteen minutes to silently listen to God. It was a nightmare! My mind wandered constantly. So whenever my mind wandered, I quoted the verse, "Be still and know that I am God." Halfway through, Lorna's cell phone rang. So I ran to answer it. As I sat there in silence, I wondered how in the world God was going to talk to me. Would he speak with an audible voice? Hardly! Would he bring things to my mind that he wanted to emphasize? I don't know. It was really strange trying to be silent and not letting my mind wander.

Whenever I read about silence, it sounds really impressive. But actually trying to be silent was a disaster. The lesson: keep trying until you get it. Of course, I'm not sure if I would really know whether I had gotten it or not.

I prayed using the Orthodox prayer rope today. I prayed the Jesus Prayer using each of the knots, and after I prayed it each time, I bowed from the waist. When I got to the beads, I prayed the prayer of the blind man from Jericho: "Jesus, son of David, have mercy on me." I then added my prayer for ALS.

I enjoyed the time I spent in focused prayer. I like the idea of asking God to have mercy on me. Today I listened to the passage from Luke describing the birth of John the Baptist. Since his parents were older, it was not at all sure that they could have children—but when John was born, the people around them said, "God had great mercy on them." So I now have a prayer to pray for my daughter and son-in-law, Heather and David, who have been trying for more than a year to have a child: "God, have mercy on David and Heather."

Actually, I should pray "Have *great* mercy" on them.

Day seventeen. I spent today at the Miami boat show with a group of friends. Since we left early in the morning and returned in the late afternoon, I did not listen to or read from the Gospels, and I didn't pray. We ate lunch at a wonderful buffet that had great-looking sandwiches, but every sandwich had meat and cheese on it. I was very tempted to eat the sandwich anyway but then I realized that I had to try and eat kosher. So I ate some rice, a salad, and cheese. It actually felt good to decline something I really wanted to eat.

Day eighteen. This morning I used the Orthodox prayer rope as I sat on the enclosed porch of our condo. The windows were open, I could feel a gentle breeze, and a palm tree right outside the window provided shade.

During the first section, I prayed the Jesus Prayer: "Lord Jesus Christ, son of God [I breathed in] have mercy on me a sinner [I breathed out]." When I got to the main bead, I prayed, "Jesus, son of David, have mercy on me." I pray this prayer as a prayer of personal healing.

On the second set of knots I prayed, "Lord Jesus Christ, have mercy on David and Heather."

Lorna and I are sitting at lunch together when the phone rings. It's Heather. She tells us that she's pregnant. I'm overwhelmed and begin to cry. So does Lorna.

Then I tell Heather about the prayer I've been praying for them, which I've only been praying for a few days! But even as I prayed the prayer, the answer was on the way. I sure wish all my prayers were like that!

> Obey these instructions as a lasting ordinance for you and your descendents. When you enter the land that the LORD will give you as he promised, observe this ceremony. And when your children ask you, "What does this ceremony mean to you?" then tell them, "It is the Passover sacrifice to the LORD, who passed over the houses of the Israelites in Egypt and spared our homes when he struck down the Egyptians."
>
> **Exodus 12:24–27**

April 20, Passover — Pesach. When the children of Israel were slaves in Egypt, God sent ten plagues so that Pharaoh would ultimately let the Israelites go. The plagues included everything from gnats to boils and were intended to soften the hearts of the Egyptians toward the idea of letting the Israelites leave to worship in the desert. The last plague was the most severe. To avoid it, Moses told the Israelites to take a lamb, kill it, and then sprinkle the blood on the doorposts of their houses.

That same evening they were to eat the Passover meal. "This is how you are to eat it: with your cloak tucked into your belt, your sandals on your feet and your staff in your hand. Eat it in haste; it is the LORD's Passover" (Exodus 12:11). During that night, the angel of death passed through all of the land of Egypt and struck down the firstborn of each household where the blood was not applied to the doorposts. God told them that they were to celebrate this feast for generations to come. In fact, it was to be a "lasting ordinance."

The exodus from Egypt becomes one of the most incredible events in Jewish history, the defining moment for the Jewish people. The only thing that will replace it is the coming of the Messiah.

> "However, the days are coming," declares the LORD, "when men will no longer say, 'As surely as the LORD lives, who brought the Israelites up out of Egypt,' but they will say, 'As surely as the LORD lives, who brought the Israelites up out of the land of the North and out of all the countries where he had banished them.' For I will restore them to the land I gave their forefathers."
>
> **Jeremiah 16:14–15**

The prophet Jeremiah is stating that for the Israelites, the day will come when their defining moment will no longer be the exodus, but rather it will be when all the people are gathered back to the land; that is, when the Messiah comes, *he* will be the central motif of Jewish history. What's interesting to me is that, from a Christian perspective, Jesus uses the Passover to inaugurate a new ceremony—a ceremony that commemorates his death, burial, and resurrection. He uses the bread to speak of his body, and he uses the wine to speak of his blood—shed for the forgiveness of sins.

I have decided that since Jesus ate the Passover meal with his disciples, I should eat the Passover meal with Jewish friends. So I made arrangements to join about 150 Jews in the Passover meal at the community in Florida. Passover begins on Sunday night, April 20, 2008.

A large rectangular table stands in the middle of the room where the leaders will lead us in the Passover meal. Around are other tables, circular and seating eight to ten people each. I arrive dressed in a suit and a tie. I take along my *kippah*—a head covering required of all male Jews. The idea of the kippah, according to some, is that we must have a covering between humans and God. We do not know, however, whether Jesus wore a head covering.

I sit at one of the smaller tables with ten others. I think I'm the only Gentile in the room. Before the meal, we make small talk, part of which is identifying where we were born and reared. Finally it's my turn. I say, "I was born and reared in Ireland—"

But before I can continue, the woman next to me bursts in, "You're the second Irish person I've met who's Jewish!"

I wonder, should I let it go? No, I need to tell the truth.

"Actually, I'm not Jewish," I say.

So the jig is up. I'm not one of them. I'm an outsider, a guest, a Gentile.

As we continue to talk I ask one of the men at the table how he manages to live as a Jew in a place like this where everything, apart from the fish, is nonkosher. "How do you deal with all the lobster and shrimp here?" I ask.

"Oh, I don't pay any attention to that at all," he says. "I eat whatever I want whenever I want to."

So the thought crosses my mind, "I'm a better Jew than he is!" but I know it's not true. I'm not a Jew at all—and he is a Jew whether he eats kosher or not. After I got over my momentary feelings of superiority, I realize that all of us pick and choose. While this Jewish man chose not to eat kosher, most of us who follow Jesus also pick and choose. We tend to do the things that are easiest for us and ignore the things that are difficult.

As I sat there at the Passover meal, I asked God to help me do the difficult things as well as the easy things.

The Passover meal is called a *seder*. The word *seder* simply means "order," and every seder follows a specific order. As soon as we sit down, each person is given a booklet, called "the family *haggadah*," a word that simply means "the telling." According to the introduction, there are over three thousand *haggadot* in many different languages. This is similar to the Sunday bulletin in Christian churches, insofar as it lists the order of service so you can follow along.

The first cup of wine

We wash our hands

We dip the vegetable and salt water and say the blessing

We break the middle *matzah* and hide the larger half, called the *afikomen*

We tell the story of Passover

The four questions are read

The second cup of wine

We wash our hands and say the blessing

We say the blessings for the "bread" and matzah

We dip the bitter herbs in the *charoset* and say the blessing

We eat a sandwich of matzah and bitter herbs

We eat the festival meal

We eat the afikomen

We say the blessing after the meal

The third cup of wine

We welcome Elijah the prophet

We sing songs of praise

The fourth cup of wine

We complete the seder

In the center of the table is a large beautiful plate, elaborately decorated, which is called the seder plate. On it is a variety of things: a roasted egg, parsley, celery or potato, a roasted bone, chopped apple and nuts, a bitter herb (whole or grated horse-radish), and another bitter herb, which is used for the sandwich. There is also unleavened bread, *matzot*, three pieces of bread that are covered.

The seder meal begins with the lighting of candles and the blessing, read in Hebrew, of the first cup of wine: "Blessed are you, God, our God, ruler of the universe, who creates the fruit of the vine." During the meal there are four different cups of wine, each of which is drunk to celebrate the four promises God made to the children of Israel:

> I will bring you out ...
> I will deliver you ...
> I will redeem you ...
> I will take you to be my people ...
> **Exodus 6:6–7**

The first cup of wine is followed by the washing of hands. During the days of temple worship, the priests often washed their hands as a symbolic reminder that we are "a kingdom of priests and the holy nation" (Exodus 19:6). Following the washing of hands, everyone dips a vegetable into the saltwater and says this blessing in Hebrew: "Blessed are you, God, our God, ruler of the universe, who creates the fruit of the earth."

This is followed by the breaking of the middle matzah. It is broken into pieces, and one piece, the largest, is set aside as the afikomen, which will be eaten at the end of the meal. The afikomen is hidden and toward the end of the meal children will go and search for it. The meal cannot end until the afikomen is found. The following blessing is then said in Hebrew: "This is the bread of poverty, which our ancestors ate in the land of Egypt. All who are hungry, come and eat. All who are needy, come and celebrate Passover with us. Now we celebrate here. Next year may we be in the land of Israel. Now we are slaves. Next year may we be truly free."

One of the tensions of Passover is between having already been set free and the need to be set free. It is a celebration of God's deliverance from Egypt, but it is also a reminder that in some ways we are all still slaves—slaves to fashion, to exercise, to money, to education, to alcohol, to drugs. The list goes on and on.

Next, the story of Passover is told. (By this time I'm starved and wondering why in the world we can't eat.) The Passover story begins with the asking of four questions:

1. On all other nights we eat bread and matzoh. On this night why do we eat only matzoh?

2. On all other nights we eat all kinds of vegetables. On this night why do we eat only *maror*?

3. On all other nights we do not have to dip vegetables even once. On this night why do we dip them twice?

4. On all other nights we eat our meal sitting any way we like. On this night, why do we lean on pillows?

This is one of the most incredible things about Judaism—you are encouraged to ask questions. This is not true in most churches. Many pastors and spiritual leaders claim to have all of the answers. In some churches you are even discouraged from asking questions. In Judaism, however, you are encouraged to ask all sorts of questions.

I have a Jewish friend in Grand Rapids. She is a faithful member of the local synagogue but has also attended Torah study at a Christian church. "When I go to the Torah study," she told me once, "Christians have such a high view of the Bible. They say, 'This is God's Word. We should treat it seriously. We should honor it and love it.' But at the synagogue people say something completely different: 'Why did God choose us? Why have we suffered so much? Why didn't God choose someone else? Why do I have to believe the Torah?'"

In Judaism, asking questions is part of the deal. In fact, Jesus himself was a great question asker. When an expert in the law asked him one question, "Teacher, what must I do to inherit eternal life?" Jesus answered not with one question but with *two*: 'What is written in the Law? How do you read it?'" (Luke 10:25–26).

It is only in really struggling with the questions that they can begin to be answered. At the seder meal, the four questions are answered this way:

> This night is different from all other nights because once we were slaves to Pharaoh in Egypt, but Adonai, our God, took us out with a mighty hand and an outstretched arm. If Adonai had not brought our ancestors out of Egypt, then we, and our children, and our children's children would still be slaves in the land of Egypt. Even if we know the story well and have told it many times, the more we tell it in great detail, the more we are to be praised. This night is also different because once we worshiped idols, but now we worship only Adonai, the one who is everywhere.[4]

The leader then goes on to explain the whole story of Passover. This was done in English at the meal I attended, but in most households the story is told in Hebrew. Then the leader calls about a dozen people forward to sing. Having grown up in large churches, I was expecting some excellent singing. But the people who sang were awful! Some sang in tune—some did not. I thought the whole thing was embarrassing, but nobody seemed to mind. They sang a song called "The Ballad of Four Songs" to the tune of "My Darling Clementine":

Said the father to his children, "At the seder you will dine,
you will eat your fill of matzoh, you will drink four cups of wine."

Now this father had no daughters, but his sons they numbered
four.
One was wise and one was wicked, one was simple and a bore.

And the fourth was sweet and winsome, he was young and he was
small.
While his brothers asked the questions he could scarcely speak at
all.

Said the wise one to his father, "Would you please explain our
loss?
Of the customs of the seder, will you please explain the cause?"

And the father proudly answered, "As our fathers ate in speed,
ate the Paschal lamb ere midnight, and from slavery they were
freed.

"So we follow their example and ere midnight must complete
all the seder, and we should not after twelve remain to eat."

Then did sneer the son so wicked, "What does all this mean to
you?"
And the father's voice was bitter as his grief and anger grew.

"If you don't consider yourself as a son of Israel,
then for you this has no meaning. You could be a slave as well."

Then the simple son said simply, "What is this," and quietly
the good father told his offspring, "We were freed from slavery."

But the youngest son was silent for he could not ask a bowl.
His bright eyes were bright with wonder as his father told him all.

My dear children, heed the lesson and remember ever more
what the father told his children told his sons that numbered four.

It was reassuring to know that the meal had to be done before
midnight! As the telling of the story grew longer and longer, I

wondered if we were ever going to eat. After several verses, the singing grew worse, and I realized that this was not entertainment. It was a celebration of something deep within the Jewish psyche. As I looked around, everybody was engaged with the song. Old, young, children, teenagers—everybody loved it.

Toward the end of the story came a beautiful section entitled *dayenu*, a word that means "that alone would have been enough, but for that alone we are grateful."

> *Adonai took us out of Egypt. Dayenu.*
> *Punished the Egyptians and destroyed their idols. Dayenu.*
> *Divided the sea and led us across on dry land. Dayenu.*
> *Took care of us in the desert for forty years and fed us manna.*
> *Dayenu.*
> *Gave us Shabbat. Dayenu.*
> *Brought us to Mount Sinai and gave us the Torah. Dayenu.*
> *Brought us to the land of Israel and built the holy Temple.*
> *Dayenu.*
> *For all these—alone and together—we say Dayenu.*

Dayenu is a powerful concept. It is learning to be grateful for what God has already done and not asking him to do more.

For me, as a follower of Jesus, it means being grateful for what God has done through Jesus Christ in restoring me to God. *Dayenu*. It is getting up every day and realizing God has given me one more day to live. *Dayenu*. In times of economic difficulty, it is realizing that I have food on my table and clothes on my back and a warm place to live. *Dayenu*. It seems to me that Western Christians are always asking God for more—more money, better health, larger houses, better jobs, a boat. I want I want I want I want.

Dayenu contradicts this kind of thinking.

Following the detailed telling of the Passover story, we drink a second cup of wine with the following blessing. "Blessed are you, God, our God, who has freed the people of Israel." Then we wash our hands again. The matzoh is distributed around the table, and a blessing is said for *maror*, which are the bitter herbs to remind us of the bitterness of slavery. Then we eat a sandwich of matzoh and maror.

Then, finally, the meal. I'm so glad to get to the meal. A couple of glasses of wine and no food make me lightheaded.

After the meal, the children are asked to find the *afikomen*, the large piece of matzoh. "The afikomen is shared just as the Pesach offering was shared in the days of the temple, to show that we are all responsible for one another. No special blessing is said because the dessert is part of the meal. We are not permitted to eat anything after the afikomen. Its taste should linger in our mouths."[5] Then the fourth cup of wine is poured, and the following blessing repeated:

> We praise you, Adonai our God, ruler of the universe, who in goodness, mercy, and kindness gives food to the world. Your love for us endures forever. We praise you, Adonai, who gives food for all life.
> May the holy one, who makes peace in the heavens, make peace for us, for Israel, and for all the world.[6]

I like the last part, when we ask God to make peace for Israel and for all the world. When God first called Abraham, he told him that through him all the nations of the world would be blessed. In this context the words refer to Israel as a people, not Israel as a nation, and the ultimate desire is for God to bring peace to the people of Israel *and* to the entire world.

As I left the room, I was profoundly moved by the fact that Jews have celebrated this meal for thousands of years. The church I served for over eighteen years was founded in 1929. We've only had our traditions for eighty years.

The Jews have had Passover for thousands of years.

I am also impressed with the fact that by serving the Passover meal, Jesus inaugurated a whole new idea—the Lord's Supper, or Communion, or Mass. Now we do not know exactly what Passover order was followed in Jesus' day—the ceremony I sat through actually dates from several hundred years after the time of Jesus—but we do know he took bread and a cup of wine. He broke the bread and said, "This is my body given for you; do this in remembrance of me." Then he took the wine and said, "This cup is the new covenant in my blood, which is poured out for you" (Luke 22:19–20).

The Passover meal I had just enjoyed represents the old covenant. It represents God's agreement with the Jews to bless them and the Jews' obligation to remember the Exodus. When Jesus celebrated the Passover he introduced a new covenant whereby both Jew and Gentile could be embraced within the new community called the Church.

Day twenty-five. I have not written in my journal for several days. I continue to listen to the Gospels—I'm halfway through John. But I need a brief rest. I'm finding that with the reading, the praying, the additional reading of other sources, and all the lists I have already made—I'm a bit overwhelmed. For the last several days I've felt buried.

So I decide not to write.

Day twenty-six. Today I finished the gospel of John. This is the eighth time I've read through—actually, listened through—the Gospels. As new as my iPod is, I realize that the early Christians also simply listened to the Gospels as they were read in public worship. In that way, I suspect, many of them memorized large parts of the Gospels. By the time I get through with this project, I hope to have memorized the Gospels as well.

Day twenty-eight. I received a book in the mail: *Praying with Beads: Daily Prayers for the Christian Year.* The introduction outlines how to pray using the Episcopal prayer beads. These beads are a relatively new phenomenon—developed in the 1980s by the Reverend Lynn Bauman. They are essentially a cross between the rosary and the Orthodox prayer rope.

The prayer beads consist of thirty-three beads and the cross. The beads represent the thirty-three years that Jesus lived on planet Earth. Above the cross is an "invitatory bead," which represents an invitation to prayer. Above this is a cruciform bead. There are four cruciform beads—one at the bottom, one at the top, one to the right, and one to the left. Between each of these are seven beads—called the week's beads. These beads recall the seven days of creation.

The rest of the book follows the church calendar and includes weekly prayers—a morning prayer, a noon prayer, and an evening prayer. The outline of prayers is as follows:

> The cross: "In the name of God, Father, Son, and Holy Spirit." (Pray while holding the cross.)
>
> The invitatory: "Merciful God, be ever with us, listening to us, and strengthening us." (Pray when you move to the invitatory bead.)
>
> The cruciform: "So if you have been raised with Christ, seek the things that are above, where Christ is" (Colossians 3:1). (Pray on each cruciform bead as you reach it.)
>
> The weeks: "I shall not die, but live, and declare the

works of the Lord" (Psalm 118:17). (Pray on each of the "weeks" beads as you move around the circle.)

The invitatory: The Lord's Prayer. (Pray on the invitatory bead when you leave the circle.)

The cross: "Thanks be to God. Amen." (Pray while holding the cross.)

I follow the daily prayers through Easter and beyond. I like the prayers because they consist of nothing but Scriptures. Sometimes I pray the morning, noon, and evening prayers. Other times I just pray the morning prayers.

I discovered on the Internet that there are many ways to use the Episcopal prayer beads. Some people pray around the circle using four basic dimensions of prayer: adoration, confession, thanksgiving, and supplication—abbreviated as ACTS. I have often used this cycle of prayers in the past even before I knew what prayer beads were:

The first section is devoted to *adoration*, so on each of the seven beads you praise God.

The second section deals with *confession*. On each of the seven beads you confess a different sin to God and ask his forgiveness.

The third section is *thanksgiving*. On each of the seven beads you give thanks to God for something different.

The fourth section deals with *supplication*—making requests of God.

On each of the seven days you ask God for something specific, primarily for other people. I find that praying the Episcopal prayer beads in this way is very meaningful to me.

When I begin with the cross I say, "In the name of the Father, the Son, and the Holy Spirit." At the invitatory bead I say, "Glory be to the father, and to the Son, and to the Holy Spirit." At the cruciform bead I say, "Lord, hear our prayer." Then I go around the circle adoring, confessing, giving thanks, and asking God for help.

Some writers suggest that you should pray through the circle three different times—one for the Father, one for the Son, and one for the Holy Spirit. They also recommend that you pray in an unhurried manner, which is also recommended whenever you pray the rosary or the Orthodox prayer rope.

As I continue my journey of praying the rosary, the Orthodox prayer rope, and the Episcopal prayer beads, I have found myself encouraged in at least three major ways. First, the physicality of these objects keeps me focused on prayer. In the past I've had a problem with my mind wandering. But holding something in my hands helps me stay focused. For the most part evangelical Christians have ignored the physical dimensions of spirituality. We reduce faith primarily to the mind and the heart. But using beads reminds me that my body is every bit as important.

Second, the repetition helps me focus. I have the weird ability to do several things at the same time—writing, listening to music, listening to the news, and so on. My mind is constantly moving in a variety of directions. But repeating the same words over and over helps me focus on one thing—prayer and the Word of God.

Third, I am deeply moved by simply praying the words of Scripture. It's a very Jewish way to pray.

Prayer has always been an important part of my life. For many years I kept a prayer journal, the first part of which contained pages of things that I prayed for every day, including family members, church staff, pastors, and friends.

It also included things that I would pray for once a week. On Monday I prayed for missionaries; Tuesday, for political leaders;

and so forth. On each page I would write out the prayer requests in longhand and date them. When God answered the prayer I would circle the entire request. After many years the journal was filled with specific prayers that God had answered.

When I was first chosen to be the new pastor at Calvary, I drove to the church, walked down the center aisle, and knelt in front of the altar by myself in the darkened auditorium. I prayed, "Dear God, please don't let this church go downhill." Not very spiritual, but it was how I felt at the moment.

Yesterday was Sunday. I was so tired that I decided not to go to church. Instead, I read through the gospel of Mark, prayed the rosary, prayed the Episcopal prayer beads, and then went to a closet in the basement and prayed the Orthodox prayer rope. It was a wonderful morning of focusing on the Bible and spending time in prayer.

It had been revealed to [Simeon] by the Holy Spirit that he would not die before he had seen the Lord's Christ. Moved by the Spirit, he went into the temple courts.

Luke 2:26–27

Day twenty-nine. When Jesus was taken to Jerusalem as a child, a righteous and devout man named Simeon lived there. God had promised Simeon that he would not die without seeing the Christ. How had the Holy Spirit revealed this to him? How did the Holy Spirit prompt him to go to the Temple on that particular day? These are perplexing questions. Maybe it has something to do with being still and letting God speak to you. I have only tried that once, and the results were not very positive. I had a hard time keeping my mind on track.

So how am I supposed to listen to the Holy Spirit? And how

do I know when he is speaking or when I've simply had too much pizza? I feel I need to focus more on the Holy Spirit and learn what it means to be prompted by the Spirit.

Today I finished the gospel of John, my ninth time through the Gospels. I also went to my closet and prayed the Orthodox prayer rope. The closet is not the most pleasing place to pray. It smells of clothes that have been hanging there for years. On the shelves are old books, and scattered around the closet are posters and framed pictures. There's only just enough room to pray, bend over, and do a full prostration.

I've been praying several things in addition to the Jesus Prayer. I did some praying for Heather. Then, each time I reached a bead I would pray, "Jesus, Son of David, have mercy on me." So I was praying for Heather as well as for healing for myself.

I've been reading the advice of the Church Fathers who recommend that you do not change the words of prayer. So I still pray the entire time, "Lord Jesus Christ, have mercy on me, a sinner."

I also did two sets of the Episcopal prayer beads and prayed the rosary as well. It took a little over two hours to do all of that praying. It also took a little over two hours to do the reading of the Gospels. This is a major chunk of my time. I am just grateful that I have the time to devote to this.

I've also spent some time with Father Daniel, the Orthodox priest.

"Thanks for taking time for me," I said to him recently, "and for sending the prayer rope."

"You're most welcome," he said.

"I've been praying through the Orthodox prayer rope, and I've also been praying the rosary."

"The rosary? That's good."

"Recently I had a really bizarre incident. I went to a local

Catholic church to pray the rosary with a small group of people. Before the last meditation, the leader asked if I would like to lead the 'Hail Marys.' So I agreed to do it. As I sat there at the back of the chapel I was focusing on the life-sized statue of Jesus behind the altar. He had his hands outstretched toward the congregation, and in his hands were the nail prints. About halfway through the 'Hail Marys' I was focused on the statue of Jesus, and for a few moments it seemed like he was alive. I've never had anything like that happen to me before."

Father Dan listened attentively. When I was finished he smiled. "God was letting you see the light under the door."

I had no clue what he was talking about.

"What do you mean?"

"God never lets anyone see the fullness of his glory. That would kill us. But every once in a while he allows us to see some light under the door. This was God letting you see a little bit of his glory under the door."

"Tell me more about the Orthodox Church and what you believe."

"Well, there's one significant difference between Western Christianity and Eastern Orthodoxy."

"Which is ..."

"In our understanding of salvation, Western Christianity follows St. Augustine. Orthodoxy does not."

I know a little about Augustine, but I wasn't sure what he meant.

He continued, "Augustine's Latin New Testament had a significant error in its translation of Romans 5:12. After mentioning Adam, the Latin text says, '... *in whom* all have sinned.' The original Greek text simply says, '... *whereas* all have sinned.' This mistake led Augustine to the belief that if we all had sinned *in* Adam, then we all inherited his guilt. This being so, Augustine viewed salvation as a legal process that dealt primarily with the issue of guilt. Consequently, the Western Church, following Augustine, stressed the legal aspects of salvation; that is, atonement, justification, and righteousness.

"The Eastern Church, however, explained salvation differently. Adam's sin had certainly separated us from God. But this separation led primarily to death. The Eastern Fathers saw that our inheritance from Adam was not guilt, but *death*. Salvation would mean Christ would have to destroy death and restore us to God. The mystery of salvation begins in the mystery of the incarnation when God became man."

"That's news to me," I said.

"From an Orthodox point of view, salvation is understood as a restoration to the unity with God that Adam had lost. In his one Person, our Lord restores that unity by being both human and divine. This is the beginning of salvation. In the mystery of the cross, grave, and resurrection, Jesus destroys the power of death. He conquers death 'by death.' The Orthodox Church doesn't deny the legal aspect of salvation, but I think it would see it as too narrow."

I wondered, what if the Western Church and the Eastern Church are two faces of the same coin? Perhaps salvation *is* a judicial act and a healing process as well. Maybe both of them are right!

May

The first few days. At the end of April and the beginning of May, Lorna and I drove our Corvette from Key Largo, Florida, to Grand Rapids, Michigan. It took several days. Along the way we stopped to see Lorna's sister and her husband, Sonny, who live in the mountains outside of Greenville, South Carolina. Sonny was in the final stages of a courageous battle with cancer. We both wanted to see him one more time.

Sonny has always had a special place in my life. After I received my master's degree from Bob Jones University, I wanted to be an evangelist, traveling the country and preaching wherever I could find a few people to listen. So I wrote to more than a hundred churches letting them know that I was available to come and preach. No one wrote back. No one invited me to speak. Since I was freshly married, I needed a job. That's where Sonny entered the picture. He offered me a job with his company — digging graves.

Most of the graves were dug with a backhoe, although some of them, mostly in remote country cemeteries, were still dug by hand. I worked on the "cover-up crew." We set up the funeral tents, put chairs under the tents, lowered the casket into the vault, helped seal the vault, and covered up the grave. I worked for Sonny for about six months and developed wonderful relationships with the other gravediggers.

One of them was named Reuben. He was southern, black, and one of the funniest guys I've ever known. We worked together on the cover-up crew. Whenever it started to get dark in one of the cemeteries, Reuben tended to get nervous. So we made a solemn pledge: we would never attempt to scare each other in a cemetery after dark.

One day Reuben said to me, "Let me see, you got a bachelor's degree and a master's degree—and you're digging graves!"

"Yep."

"What a waste of money and education!"

"I guess you're right."

"You know what we ought to do?"

"What's that?"

"We need to go on the road and have you preach. We could rent arenas in major cities all over the South. I'll be your promoter and you do the preaching. We'll split the take half and half."

We both laughed, but somehow I knew he was half serious.

Every time I see Sonny now, we talk about "the good old days" of digging graves. I haven't seen Reuben since those days, nor any of the other guys I worked with for those six months, but Sonny usually catches me up on the news. He's sort of the middleman between me and that part of my life. To this day I feel a deep connection to those guys that I used to work with. So now I had the chance to talk to Sonny one last time about the "good old days."

And we did.

We had a wonderful visit at their place in South Carolina. We even went out to eat that night. As we drove away from their house, I had this strange feeling that it would be the last time I would see Sonny alive. And I was right.

At the gated community in Florida, I'm the only one with a long beard. In Grand Rapids, I'm one of the few who has a long beard. Whenever I see someone else with a long beard either in Florida or in Grand Rapids, I look at them and nod. Most of the time they nod back. It's a ritual.

At a gas station in South Carolina, however, I nodded at one man with a long beard, and he glared at me like I was nuts. No return nod. No mutual acknowledgment of our beardedness. The reason? Nearly every man in the mountains has a long, bizarre, and unkempt beard. I fit right in—except for the nodding part.

On our way through Kentucky, Lorna and I stopped at the welcome center on the border. In addition to maps and brochures, the center displays artwork and crafts by Kentucky artists. As we were walking up to the door, a woman who worked at the center was just leaving the building. She looked me in the eye and said, "You'll fit right in!"

I thought it was a strange thing to say—I mean, I'd never met this woman before, and ordinarily people usually say, "Hello," or something like that. But she said, "You'll fit right in!" Then, as I saw my reflection in the glass door of the center, I saw what she meant. It was the beard. I looked as though I had just come down from the mountain.

Woe to you, teachers of the law and Pharisees, you hypocrites!... You have neglected the more important matters of the law—justice, mercy and faithfulness. You should have practiced the latter, without neglecting the former.

Matthew 23:23

Day seven. The kingdom of God is one of the major topics in the teachings of Jesus. I've gone through all the Gospels and written down every reference to the kingdom of God—there are dozens of them. Sometimes Jesus says that the kingdom of God is near. Other times he says that the kingdom of God is already in our midst. He tells his disciples to pray for the kingdom to come, and as he is about to ascend to heaven, the disciples ask him if the time has come when Jesus will restore the kingdom to Israel. So the kingdom is near, already here, and somewhere off in the future.

Clearly, Jesus came to announce the kingdom. He wants us to reflect the values of that kingdom. It's a place where justice prevails, where mercy prevails, and where faithfulness prevails. Such is the kingdom of God. When we pray for the kingdom of God to come, we are praying that these values of God will be lived out in our lives and in our communities.

Now I need to go back to the issue of the suits. I've already agreed to give away half of my suits. This comes from the preaching of John the Baptist, who told people if they have two coats to give one to the person who has no coat. First, I need to find people who have no suits. Second, I need to give them half of my suits. My wife accepts the responsibility of finding people who have no suits. She called the president of the Grand Rapids Theological Seminary, and he agreed to accept all my suits and to give them to students in the seminary who don't have any.

So I went to my closet and began the painful process of choosing which ones to give away. It was difficult. First I chose a light brown summer suit, which I love. Since it was one of my favorites, I decided that I had to get rid of it. After a long struggle, I identified other suits — more than half of them, in fact — to give away. I ended up keeping only four.

Why was it so difficult? I'm not sure. Perhaps it relates to the fact that when I grew up, our family didn't have much money. When we came from Ireland, all our belongings fit into three trunks. I still have one of those trunks sitting by the front door of our house to remind me of my roots. Consequently, everything I have I cherish, including clothes.

Or perhaps it's simply the result of materialism. The more you have, the more you want, and the more you want, the more you get.

The truth is that I have far more clothes than I need. I'm reminded of the words of Jesus, "No one can serve two masters. Either he will hate the one and love the other, or he will be devoted to the one and despise the other. You cannot serve both God and

Money" (Matthew 6:24). It wouldn't be too much of a distortion to say, "You can't serve both God and suits."

This journey of trying to live like Jesus has revealed to me how many of my inner motives are very unlike Jesus'. When he was questioned about the fact that his disciples violated the tradition of the elders by not washing their hands before they ate, he articulated the fact that food does not make a person unclean. Rather, the food goes into the stomach and then out of the body. What makes a person unclean comes from the heart. "For out of the heart come evil thoughts, murder, adultery, sexual immorality, theft, false testimony, slander. These are what make a man 'unclean'; but eating with unwashed hands does not make him 'unclean'" (Matthew 15:19–20).

Day ten. Today I went by to see my friend Joe Stowell, who just became the new president of Cornerstone University in Grand Rapids. Joe and I have been friends for many years. Shortly after I came to Calvary Church in 1987, Joe became president of the Moody Bible Institute. Moody is not only a leading college that focuses on training people for the ministry, it also owns an array of radio stations as well as a major Christian publishing house. Joe has invited me to speak at Moody numerous times, and I've asked him to speak at Calvary quite often.

Several years ago Joe resigned from Moody. On that day, he called me and said, "Thank God I'm free!" He said he'd lost his passion and decided that the best thing he could do for himself and for the school was to resign.

Joe then became one of the teaching pastors at Harvest Bible Church in Chicago, and he also worked with Radio Bible Class, doing some of their worldwide television broadcasts. He's now in his early sixties, and I assumed that he'd spend his retirement teaching the Bible, writing books, and doing radio and television shows. But through a series of unusual circumstances he decided to accept the presidency of Cornerstone University.

I dropped by one day recently to see him. He was delighted to see me.

"I just came by to offer you my sympathies on your new position and to pray with you," I said, laughing, "And also to ask you: what in the world were you thinking?"

Joe laughed too. Originally he was asked to be the interim president, but he thought, why not consider being the permanent president? At least that way he could make the long-term decisions that most universities need.

He said he was in Detroit for a funeral when the chairman of the search committee called him. "On your way back to Chicago," this person asked, "could you meet me in Kalamazoo for dinner?"

"Of course." Joe said. At least he'd get a free meal. On the way to Kalamazoo, Joe and his wife made a list of his personal characteristics and passions. If he were going to accept the presidency, then he wanted the search committee to know what values would drive him. At dinner the chairman of the search committee began telling Joe all of the characteristics they were looking for. As Joe listened, he realized that they were the very same characteristics Joe and his wife had written down on the piece of paper tucked in his coat pocket.

So he agreed to become Cornerstone's new president.

As we sat in his office, he began to tell me about his priorities as the new president. One was to raise the whole spiritual temperature of the entire campus: students, faculty, administration, and staff.

"I'm looking for a vice president for spiritual formation," he said. "This person would be responsible for the spiritual atmosphere of the campus. All the staff working in student develop-ment would answer to this person, and this person would also work with faculty, administration, and staff in the whole area of spiritual formation."

As I sat there, my heart began to beat faster. This has long been one of my passions. My doctorate from the University of Virginia was in higher education, and all during my years at Calvary Church, I wondered why I'd spent all of that time earning that doctorate. As I listened to Joe, I realized that I would be the ideal candi-date for the position. I was passionate about spiritual formation — and I was in the middle of a year-long journey of trying to live like Jesus.

Finally Joe looked at me with a twinkle in his eye. "Think you'd be interested?"

"What do you mean?"

"Could you give us a year of trying to turn our hearts toward becoming devoted followers of Jesus?"

"You know I can't work full-time."

"I'd rather have *you* half-time than anyone else full-time."

I've always had deep respect for Joe, and I was excited about the prospect of being involved in the area of spiritual formation. But then doubts crept in. Would I have to sit through endless meetings, for instance? I knew from past experience that a large part of university life is constant meetings.

"Let me think it through and pray about it," I said.

After we prayed together, I left. As I drove back home, my mind was racing. I began to list all the reasons why it wasn't a good idea. First, my health. Taking on this responsibility would not be good for my health. Or would it? Maybe having something to do on a regular basis and an office to go to and responsibilities to attend to would actually be good for me.

Second, Cornerstone has fundamentalist and legalist roots. Then again, it has changed a lot since Joe became president; it was a major step forward for the institution. Still, their lifestyle statement requires that all faculty, administration, staff, and students refrain from drinking. Jesus did *not* refrain from drinking.

At that point, I knew I needed to do three things:

First, I needed to talk it over with my wife.

Second, I needed to talk with my accountability group—a small group of men whom I've been meeting with monthly for many years. They are most helpful when it comes to decisions like these. One of the men has been my neurologist for the past nine years, and he could advise on the health effects of the job.

Third, I needed to talk with my kids.

Day eleven. I'm very interested in the position at Cornerstone, but new responsibilities will seriously impact my ability to listen to the Gospels and live out their teaching. So I decide that whenever I'm in the car, I will listen to the Gospels on my iPod instead of listening to National Public Radio. Even though most of my drives are short and will break up my listening to the Gospels, it will be good for me.

Today I ate lunch with my accountability group, men that have walked with me in the best of times and the worst of times. They love me but they are also honest. On many occasions they have advised me not to do something I've wanted to do—and most of the time I listen to them.

I told them about the opportunity at Cornerstone, and, miracle of miracles, they were supportive. My doctor liked the idea of limiting it to one year; that way, if it begins to damage my health, I can step away more easily. The others, knowing that I should avoid all activities that drain my energy, felt that working at Cornerstone, for the most part, would only enhance my energy. They thought it would be good for me.

I also talked with my kids. My youngest son, a student at Cornerstone, thought it was a great idea. My daughter (who worked at Cornerstone) and son-in-law (who is a student at the seminary) both felt that it's a good situation, and my oldest son and his wife were supportive but concerned that I not get overly involved. My wife was generally supportive as well. She thought it would be good for me to get out of the house and have specific responsibilities. She thought it was great that I'd have an office, a role, and, most of all, influence over students.

The one reservation I have is that this comes in the middle of my year of trying to live like Jesus. Cornerstone will limit my ability to do that. But maybe that's a good thing. After all, most people who want to try and live like Jesus do not have the flexibility that I do — they have jobs. Maybe I'll learn even more about living like Jesus if I have a job and responsibilities. Unfortunately, I'm spending more time thinking about the position at Cornerstone than about how to live like Jesus.

When he was accused by the chief priests and the elders, he gave no answer. Then Pilate asked him, "Don't you hear the testimony they are bringing against you?" But Jesus made no reply, not even to a single charge — to the great amazement of the governor.

Matthew 27:12–14

Day sixteen. I have not written in my journal for a while.

Recently my son had his own show on the Discovery Channel. He raised some important historical questions that were in conflict with the biblical story. At the end of the program he identifies himself with Thomas — someone who has questions and doubts but is still a devoted follower of Jesus. As a result of the questions he raised, however, he was asked to resign his teaching position at a Christian school.

I talked with the *Grand Rapids Press* and was quoted several times in one of their articles about his firing. Of course, my son refused to comment—even to the *Press*. I also preached at Calvary Church the Sunday after the program and spent a few minutes talking about the situation.

My son was upset that I mentioned the situation publicly. He told me that I'd made the situation worse, not better, and that I had no business mentioning it at Calvary. After reflecting on what he said, I went to see the pastor the next day and apologized and asked him to relay my apology to the church elders. I knew I was wrong. I made a serious mistake. I was so passionate about defending my son that I never asked, "What would Jesus do?" Had I asked that question I would have kept my mouth shut.

After all, when Jesus was tried before Pilate and others, he did not answer their questions. Although many false witnesses were brought against him, he refused to answer or respond to their testimony. The Jesus thing to do would have been not to comment —like my son did!

Last night I had dinner with several people. Everyone was drinking, so I drank a beer before the meal and had wine during the meal. It was a wonderful dinner, but I clearly violated my diet. Fortunately I'd read earlier in the day that when Jesus sent out his disciples he told them to eat whatever was set before them without asking questions. When he sent out his seventy-two disciples to preach the good news of the kingdom all over Israel, he told them to stay at whatever house invited them in: "Stay in that house, eating and drinking whatever they give you." And he goes on to say, "When you enter a town and are welcomed, eat whatever is set before you" (Luke 10:5–8).

Of course if they were going to Jewish villages, the "whatever was set before them" would be kosher. So at this point I take a little liberty with the text. What if something was set before them that was not kosher? In that case, as I read the text, Jesus is saying that they should eat it. So I had cheese and meat and conch fritters.

I'm seriously considering accepting the position at Cornerstone. All of the student personnel staff would answer to me, and I'd help oversee the chapel program. I'd deal with the faculty and staff to promote spiritual growth. But do I want to take on this kind of pressure and responsibility? On the other hand, it's a wonderful opportunity to influence young people who will, in turn, go out and make a difference for Christ.

I talked with some people a few days ago about next year's schedule at the community in Florida. They felt it was important to have someone there to teach the Bible during "snowbird season," that is, when people from cold climates "winter over" in Florida, generally from November through the end of April, and I agree with them.

In the course of the conversation I found out that they have already been looking for someone and have at least one résumé. I told them that at best I could only be there two or three months after the new year. Lorna and I both feel that this is a clear leading not to go back to that community. Still, I will miss my interaction with the people there. They want someone who feels "called" to ministry at the community, and I'm just not sure I feel called.

Day seventeen. Joe called me to talk about the details of the position. I think it's significant that he called me the day after I had talked with the people at the community. One of the problems with working at Cornerstone is that it will mess up my commitment to be and act like Jesus. Let's face it—Jesus was called a glutton and a drunkard. He partied with pagans. If I accept the position at Cornerstone, I'll have to accept their lifestyle code—

which means no more drinking. That will limit my ability to be and act like Jesus!

Day eighteen. I called Joe and told him I'd accept the position of vice president of spiritual formation. He was delighted! He was praying that I'd accept.

"Before we work out the details," I said, "you need to know that I can't work full-time. I can give you two or three days a week at best. Also, if the job starts seriously impacting my health, I may have to step down."

"Not a problem," said Joe. "I've already told you that I'd rather have you part-time than anyone else full-time. You've made my day. I'm excited to be working with you as we explore the whole area of spiritual formation. I'd like to announce that you've accepted this position during the last chapel of the semester, just before graduation."

That was fine with me. The chapel is still several weeks away, and that gives me time to work through the details and begin to meet with the staff in student development. I also know that I'll have to be quiet about my project of living like Jesus. I know that praying the rosary will be completely alien to what most of the people at Cornerstone consider to be prayer. The Orthodox prayer rope will be completely foreign to their experience as well. I will no longer be able to go to cocktail parties or go to the bar for a beer. So for the sake of the students, faculty, administration, and staff, I'll need to be careful. By joining the administration at Cornerstone, I'm accepting some of the limitations of organized religion.

It seems to me that Jesus and his first disciples were a whole lot different than organized religion and religious institutions today.

One of the favorite pastimes of evangelicals is deciding who is "in" and who is "out"; that is, they love to decide who's been converted and who hasn't. Having grown up as a Protestant in Northern Ireland, I was convinced that no Catholics would go to heaven. They were "out." Conversely, most Catholics believed that no Protestants would go to heaven. They were "out." On one occasion, Reverend Ian Paisley, a fiery Protestant minister and political leader, refused to shake the hand of the Archbishop of Canterbury. When asked why, he said, "I will not shake the hand of the man who shook the hand of the pope!"

I grew up among the Plymouth Brethren—a very small, narrow, and exclusive group. One of the jokes that went around about the Plymouth Brethren was the following: Saint Peter was showing some new arrivals around heaven. There were people all over the place. Finally they turned a corner and saw a small group of people off by themselves. "Who are they?" the new arrivals asked. "They're the Plymouth Brethren," said Peter. "Don't disturb them—they think they're the only ones up here!"

> Once again, the kingdom of heaven is like a net that was let down into the lake and caught all kinds of fish. When it was full, the fishermen pulled it up on the shore. Then they sat down and collected the good fish in baskets, but threw the bad away. This is how it will be at the end of the age. The angels will come and separate the wicked from the righteous and throw them into the fiery furnace, where there will be weeping and gnashing of teeth.
>
> **Matthew 13:47–50**

This story is about judgment. The fishermen cast their net into the lake and caught both good fish (the kosher) and bad fish (the nonkosher), which they separate. The end of the age, says Jesus, will be like that. The angels of God will separate the good fish from the bad fish—the righteous from the wicked, and the wicked will be thrown into a place of suffering and sorrow.

So what are the implications? I think it means that deciding who is "in" and who is "out" is entirely up to God and the angels. Not us. And for that I am deeply grateful.

In Northern Ireland, Protestants believe that Catholics can't be saved because they pray to Mary, go to confession, think that the bread and wine become the literal body and blood of Jesus, and are loyal to the pope. Catholics believe that Protestants can't be saved because they're not part of the Catholic Church. Since I've been babbling on the fringes of the Catholic Church by praying the rosary and seeking the advice of a priest, perhaps my own salvation will now be called into question.

Peter denied Jesus three times. Thomas was filled with questions and doubt. Judas went so far as to betray him. The rest of the disciples ran away in Jesus' greatest hour of need. No church would accept such people as spiritual leaders, and no Christian college would accept such people as teachers.

But as religious institutions grow, they develop not only a consistent theology but norms of acceptable and unacceptable behavior as well. When you join that community, the understanding is that you have to agree with their theology and be willing to adjust your behavior to accommodate what they believe is good and bad.

In the 1960s and '70s, for example, long hair was the norm for guys in the hippie movement, so many Christian colleges prohibited guys from wearing long hair. The problem, though, was that people began to judge each other on the basis of hair length. Long hair equals unspiritual. Short hair equals spiritual. Over time churches and schools developed dress codes, prohibited alcohol and certain types of music, and so on. I understand why these institutions formulate their theological statements and behavior codes, but it all seems quite far from the spirit and teaching of Jesus.

So, for the sake of encouraging others in their spiritual formation, I'll have to be willing not to talk about some of these controversial issues. A part of me wants to talk about these issues and create a certain amount of healthy controversy; that's just part of my nature. But I know that for the sake of the school, and for the sake of spiritual formation, this wouldn't be wise. I'll have to take a deep breath and swallow the stuff I don't like about Cornerstone in order to have an influence over students. I hope that in swallowing this stuff I won't become un-Jesus-like.

Day nineteen. I continue to listen to the Gospels and pray the rosary every day—and something strange is beginning to happen. The more I pray the words of the Gospels, the more I feel that I'm really praying.

Day twenty-one. Today Joe Stowell and I did an interview with the *Grand Rapids Press* about my new position at Cornerstone. We sat together in a conference room in the administration building—at the end of a long table. A photographer was there, as well as a reporter. Joe told them that I would become "Jesus on the campus" and would walk around wearing sandals. It was a joke, of course.

But for weeks after the interview, people assumed that I would actually be walking around campus wearing a robe and sandals. They had taken Joe literally. Even though I am trying to live like Jesus, wearing a robe and sandals doesn't make me any more like Jesus than wearing a suit and tie made me a preacher.

One of the changes I made at Cornerstone was to revise the dress code for the people in my area. In the past, when they were meeting with administrators, they were required to dress up; a tie for the men and dresses for women. Now I allow them to wear jeans and T-shirts—even if they're meeting with other administrators.

Maybe robes and sandals wouldn't be such a bad idea after all.

June

This is the month I have been waiting for all year. I'm leading a group of fifteen people on a tour of Israel. I love Israel! It's where Jesus lived, walked, breathed, ate, drank—and partied with sinners. My preference would have been to move to Israel for a year and walk everywhere Jesus walked, but that's not possible.

I'm on the plane from Newark, New Jersey, to Tel Aviv. After a meal and before I go to sleep, I think about how grateful I am for another opportunity to lead a group to Israel. It will be life changing for every one of us.

Of course, I didn't always feel this way. After hearing so many pastors say, "Going to Israel will revolutionize how you read the Bible—you'll never be the same again!" I simply refused to go. I figured you could follow Jesus and love the Bible without ever going to Israel. Although I had many opportunities, I declined them all.

Then, fifteen years ago, I finally went—and I've been going back ever since.

I am deeply indebted to Ray Vanderlaan, who leads tours to Israel, and though I never went on one of his tours, my oldest son did, and he was profoundly moved by Ray. Shortly after my son toured Israel, he quit his job as the minister of music at Mars Hill Bible Church and went to Israel to study. He earned a master's degree at Jerusalem University College in the history and culture of the first temple period. He came home for a year and then went back to Hebrew University in Jerusalem for another year of study. He and I have conducted several tours to Israel together. As I think about all the sites we will visit and the insights we will get from the Bible, I'm indebted to both Ray Vanderlaan and my son. The rabbis say that when you give credit to someone, you bring in the kingdom of God. So I'm praying that on this trip God's kingdom will arrive because without Ray and my son it wouldn't have happened.

––––––––––

Day one in Israel. At our hotel I arrange for the front desk to give us a wake-up call at 6:30 a.m. Then we'll breakfast at 7:00 a.m. and be on the bus at 7:30.

As my wife and I walk into the dining room for breakfast, I realize something incredible: I don't have to think about what to eat. Everything is kosher. At home my kosher breakfast usually consists of a protein drink and a bunch of vitamins, but lunch and supper are always a challenge.

But the joy of eating in Israel is that you don't have to think about what you're eating. And that's really exciting!

We get on the bus and head to our first site—Bet Shemesh, the city where the ancient Hebrews brought the Ark of the Covenant after the Philistines had captured it. It's also in the valley where the story of Samson and Delilah took place. We plan to read through four or five chapters of that story at the site.

But on the way, I want to make a special stop. The bus pulls over, and we all empty out and walk several hundred yards to a large olive grove. There I have everyone gather around an olive tree, and I ask someone to read Jeremiah 11:16 (every morning when we get on the bus I distribute about twenty different texts for us to read during the day): "The Lord called you a thriving olive tree with fruit beautiful in form."

Israel is a thriving olive tree, and we are now surrounded by thriving olive trees.

"So what do we use olives for?" I ask.

I get a variety of answers. Cooking. Healing. Anointing.

But no one guesses the main purpose of olives in the ancient world. Olive oil was used for lamps. It gave light.

"So why is Israel called a thriving olive tree? Because God wants to use her to give light to the world. Look at the leaves on the olive tree. The top side of the leaf is darker than the bottom side. Pull off a leaf and look."

People take leaves from the tree and look at them. Some of them keep the leaves and make them part of their journal of their journey in Israel.

"When the wind blows and the sun shines on the leaves, it looks like a lamp."

Then I ask someone to read Romans 11:17–21, a passage from the apostle Paul that deals with the subject of Israel—the Jewish people:

> If some of the branches have been broken off, and you, though a wild olive shoot, have been grafted in among the others and now share in the nourishing sap from the olive root, do not boast over those branches. If you do, consider this: You do not support the root, but the root supports you. You will say then, "Branches were broken off so that I could be grafted in." Granted. But they were broken off because of unbelief, and you stand by faith. Do not be arrogant, but be afraid. For if God did not spare the natural branches, he will not spare you either.
>
> **Romans 11:17–21**

"Look around on the ground," I say. "Do you see any wild olive shoots?"

"They're all over the place," several people say.

"If you're a Gentile—and all of you are—then this is what you are. You're a wild olive shoot. And God, through faith, has grafted you into the olive tree. Paul warns us not to be arrogant. He reminds us that we share the nourishing sap from the olive tree, which is Israel. Abraham, Isaac, and Jacob are the forefathers of the Jewish nation. They are also our forefathers as well. Our journey together for the next several days in Israel will be a journey of discovering the roots of our faith. And the root of our faith is Israel."

We talk for a few minutes, and then I ask them to gather in the circle to do the Shema prayer: "Hear O Israel, the Lord is our God, the Lord is one. Love the Lord your God with all your heart, with all your soul and with all your might." I tell them that we will begin and end every day by saying the Shema.

We get on the bus and resume our drive. As I sit there in the front row I realize that my commitment to live like Jesus for a year is really an exploring of the trunk and roots of the tree into which I've been grafted. Some Christians divide the Old Testament from the New, as though the word *old* implies that it's no longer relevant. But Paul reminds us Christians that we are deeply indebted to our Jewish friends. We are simply a wild olive shoot grafted into the tree.

We visit several more sites and end the day at Bet Guvrin. There is one thing I specifically want them to see at this site: an underground olive press. We walk for about three-quarters of a mile, and then we descend some steps into several connected caves. Each September, at harvest time, a farmer would beat the olive trees with a stick to make the olives fall to the ground. Then he would take out the pits and bring the olives to the press. The first step was to place the olives in a large circular vat and roll a huge stone over them to crush them. Then they were collected and put in baskets. The baskets were then taken and placed under pressure created by a huge stone manipulated by a complicated pulley system. This would be the first press of the olive oil. Then the baskets were taken back to the circular vat where the stone was rolled over the olives once again. They were then put back in the baskets and pressed one more time.

Olive oil was also used to anoint kings. Saul was anointed king of Israel, and so was David. The word *Christ* is the equivalent of the Hebrew term *Messiah*, which literally means "the anointed one." Jesus is the Messiah—the anointed one.

But if that is so, then exactly *when* was Jesus anointed?

Perhaps his anointing was in the Garden of Gethsemane. The word *Gethsemane* is from the Hebrew *gat shemenah*. *Gat* means "a press"—just like the olive press where we were now standing. And *shemenah* means olive oil. When you put them together, *Gethsemane* means "a press for olive oil." So perhaps Jesus may have been anointed in a garden that contained an olive press, just like this one. But his anointing was not with oil.

Rather, he sweat great drops of blood.

We get back on the bus and drive down to the Dead Sea, near our hotel. I encourage everyone to take a few minutes and go down to the water—just to float. All the salt in the water makes floating especially easy. Of course I've never floated in the Dead Sea myself. Why? Since everyone loves it so much—I'm against it. I know, poor excuse!

Before dinner we all meet at the bar. Some order wine, some cocktails, and I order a beer. Several people have already downloaded their photographs for the day onto a computer, so we can all watch a slideshow. It's a wonderful way to conclude the day. Then we meet for dinner at the hotel restaurant, where there's a huge salad bar, all sorts of hot entrées, and a massive dessert section as well. And again, everything is kosher—hallelujah!

Day two in Israel. We spend the entire day in the desert. I love the desert. It's my favorite part of Israel. I love its solitude and vastness.

One of the places we visit is Tel Arad. It has two major sections. The first dates back to the early bronze age, 3000–2300 BC. The other is a major fortress that existed during the divided kingdom. Inside is an ancient Israelite temple. Throughout ancient Jewish history, an ongoing struggle took place to centralize worship in Jerusalem. If you had lived in Tel Arad at that time, you would have found it highly inconvenient to travel all the way to Jerusalem to worship, so temples were built all over the land, including the one here at the fortress. The altar in its open courtyard has the exact dimensions as the one in Jerusalem.

I have everyone sit down around the altar, and I tell them about Yom Kippur—the Day of Atonement. On that day the high priest, wearing white linen garments, is allowed to enter the Holiest of Holies and sprinkle blood on the Ark of the Covenant for the forgiveness of people's sins. He casts lots for two goats—one dedicated to God and the other dedicated to *Azazel*, probably meaning a cliff. The goat dedicated to God has a red rope placed around its neck. It will be killed and its blood used to make atonement for sin. The other goat has a red rope tied around its horns, and it will be led out into the desert and pushed over a cliff to die.

The high priest confesses to God his own sin and the sins of the people: "I beg of you, Hashem, I have acted wickedly, rebelled, and sinned before you, I and my household. I beg of you, Hashem, forgive now the wicked acts, rebellions, and sins, for I have acted wickedly, rebelled, and sinned before you, I and my household, as it is written in the Torah of your servant Moses." Before the high priest enters the Holiest of Holies he sprinkles blood from the first goat. Then he takes a shovel with coals from the altar, a ladle containing incense, goes into the Holiest of Holies, puts the incense on the coals, and fills the place with smoke.

The final act of the day is to confess the people's sins over the second goat, the one that will be pushed over the cliff. Taking the goat out to the wilderness represents the fact that the people's sins are carried away. (I suppose it is then pushed off the cliff because it would be really bad if the goat carrying away the people's sins wandered back to the village!)

The sages struggled with the idea that a goat could carry away people's sins. How is it possible for a goat to bear all the sins of the entire community? Their answer is *hoq*, a word that means "beyond human understanding."

After working our way through Leviticus 16 and acting out every part of the story, we then look at several passages in the book of Hebrews that talk about the fact that Jesus Christ has offered himself as a sacrifice for our sins, once and for all. He did it once. He did not repeat it every year on the Day of Atonement. And he did it for all. He did not offer himself as a sacrifice only for the Jews, but for all of us.

One Sunday at Calvary Church I preached about the Day of Atonement from the book of Leviticus. I had a farmer bring two huge goats to be part of the service. People loved it. I cast lots for the goats. I tied a red ribbon around the neck of one and another ribbon around the horns of the other. Then I confessed the sins of the community over the head of the second goat and led it down the center aisle and out of the building.

The only problem was that since we had three morning services, I had to keep the goats in the back hallway between services. You can't potty-train a goat. They peed and pooped all over the back hallway.

At their next meeting the deacons expressed their concern about what had happened that Sunday morning, so they passed an official church policy called "The Large Animal Policy." I was called into that deacons meeting and promised never to do it again—until ... I did it again!

At the end of our session I tell the people that on the Day of Atonement only sins that are committed against God will be forgiven. Sins committed against another person require you to go to that person and ask their forgiveness. At the conclusion of this session I read Leviticus 16:30: "Then, before the LORD, you will be clean from all your sins." There are two ways to read this statement. First, it could mean that since all sins are committed before the Lord, then all sins are forgiven, including those committed against another person. Or it could mean that only sins committed before the Lord will be forgiven—not sins committed against another person, which is how rabbis read this statement. So on the Day of Atonement only sins committed against the Lord can be forgiven.

Years ago, a young African pastor who was attending Calvin Theological Seminary used to come to Calvary with his wife and children. We looked out for them, took care of them, and loved them. They became a vital part of our congregation. But finally they had to go back to Africa. At the last Sunday evening service before they left, I asked the young pastor if he'd like to say anything to us.

"Of course," he said.

I assumed he would thank our congregation for their love and support during the three years he was with us. But no. He said, "As I leave, I want to ask your forgiveness for ways in which I may have offended you in what I said or did. And be assured, in whatever ways you have offended me in what you have said and done, I forgive you." Then he went and sat down. That was it!

When I resigned from Calvary several years ago after eighteen and a half years of ministry, I made a short video to be played after

I left the building. The last Sunday night was a joyous celebration of what God had done in our church. At the end of the service, my wife and I and our children and grandchildren left before the crowd was dismissed. I really didn't want to stand around to shake hands and hug everybody.

After I walked out of the building, they played the video. It was very brief. I asked the congregation for their forgiveness for ways in which I had offended them by what I had said or done. I assured them that as I left, I had forgiven them for ways in which they had offended me in what they had said or done.

But if I drive out demons by the finger of God, then the kingdom of God has come to you.

Luke 11:20

Day three in Israel. This is our last day in the desert. Today we will visit Masada and Qumran and then drive all the way up north to the Sea of Galilee. On the way to Masada, we stop by the side of the road and walk out into the desert. We need to do the Shema, but first I want to share some insights from the gospel.

I read Luke 11:20, in which Jesus has just been accused of driving out demons in cooperation with Satan himself. He then states that he drives out demons by the finger of God, and as a result, God's kingdom has come to them.

This is a reference to an important passage in the Hebrew Bible in which God sends Moses down into the land of Egypt to lead the Israelites out of slavery. He gives Moses three signs to prove to the people that God has sent him. First, when he throws down his staff, it will turn into a snake. Then, when he picks the snake up by the tail, it will become a staff again. Second, when he puts his hand into his cloak and pulls it out again, it will have leprosy. When he puts it back and pulls it out again, it will healed. Third,

131

when he takes water from the river and pours it out, it will turn to blood.

Sure enough, when Moses stands before Pharaoh he throws down his staff and it becomes a snake. The Egyptian magicians, however, are able to do the same thing. They throw down their staffs and they become snakes. So Pharaoh is not impressed. Then Moses stretches his staff over the River Nile and it turns to blood. The magicians do the same thing. A week later, Moses stretches his staff over the streams, canals, and ponds and makes frogs come up from them, and they fill the land of Egypt. Again the magicians do the same thing. Finally Moses takes his staff and strikes the dust of the ground and the dust becomes gnats. The magicians are unable to repeat this miracle. So they say to Pharaoh, "This is the finger of God" (Exodus 8:19).

The rabbis ask the question, "Which finger?" Does God use his thumb? His index finger? His middle finger? His ring finger? His little finger? The rabbis conclude that God only uses his little finger. When we are facing incredible odds, they reason, all we need is the little finger of God. And Jesus overcame all the power of Satan and his demons with that same little finger.

"So as we say the Shema this morning in the desert," I say to the group, "I want you to lift your hands and point your little finger to heaven and say with me, 'Hear O Israel, the Lord is our God, the Lord is one. Love the Lord your God with all your heart, with all your soul, and with all your mind.'"

I hate to leave the desert. The desert is where God and Israel fell in love with each other, where Israel became God's bride. "I remember the devotion of your youth, how as a bride you loved me and followed me through the desert" (Jeremiah 2:1). We know that God had already established his covenant with Abraham, but this text reminds us that it was in the desert that God married Israel. It is also where John baptized Jesus and where Jesus was tempted for forty days and forty nights. As much as I hate to leave, we need to get to Galilee.

Days four and five in Israel. Today we make the transition from the desert to the region of Galilee. We also make the transition from the Hebrew Bible to the life of Jesus, which makes me particularly excited.

After breakfast we drive to the foot of the Mount of Beatitudes. That is where it is believed Jesus delivered the Sermon on the Mount (Matthew 5–7). We make a fifteen-minute hike up the side of the mountain to a place that's flat and has a Catholic altar. Behind the altar is a large shade tree, where we catch our breath and drink water (very important to remember to do in this hot climate). Then I ask everyone to sit in a circle.

On the Mount of Beatitudes, without any explanation or introduction, I deliver the entire Sermon on the Mount from memory. Later, many people will tell me that this was the most moving part of the entire trip. Sitting there on the side of the hill, looking out over the Sea of Galilee, and listening to the words of Jesus—it's all pretty overwhelming.

I actually memorized the Sermon on the Mount several years ago, after I'd read somewhere that it's a disciple's responsibility to memorize, word for word, the teachings of the rabbi. Jesus' disciples would have memorized all of his teachings and all of his parables.

So how much of Jesus' other teachings have I memorized? The answer is not much! This year I started to memorize the gospel of Mark but didn't get very far. I've been so busy just reading the Gospels and trying to live them that I really don't have time to memorize them. Still, I know the Sermon on the Mount by heart.

Some scholars think that Jesus didn't deliver this sermon all at once, that it's simply a compilation of many of Jesus' teachings. I happen to believe that he did deliver it all at the same time, but I agree that it's a compilation of his teachings as well. It's the heart and soul of the teachings of Jesus. Maybe this year I should've just focused on the Sermon on the Mount. It's like a summary of his teachings. If I could just live the Sermon on the Mount, I know I'd be a whole lot more like Jesus.

After I finish the Sermon on the Mount, I ask people to stand for the Shema. "But I want to add another statement to the Shema," I say. "It comes from the teachings of Jesus. When Jesus was asked which command is the greatest, he responded by quoting the Shema: 'We are to love the Lord our God with all of our heart, soul, mind, and strength.' But I want to add another phrase that Jesus added: 'And we are to love our neighbor as ourselves.'" So we all stand, raise our hands with our little fingers to the sky, and say, "Hear, O Israel, the Lord is our God, the Lord is one. Love the Lord your God with all your heart, with all your soul, and with all your might. And love your neighbor as yourself."

If we could just focus on these two commandments it would profoundly impact our lives.

Love God and love your neighbor.

That's it.

For the rest of today and all day tomorrow we will visit a variety of sites in the Galilee region, ending at the Jordan River where the group will have the opportunity to be baptized—just as Jesus was. A little farther away there's an official place, south of the Sea of Galilee, where groups of people can be baptized. But it's owned by a church, and you have to pay a fee and get a white robe before walking down the gentle slope into the slow-moving river. You can be baptized like that at any of three or four places along the river, and people can witness your baptism from rows of benches.

You can also purchase a videotape afterward. On the way out you have to walk through the bookstore and gift shop, where they hope to sell you a bunch of stuff.

I'm bothered by the commercialism.

At another site north of the Sea of Galilee, where I plan to baptize our group, the Jordan runs extremely fast. You have to be very careful stepping into this part of the river because you can be swept downstream if you stumble. Today I will have two people help me so that no one gets swept away!

I like this spot because it's not commercial.

I like it because the river is rugged and natural.

I like it because no one else is around.

We began our teaching at the Jordan River with the creation narrative.

> In the beginning God created the heavens and the earth. Now the earth was formless and empty, darkness was over the surface of the deep, and the Spirit of God was hovering over the waters.
> And God said ...
>
> **Genesis 1:1–3**

I point out two significant things about these verses. First, the Spirit of God is hovering over the waters. Second, God speaks. I remind everyone that at the baptism of Jesus the same things happened. The Spirit of God descended and hovered like a dove above Jesus and above the water of the Jordan River. Second, God speaks from heaven, "This is my son with whom I am well pleased." So there is a sense that just as God created the world, so too he is now beginning a new creation through Jesus Christ.

We also talk about the crossing of the Red Sea. The children of Israel crossed on dry land, but when the Egyptians tried to pursue them, the waters poured in and the Egyptians were drowned. We also talk about the time the children of Israel came to the

Jordan as they were about to enter the Promised Land. The river was at flood stage—similar to what we are witnessing right now. Again God intervened, and they crossed on dry land. The apostle Paul picks up these ideas when he talks about Christian baptism: "We were therefore buried with him through baptism into death in order that, just as Christ was raised from the dead through the glory of the father, we too may live a new life" (Romans 6:4). The idea of baptism is that when we do step down into the waters, we are stepping down into death. When we come up again, we are coming up to live a new life.

Then I offer baptism to anyone who wants it. Nearly everyone decides to be baptized. Even though many have been baptized before, just walking through the land, reading the stories that happened at each site, and studying the teachings of Jesus make these people cultivate a passion to live a new life. So for about an hour we baptize everyone. It's informal. It's communal. And it's powerful. We decide to stay there for another thirty or forty minutes. It's so peaceful even though the river is raging.

Day six in Israel. Today we leave Galilee and head up to Jerusalem. Even though it's south of where we are, the proper theological way to speak of going to Jerusalem is "up." On the way we stop at Mount Carmel, where the view is stunning. It overlooks the entire valley of Armageddon. Straight ahead is an Israeli airbase, with planes taking off and landing constantly. On Mount Carmel we study the story of Elijah and the prophets of Baal.

According to the book of Revelation, the valley of Armageddon is where the final great battle on planet Earth will take place: "Then they gathered the kings together to the place that in Hebrew is called Armageddon" (Revelation 16:16). *Armageddon* is a Hebrew word that simply means "the mountain of Megiddo."

> As Jesus was sitting on the Mount of Olives, the disciples came to him privately. "Tell us," they said, "when will this happen, and what will be the sign of your coming and of the end of the age?"
>
> **Matthew 24:3**

The story begins with the disciples admiring the beautiful stones that make up the ancient temple at Jerusalem. Jesus tells them, "I tell you the truth, not one stone here will be left on another; every one will be thrown down." This is shocking news to the disciples. So when they sit down on the Mount of Olives, they ask Jesus when this will take place. The Matthew account includes the question, "What will be the sign of your coming and the end of the age?" The Luke account simply states, "When will these things happen? And what will be the sign that they are about to take place?" The short version of this discourse occurs in Mark, where the disciples ask, "When will these things happen? And what will be the sign that they are about to be fulfilled?" So Luke and Mark focus exclusively on the fact that the temple will be destroyed, and the disciples want to know when this will happen. The Matthew account is concerned with the same question, but it also includes signs of the "second coming" and the "end of the age."

Some scholars believe that all three accounts deal with events that were fulfilled in AD 70 when the Romans destroyed the temple and threw down all the stones. And it appears that the Mark and Luke accounts accurately reflect this perspective. Matthew talks about Jesus' coming again and the end of the age. From a Jewish point of view, the end of the age could refer to the destruction of the Temple; after all, the temple has still not been rebuilt. So perhaps the entire sermon predicting the signs that lead up to the destruction of the Temple has already been fulfilled.

Another interpretation is that Jesus is talking about both the destruction of the Temple and the signs that will accompany the end of the age. This is what I have always believed. In fact, I have preached many sermons on the Olivet discourse using the book of Daniel and the book of Revelation—both books are apocalyptic in nature. Some of the signs that I have identified from the Matthew account are as follows:

1. Wars and rumors of wars
2. International conflict
3. Famines and earthquakes
4. Persecution of believers
5. False prophets
6. The increase of wickedness
7. Believers will grow cold in their love for God
8. The gospel will be preached in the entire world and then the end will come

About ten years ago I wrote a book for Zondervan called *Fifty Reasons Why Jesus Could Come by AD 2000*. I was slightly off! I think Zondervan wanted to capitalize on the uncertainty leading up to the year 2000, but I've always believed—and still believe— that Jesus could come at any moment. I think his early followers were expecting him to return, and every generation of Christians since then has expected that Jesus could return at any moment. I was trying to write a book that articulated at least fifty reasons why Jesus could come at any time.

Of course, I'm trying to defend myself, and there's really no defense. I was wrong.

But I'm still waiting for the coming of Jesus.

Which brings me back to the Olivet discourse. It is possible that all of the signs that Jesus listed have already been fulfilled. Perhaps Jesus had in mind the destruction of the Temple, but it is also possible that he was speaking on two levels—the level of the Temple's destruction and the level of the end of the world and his second coming. I still believe the latter. But I'm not as convinced as I once was.

When Jesus was about to ascend to heaven, the disciples asked him, "Lord, are you at this time going to restore the kingdom to Israel?"

Jesus responded, "It is not for you to know the times or dates the Father has set by his own authority" (Acts 1:6–7). So if it is not for me to know, then I shouldn't speculate. I recently heard one televangelist who is known for his end-of-the-world scenarios say, "I know people say you can't know the time or the dates for the coming of Jesus, but that's a bunch of baloney!"

I thought, "What a total idiot!"

Then I realized, "That's not a very Jesus-thing to say!" Jesus himself said, "Anyone who says, 'you fool!' will be in danger of the fire of hell" (Matthew 5:22). Of course, I didn't call him a fool—but I did call him an idiot. If a "fool" and an "idiot" are synonymous, then I'm in danger of the fire of hell. Not a pleasant thought.

Some of my friends have suggested that we don't know the day or the hour, but we can know the general period of time. Give me a break! Nearly every generation of Christians has believed that they were living in the last days. And so far, all of them have been wrong. I still believe the same thing I've always believed about the coming of the Lord, but I'm more hesitant now than ever before to be emphatic about it. I like the words of Abraham Heschel, a famous Jewish writer who passed away a few years ago: "I will not trouble myself with things too difficult for me to understand" (referring to Psalm 131:1). This is one of my eldest son's favorite quotes.

We leave Mount Carmel and drive to Caesarea, which is on the seacoast. There's a wonderful amphitheater there as well as the ruins of a large city built by Herod the Great. We walk down among the rocks to the edge of the water, where I have someone read some of the last words of Jesus: "But you will receive power when the Holy Spirit comes on you; and you will be my witnesses in Jerusalem, and in all Judea and Samaria, and to the ends of the earth" (Acts 1:8).

We're now on our way up to Jerusalem. We've spent time in the Judean desert. We've driven past Samaria. As we stood on the rocks with the waves crashing around us, I say, "Look out at the ocean. From the ancient point of view, you're looking at the ends of the earth. For several days we've studied the life and teachings of Jesus. But now, at this place, Jesus tells his disciples that they are to witness for him not only in Jerusalem and Judea, but in Samaria and ultimately to the ends of the earth. I can't even imagine what must have gone through the disciples' minds. When they signed up to follow Jesus I'm sure they had no idea he'd force them so far out of their comfort zone. Here he is, sending them into the whole world!"

Days seven, eight, and nine in Israel. We began our first day in Jerusalem on the Mount of Olives. It overlooks the holy city of Jerusalem, and it's an incredible sight. We then walk from the Mount of Olives down to the Garden of Gethsemane.

The church associated with the Garden of Gethsemane is on the left, but we have received special permission to go into a garden on the right that will not be as crowded. In fact, we are the only ones there. I have someone read, without interruption, the story of Jesus in the garden. Then I ask people to spread out over the garden and spend forty-five minutes in silent reflection. During this time I pray the Orthodox Jesus Prayer: "Lord Jesus Christ, son of God, have mercy on me, a sinner." I pray it over and over and over. I spend the entire time focused on this prayer. By the end I am overwhelmed with gratitude for what Jesus did in the garden and on the cross.

We leave the garden and walk to the Old City. The first place we stop is Bethesda, where the ruins of the ancient pool can still be seen. We read the story of the invalid Jesus healed by the pool. After healing him, Jesus tells him, "Get up! Pick up your mat and walk."

It was the Sabbath when Jesus healed the man, and Jewish law forbids any work on the Sabbath. Picking up your mat would have been considered work. So the Jews were upset with Jesus.

I talk about the subject of divine healing and suggest that it's possible to be cured but not healed, and I suggest that it's possible to be healed but not cured. In the Gospels is the story of ten lepers Jesus cured, only one of whom comes back to thank Jesus.

All of them were cured, but only one was healed.

Paul writes about what he calls his "thorn in the flesh." Three times he prayed to God to remove this thorn, but God doesn't do it. Then Paul discovers that God's grace is sufficient to sustain him even in the face of suffering. So he writes that he will glory in his weakness because in his weakness God's grace is more than sufficient.

Paul was not cured, but he was healed.

When Jesus sent his disciples out to perform miracles and heal, they anointed people with oil and prayed over them. So I offer to anoint the people in our group and pray for their healing as well. Several respond immediately, so I anoint them with oil and pray over them.

After the teaching and the anointing, we go into the adjacent church, where we gather on the steps of the altar and sing the doxology. The church has brilliant acoustics. The sound is unbelievable. It echoes everywhere.

Shortly after I was diagnosed with ALS, I had a difficult time giving thanks. After all, I thought, I had little to be thankful for—I had a terminal, incurable disease. But about a year after my diagnosis, I led a tour to Israel and we came to this church. One of the songs we chose to sing was "Give Thanks with a Grateful Heart." For the first time in a year, I was able to sing and give thanks to the Lord—not for the disease, but for his goodness and kindness in the midst of my struggle.

The next several days are filled with visiting various sites. We go to Bethlehem. We go down into the desert to En Gedi. We walk all over the Old City. On the last day we go to the Holocaust Museum because I want our group to understand the long, difficult, and painful struggle for Jewish existence.

In the desert we were basically alone. In Galilee we saw a few other groups at the sites we visited. But in Jerusalem people are everywhere. Jerusalem is like a "religious flea market."

Back in Grand Rapids. We flew through the night back to the U.S. The next day I went to my office at Cornerstone. I went out to lunch with several of the key people on our staff. At the restaurant, for the first time in over a week and a half, I had to make decisions about what to eat. In Israel, everything was kosher. But now, back at home, every meal will be a challenge. It must be hard for Jews in the United States to obey the laws of kosher. I doubt they eat out very much.

July

I read the Gospels.
I ate kosher.
I took the month off.

August

The Lunatic in My Head

I'm tired of reading the Gospels.

At this point in my journey I've listened to the Gospels almost thirty times. Since I began working at Cornerstone, I've had to fight to find the time, but in the car, on my way to and from work, I listen to the Gospels. Whenever I go for coffee, I listen to the Gospels. Every spare minute, I listen to the Gospels.

And I'm tired of it!

So I decide to sit on the porch today with my iPod, and for the first time in months I listen to something other than the Gospels —I listen to Pink Floyd, to their album *The Dark Side of the Moon*. The words to one song, called "Brain Damage," grab my attention. It's a song about "lunatics." The opening line states, "The lunatic is on the grass," but the verse that really captures my attention begins, "The lunatic is in my head." The end of that verse says, "There's someone in my head but it's not me."

I've been thinking about my journey this year. I'm eating kosher, keeping the Sabbath, wearing an undershirt with tassels, observing the feasts and festivals, and praying like Jews pray. I'm also praying the Catholic rosary, the Orthodox prayer rope, and the Episcopal prayer beads. I'm a confused individual!

And now, as I look toward the election in November, I'm seriously thinking of voting for Senator Obama. So maybe there is a "lunatic ... in my head." Perhaps there is "someone in my head [that's] not me."

Or maybe the someone in my head is Jesus—and that's exactly what my year is about.

From now on, I don't plan to keep a record of my days. Maybe I can blame it on Cornerstone. I will continue to pray the Orthodox prayer rope, but I've decided to drop the rosary for Cornerstone's sake. I will continue praying the Episcopal prayer beads, eating kosher, observing the Sabbath (when it's convenient), wearing the tzitzit (from time to time), reading the Gospels (though the pace has slowed considerably), and, in general, attempting to live out Jesus' teachings.

So that's what's been going on in my head. I'd like to think it's Jesus.

The Sabbath

I desire mercy, not sacrifice
Matthew 12:7

It's the Sabbath. Jesus and his disciples are going through the fields and some of the disciples are hungry and begin to pick grain and eat it. The religious leaders immediately say, "Look! Your disciples are doing what is unlawful on the Sabbath." Of course, the religious leaders are right. Picking grain, rubbing it together, blowing away the chaff, and eating it would be considered work, which is not allowed on the Sabbath. Jesus reminds them that even priests work on the Sabbath and are thereby violating it, yet no one accuses them of breaking the Sabbath. He then tells the religious leaders that God desires mercy, not sacrifice, and concludes with the statement that God is "Lord of the Sabbath." Jesus then goes on to heal a man on the Sabbath, which infuriates the religious leaders even more.

I've been trying to keep the Sabbath, though I haven't been successful. Jesus is stating that something is more important than keeping the Sabbath—that is, showing mercy. Jesus had mercy on his disciples because they were hungry. He had mercy on the man who was healed on the Sabbath. And Jesus expects us to have mercy as well. This is a great reminder to me as I struggle with keeping the Sabbath. Jesus is more concerned that I show mercy to others than that I try to keep all the rules of the Sabbath.

And for that I say, "Praise be to God!"

Jesus' Prayer

> Abba, Father, everything is possible for you. Take this cup from me. Yet not what I will, but what you will.
>
> **Mark 14:36**

After the Last Supper, Jesus takes his disciples to the garden of Gethsemane. He tells them to sit down. Then he says to Peter, James, and John, "My soul is overwhelmed with sorrow to the point of death. Stay here and keep watch." In Luke's account it states that when Jesus prayed "his sweat was like drops of blood falling to the ground" (22:44). Jesus knows that he's about to be arrested. He knows that Judas has already betrayed him. He knows that after his arrest his disciples will forsake him. He knows that Peter will deny him. He knows that he will be crucified. He knows that he will die for the sins of the entire world.

And so he prays with passion.

Abba, Father

He opens his prayer with this statement: "Abba, Father." He addresses God as his *Abba* ("daddy" in Aramaic). God is our father as well; many people, however, do not have a good earthly father and therefore struggle with the idea of God as a father. What kind of father is God?

Jesus tells the story of the prodigal son to help us understand.

A father has two sons. The younger comes to the father and says, "Father, give me my share of the estate." In the culture of Jesus' day this would've been a huge insult. Normally you divide the inheritance after the father dies. So what the son is really saying is "I wish you were dead!" The amazing thing is that this father agrees to divide the inheritance and gives the younger son his portion.

The younger son goes off to a distant country and squanders his wealth in wild living. After a severe famine, the son no longer has any money, so he hires himself out to feed pigs (unclean, nonkosher animals). He's so hungry that he even longs to eat "pig food." One day he realizes that the servants at his father's house are better off than he is. So he decides to go back home, apologize for what he has done, and tell his father that he no longer deserves to be his son. He will ask his father to hire him as a servant.

So he heads home.

When the father sees him at a distance, he's filled with compassion. He runs to his son, throws his arms around him, and kisses him. The son immediately confesses his sin. Then the father says to his servants, "Quick! Bring the best robe and put it on him. Put a ring on his finger and sandals on his feet. Bring the fatted calf and kill it. Let's have a feast and celebrate. For this son of mine was dead and is alive again; he was lost and is found."

So what kind of a father is God?

He sees me.

He is filled with compassion for me.

He runs to me.

He throws his arms around me.

He puts a robe around me.

He puts a ring on my finger.

He puts sandals on my feet.

He parties with me.

This is the kind of God that Jesus prays to. The ancient world saw many gods, and humans were responsible to perform certain religious duties to appease them. But the God of the Bible is the complete opposite. He is a God who runs toward us. He is a God who embraces us and celebrates with us.

As I face my own suffering with ALS, I am deeply encouraged that God is my Abba—my daddy. He loves me and cares for me. He runs toward me and embraces me. He celebrates each day with me.

Everything Is Possible for You

While our kids were growing up we lived on a strict budget. When one of the kids would say, "Let's go out to eat tonight," we'd respond, "It's not in the budget." We limited the amount of money we spent on eating out, on vacation, on Christmas gifts, and so on—because we had agreed to live within our means. I wanted to do more for the kids, but we couldn't afford it.

But it's not that way with God. As Jesus prays in the garden, he says, "Everything is possible for you."

I am grateful that nothing is impossible with God. Even with the disease I have, I know that he possesses all the power to heal it. Even though I don't know of a single person who has been healed of ALS, I still believe that God is able to do it. He is omnipotent —all powerful. It's always in his budget.

Take This Cup from Me

Jesus doesn't want to face the suffering that lies ahead. He knows what that suffering will mean. He knows that he will feel forsaken by God, and so he makes a simple request: "Take this cup from me."

I've met a number of people over the years who have been diagnosed with terminal diseases who say, "I am grateful that God gave me this disease. It has changed my way of thinking and living."

Unfortunately I've never been able to say that. First of all, I don't believe that God gave me this disease. I believe I was genetically predisposed to ALS and something triggered it. Because I was predisposed, I was unable to fight it off. I believe that this disease is part of the brokenness of the world in which we live.

Second, instead of being grateful for the disease, I feel more like Jesus in the Garden of Gethsemane when he said, "Take this cup from me." I know that ALS has profoundly impacted me. I know it has shaped and reshaped my thinking and living. I know it has deepened my walk with God. But frankly, I'd rather be healthy and whole. So I resonate with Jesus' prayer.

Yet Not What I Will, but What You Will

This must have been a difficult prayer for Jesus. He has already reminded God that nothing is impossible for him. He has already asked God to take the cup from him. But he concludes by surrendering his will to the will of the father. It's not what Jesus wants — it's what God wants.

For me, the same is true. It's not what I want — it's what God wants. Every day I have to surrender my will to the will of the father. I keep reminding God that nothing is impossible with him, and I keep asking God to take this cup from me. But I also surrender my will.

Now I'm not trying to compare my ALS with the sufferings of Jesus. I realize there's no comparison. But as Jesus faced his suffering and prayed in the face of that suffering, I am encouraged by what he prayed. I plan to use it as a model for my own praying. So what is my prayer?

> *Daddy, I know you love and care for me.*
> *I know that nothing is impossible for you. You could heal me*
>   *in an instant.*
> *Please take this cup from me. Please heal me of ALS.*
> *But it's not what I want that matters, it's what you want.*

God's Commands

One of my favorite fast food restaurants is Qdoba, which has good fresh Mexican food. When I go there I always order the same thing—chicken, rice, poblano pesto sauce, medium salsa, sour cream, and cheese. But this year I have had to adjust what I eat. Chicken, sour cream, and cheese do not go together. So I order the meal without the sour cream and cheese, and it's nowhere near as good. I've also gone from the medium salsa to the mild salsa since I don't have the sour cream to moderate the spiciness of the salsa. And every meal is like this.

So why does God give these strange regulations? After all, shrimp and lobster are wonderful! And there's nothing like a breakfast of fried eggs, grits, bacon, sausage, and country ham. As I've mentioned before, some people argue that these regulations were for health restrictions. Others argue that it has something to do with separating the people of God from pagan practices.

But the Bible makes it clear that the ultimate reason is holiness. The word *holiness* implies a complete separation from pagan practices. Even in their eating habits, the people of Israel were to be separate from the culture and separate to the Lord.

During the time of Jesus, the religious leaders would not eat unless they had first ceremonially washed their hands. Failure to do this would make their hands "unclean" or unkosher. This washing was based on tradition, for nowhere does the Hebrew Bible require people to wash their hands before they eat. On the Day of Atonement, however, the high priest is required to wash with water several times: "He shall bathe himself with water in the holy place and put on his regular garments" (Leviticus 16:24). Perhaps this is the basis for the hand-washing tradition.

The religious leaders noticed that Jesus' disciples didn't wash their hands before they ate, so they asked Jesus, "Why don't your disciples live according to the tradition of the elders instead of eating their food with unclean hands?" (Mark 7:5).

From a Jewish point of view, this is an important question. Jews believed that God gave Moses the Torah on Mount Sinai. In addition to the written Torah, however, there was also the oral Torah—rules developed over time by the elders of the community, rules that were just as binding as the written Torah. So the religious leaders were essentially asking why Jesus' disciples didn't obey the oral Torah.

In response, Jesus quoted from the prophet Isaiah. "These people honor me with their lips, but their hearts are far from me. They worship me in vain; their teachings are but rules taught by men" (Mark 7:6–7). It's interesting that Jesus responded to the traditions of the elders by quoting from the Hebrew Bible. Isaiah is clearly condemning people for worshiping God based on human rules and regulations. Jesus then went on to say, "You have let go of the commands of God and are holding on to the traditions of men" (Mark 7:8).

And what are those commands?

> You have heard that it was said, "Love your neighbor and hate your enemy." But I tell you: Love your enemies and pray for those who persecute you, that you may be sons of your Father in heaven. He causes his sun to rise on the evil and the good, and sends rain on the righteous and the unrighteous. If you love those who love you, what reward will you get? Are not even the tax collectors doing that? And if you greet only your brothers, what are you doing more than others? Do not even pagans do that? Be perfect, therefore, as your heavenly Father is perfect.
>
> **Matthew 5:43–48**

The kingdom that Jesus promotes is an upside-down kingdom. Sometimes it doesn't make sense. Loving your enemies is not logical—it's the opposite of human nature. Moses, who led the children of Israel out of Egyptian bondage and through the desert for forty years, makes one last speech to the tribes before they enter the Promised Land. He says, "The eternal God is your refuge, and underneath are the everlasting arms. He will drive out your enemy before you, saying, 'Destroy him!'" (Deuteronomy 33:27). This makes sense—destroying your enemy. God had told them that when they entered the land they were to completely destroy all of the inhabitants—men, women, children, and cattle.

This command has always bothered me. I know the traditional evangelical position: that if they had not destroyed the inhabitants of the land they would have ended up intermarrying with them, worshiping their idols, and losing their uniqueness as the people of God. Since the Messiah was still to come through the Jewish people, the very future of the Messiah was at stake. I agree that there is a grain of truth in these statements.

Still, it bothers me, and when I get to heaven it's on my list of questions to ask God.

Israel has always had its enemies—ancient and modern. From Pharaoh to Hitler, they have all desired the extinction of the Jewish people. For the Jews, fighting back was a matter of personal survival. Even David prays for the extinction of his enemies: "Arise, O LORD! Deliver me, O my God! Strike all my enemies on the jaw; break the teeth of the wicked" (Psalm 3:7). There are many similar psalms—called "imprecatory psalms." Then Jesus comes along and argues that in his kingdom we are "to love our enemies."

From a Jewish point of view, this is ridiculous!

A few days after 9/11, I was at ground zero for several days, encouraging and praying with the rescue teams. It was an overwhelming experience. The size of the devastation cannot be described. Even the videos and photographs don't do it justice. During those days, the search-and-rescue teams were still hopeful of finding survivors; when they came up out of the rubble, I'd gather the group together and we'd pray.

Sometimes we would get police officers together and pray with them. We prayed that they'd find more survivors. We prayed for the families who had lost loved ones. We prayed for those involved in the search and rescue. We prayed for our country as well. It was one of the most profound experiences of my ministry life.

One night around midnight, I was standing with an Irish cop who had lost several friends in the attacks. He said, "There's no way to describe how I feel. Whoever did this, I think we ought to take a nuclear bomb and drop it on their country." And I felt the same way—maybe not a nuclear bomb—but we certainly should go after our enemies.

After all, it's the right thing to do. We should resist our enemies. We should fight our enemies. We should defeat our enemies. If we don't, they will continually come back to wreak devastation on our country.

But that is not the way of Jesus.

So how do we love our enemies?

My youngest son served two tours of duty in Iraq, compliments of the United States Army National Guard. During his last tour, one of his good friends was killed in action. He'd been with my son on the first tour and volunteered to go back a second time, just like my son. During that tour, this friend volunteered to be a gunner on a gun truck. He provided security for the convoy. During one mission the gun truck was hit by a roadside bomb, and my son's friend was killed. A few weeks before he died, he had written home saying, "If I die over here, please know that I died doing what I love."

My wife and I decided to go to the church to meet with this soldier's family before the burial service. As we pulled up to the church, a number of motorcycles were already parked there. As we walked up the steps of the church, several tough-looking, tattooed, long-haired veterans were there to make sure that protesters were kept at a distance. During those days a church group from Texas was protesting, saying that the killing of soldiers in Iraq was the result of the moral and spiritual decline of America. They seemed almost happy when our soldiers were killed. These veterans had made a commitment to protect the family from the protesters.

As we walked into the church, we could see the coffin down in front, covered with an American flag. Next to the coffin were the soldier's boots. It took every ounce of control I had not to break down and sob. My wife and I were some of the first to greet and talk with the family.

What do you say?

"I want you to know that my wife and I are praying for you and your family. My son was with your son on the first tour and also was on the second tour."

"Thank you for coming," the mother said. "Your son will be fine. He'll come home."

How did she know that this was what I was thinking? *What if it were my son?* You try not to think about losing your child; you put it out of your mind. But when you don't hear from your son for several days, you begin to wonder.

When we got back in the car I started to cry. It was one of the most difficult things I had ever done. I hadn't really wanted to face the family of the dead soldier, but I knew I had to.

As I sat there in the car, I had an overwhelming feeling of anger toward those who had killed my son's friend. The people who made the roadside bomb. The people who planted it. The people who had detonated it. I wanted them to be brought to justice. I wanted them to suffer for what they had done. I wanted them to know that there was a family in Michigan who was completely devastated because of what had happened.

But this is not the way of Jesus.

Jesus says, "Love your enemies."

So I prayed, "God, help me to love the people who killed my son's friend."

Of course this is not easy to do.

On one occasion, an expert in the Torah stood up to test Jesus. "Teacher, what must I do to inherit eternal life?" Notice that he did not ask, "Teacher, what must I *believe* to inherit eternal life?" That would have been an evangelical's question. We tend to be interested in *what* you believe and in *whom* you believe. But this is not the question that the expert in the law asked. He wanted to know what he needed *to do* to gain eternal life. Jesus did a very Jewish thing. He answered the question with two more questions: "What is written in the Law? How do you read it?" Then he answers by repeating the words of the Shema found in Deuteronomy 6: "Love the Lord your God with all your heart and with all your soul and with all your strength and with all your mind, and, love your neighbor as yourself." In essence, Jesus was saying, "Do this and you will live."

But the expert in the law was not through. If we are to love our neighbor, then who is our neighbor? Jesus answered by telling the story. My preference would have been for Jesus to give a list of people who qualify as "our neighbor." Then I could simply evaluate my life based on the list. But this is not what Jesus does.

Instead he tells a story about a man who, while making his way from Jerusalem to Jericho, gets robbed, beaten, and left almost dead. A priest (someone who served in the Temple) and a Levite (the priest's helper) come by. When they see the man lying on the road they cross to the other side.

Most preachers on this passage argue that what the priest and Levite did was terrible. They passed by a man in need. But if you were a Jew standing in that crowd while Jesus told this story, you would have understood that the priest and the Levite did *exactly* what they were supposed to do. If the man was dead and they had approached him, they would have been unclean. They would not have been able to participate in the Temple worship for a period of time.

So they did the right thing. They passed by on the other side.

Then a Samaritan comes along. If you were standing in the crowd listening to Jesus that day, just the mention of the word *Samaritan* would have made your blood boil. Jews and Samaritans had nothing to do with each other. They hated each other. They were enemies. In the gospel of John, when the Jews want to demean Jesus, they say, "Aren't we right in saying you are a Samaritan and demon possessed?" (John 8:48). It was the ultimate insult. They were calling Rabbi Jesus demon possessed—and a Samaritan.

Then, in the story, a series of actions are associated with the Samaritan: he saw the man on the road. He took pity on him. He went to him. He bandaged his wounds. He poured on oil and wine. He put the man on his own donkey. He took him to an inn. He took care of him. He offered the innkeeper money to look after him.

Then Jesus asks this question. "Which of these three do you think was a neighbor to the man who fell into the hands of robbers?"

The expert in the law replied, "The one who had mercy on him."

Jesus says, "Go and do likewise" (Luke 10:25–37).

The point of the story is that your enemy is your neighbor.

This month I preached from this text in the African American church where we occasionally attend. After I retired I knew that I could no longer keep attending Calvary Church. After all, I'd served there for eighteen and a half years. I didn't want to be part of the process of looking for a new pastor, nor did I want a constant stream of people asking me how I was doing.

For a while my wife and I attended a large African American church in our community. The pastor has been a good personal friend for many years. We doubled the minority population — from two white people to four. From time to time the pastor still asks me to preach.

When I got to the end of my sermon I walked off the platform and stood in the middle aisle. "In case you haven't noticed," I said, "I'm not African American! So tell me, who are your enemies?"

People in the African American church are extremely responsive. Ask a question, and several people will yell out the answer.

"Racists!"

"God says you are to love them," I said.

"The KKK!"

"God says you are to love them."

"The Republican administration."

"God says you are to love them."

And the list went on and on. After each statement, I said, "God says you are to love them."

We know clearly what God commands. The Jewish leaders had forgotten these commands and were holding onto the traditions of men. It's easy for us to look back and condemn them for this, but before we do, we must look at ourselves. In what ways have we forsaken the commands of God? In what ways do we hold to human traditions? I'm afraid that in some cases we are more passionate about human traditions than about the commands of God.

So what human traditions does the evangelical church hold sacred? I could name a bunch. But the problem with naming them is that we think by naming them we're above them. The truth is, we all tend to conform to human traditions and forsake the ultimate commands of God.

But Jesus isn't through yet. He goes on to say that nothing outside a person makes them "unclean" or unkosher, but rather it's what comes out of a man—from the inside—that makes him "unclean." He states that nothing we put into our bodies makes us unclean because it goes into the stomach and out of the body. Rather it is what comes out of the heart that makes a person unclean. The narrator adds an interesting statement at this point: "In saying this, Jesus declared all foods clean" (Mark 7:19).

Thank you, Lord.

I love bacon. I love shrimp. I love meat with cheese. And I am free to eat all of them at the same time or separately. It doesn't matter (though I still plan to eat kosher for the rest of the year).

Then Jesus says the following: "For from within, out of men's hearts, come evil thoughts, sexual immorality, theft, murder, adultery, greed, malice, deceit, lewdness, envy, slander, arrogance and folly. All these evils come from inside and make a man unclean" (Mark 7:21–23).

So while I'm focusing on all the details of living the way Jesus lived, I must not forget that the real issue is not on the outside—it's on the inside. Wearing tassels, eating kosher, observing the Sabbath, and going to the synagogue are all on the outside. So is reading the Bible, going to church, listening to sermons, and listening to Christian radio. These are all on the outside. What Jesus demands is purity inside. And the hard issues are the most difficult to deal with.

Adultery

When I was in college my roommates and I decided that we all had problems with lustful thinking, the very thing that Jesus talks about in this passage. So we decided that every time we had a lustful thought, we would immediately stop and read a chapter of the Bible. I would be walking across campus and there notice one of my roommates sitting on a bench reading the Bible. "I know his problem." I'd smile, nod, and keep on walking. Of course all of my roommates saw me at various places across the campus reading the Bible as well. That month all of us read huge chunks of the Bible!

In the Sermon on the Mount Jesus states that anyone who looks at a woman lustfully has already committed adultery with her in his heart. But what does it mean to look at a woman lustfully? I have often heard preachers state that the first look is okay but if you keep looking then you have sinned. This is especially a challenge when you are only a few clicks away from pornographic material on the Internet. The temptation is always there. For men it's an ongoing struggle, and increasingly for women as well. You can read the Bible, pray, go to church, be in a small group, have accountability partners, and be a spiritual leader—and at the same time be addicted to pornography. And Jesus says, "If you are, you're unclean."

Theft and Greed

These ideas go together. Greed is the constant desire for more and more of what we do not have. It is one of the reasons our economy is in such terrible shape—the greed of those who led major corporations. But greed is not something that only the rich struggle with. It is something we all struggle with.

Murder

In the Sermon on the Mount Jesus states that if you hate your brother you are guilty of murder. Some of my conservative friends hate homosexuals. They say, "Love the sinner but hate the sin," but the truth is, they hate both—the sinner and the sin. It's easy to hate those with whom we have little contact. But when you hate anyone, including homosexuals, you are guilty of murder.

Malice, Deceit, Envy, and Slander

All these go together as well. They involve what we say about other people, and when we skew the truth to our own advantage while at the same time putting others down, we are guilty of being unclean.

Lewdness

When I was growing up many pastors were upset with the kind of language used on television. They argued that if we began laughing about sin, pretty soon we'd begin to commit sin. At the time I thought it was far-fetched. But they had no idea how bad television would get. It's lewd. And being lewd, it's unclean.

Arrogance and Folly

Whenever I think that I am more spiritual than others, then I am arrogant. Whenever I think that what I'm doing qualifies me to be in the closer relationship to God, I am arrogant. Arrogance and folly mean that I am unclean.

> *Lord, while I am devoting this year to living like Jesus, remind me that what I'm doing is not all that important.*
> *Remind me that you do not look on the outward appearance, you look on the heart.*
> *And purify my heart.*
> *Keep my heart clean.*
> *Keep my insides kosher.*

I was sitting at home late one afternoon when the doorbell rang. I went to the door, opened it, and an older African American man was standing on the porch. His hair was messed up. His clothes were old and dirty. He had a crumpled piece of paper in his hand.

"Could you please help me?" he said. "I'm a Vietnam veteran, and I have an appointment in Lansing with the Veterans Administration for medical reasons. I don't have any money to take the bus." Before I could answer he held up the crumpled piece of paper and let me see it. "This shows my appointment in Lansing. But I don't have any money to get there. Could you help me?"

So I reached into my pocket and gave him all the cash I had, fifteen dollars. In the past I probably would not have given him cash. Last year I was walking through the neighborhood and bumped into a man who asked for money so he could get a ticket to Detroit. I told him to wait there and I'd go get my car to take him to the bus station and buy him a ticket. But the bus station was closed, so I wasn't able to buy him a ticket. Then I drove him to the other side of town and dropped him off at a friend's house. I told him that the next day I'd be happy to take him down to the bus station and buy a ticket, but I never heard from him again. My cynical side thought that he really didn't want a ticket to Detroit —he wanted money for alcohol or drugs.

So as I stood on the porch looking at this veteran, I thought the same thing. He wanted money for alcohol or drugs.

But I gave him the money anyway. This is very much in keeping with Jesus' teaching. Jesus told us to give to anyone who asks. This guy asked. I have a responsibility to give.

And with a "thank you very much" and a "God bless you" he left. I doubt he ever made it to Lansing. But maybe he was telling the truth.

September

Going to Bars

I decided to go to a bar with a friend. He's a youth pastor at a local church, and he's joined me this year in trying to live like Jesus. In January he started growing his beard, eating kosher, and reading through the Gospels too. But he only lasted a few weeks. He told me, "I can't keep this up. I work at a church full-time—so I can't live like Jesus!"

We go to one of the downtown bars in Grand Rapids. I'm a little nervous. Most of my bar experiences have been in Florida, not Grand Rapids. I'm still afraid someone will see me drinking a beer—especially someone from Cornerstone. But we each order a beer.

Some of my best experiences in living like Jesus have come because of alcohol! Jesus was accused of being a glutton and a drunkard, and you can't be accused of that unless you eat food and drink wine. (The Greek word for *drunkard* means "wine imbiber.") Jesus often attended parties with people who were offensive to the religious establishment.

So if I am to follow Jesus, I have to do the same!

First Time

At the beginning of the year I went to a beach bar in Florida, right on the ocean—just to see what would happen. I bellied up to the bar and ordered a beer. To my right were several guys who had just played golf. They were arguing about who owed what to whom. To my left was a man from Houston, short, balding, and wearing a Pittsburgh baseball cap. He spent several hours at the bar each day, and the more he drank, the louder he talked.

We struck up a conversation.

"Where you from?" I asked.

"Originally from Colorado, but now I live in Houston. I have a place here in Florida. Where you from?"

"Grand Rapids, Michigan."

"It's really cold up there. Bet you're glad to be here in the warm sun."

"I am. Did the hurricane hit you last fall?"

"Not really, but it hit a lot of my friends. Their houses were damaged."

The conversation continued back and forth. We talked about sports. We talked about regions of the country. We talked about his job (I was glad he didn't ask me what I do). We talked about the weather. We talked about the news. And as we talked, we drank beer.

At the end of the conversation he got up to leave. We shook hands and said good-bye. I was disappointed that we never got around to talking about God, Jesus, or the Bible, but then, I haven't been to bars very often. The only time I go to a bar is when I go back to Ireland. I usually go down to the pub several times and order a pint of Guinness. Apart from that, this was a new experience.

Second Time

Several days later I went back to the same bar, sat at the counter, and ordered a beer. I've learned to order light beer because it has less alcohol; usually I can drink a couple. After getting the beer, the bartender started to talk to me. He was short, Jamaican, and in his fifties. He had a small mustache that was slightly gray. He was wearing a Hawaiian shirt, and his laugh was contagious.

"I like your beard," he said. "How long you been growing it?"

"I started January first of this year. I'll let it grow until December thirty-first, and then I'll cut it."

"Why you growing it?"

This was the opportunity I'd been looking for.

"I made a commitment on January first to spend the whole year trying to live like Jesus. So the beard is part of the gig."

"A year of living like Jesus? What does that mean?"

"Well, I'm a Jesus follower. I decided to devote a year to focusing on Jesus and his teachings. So I'm eating kosher, observing the Sabbath, growing a beard, and observing Jewish feasts and festivals. I'm reading through the Gospels, Matthew, Mark, Luke, John, every week. I'm trying my best to obey all of Jesus' teachings."

At this point you could see the shock come over the bartender's face. I suspect he'd served beer to thousands of people, but I doubt anyone had ever said, "I'm trying to live like Jesus." I didn't tell him I was at the bar in the first place because that was part of trying to live out Jesus' teachings. I thought that might be a bit too much for him.

After staring at me for a few moments and gathering his thoughts, he continued: "Dude, that's unbelievable. So what are you learning?"

"I'm learning that trying to follow Jesus is a full-time job. I'm learning how difficult it is to actually follow his teachings."

"So what's so hard about it?"

"That's a great question. How about loving your enemies? How about caring for the poor, the crippled, the blind, and the lame? How about clothing the naked, visiting those in prison, visiting the sick, feeding the hungry, and giving water to the thirsty?"

"Right on."

We talked about Jesus and his teachings between his serving other people at the bar. He kept coming back for more conversation. Later, as I drove home, I thought, *Who's going to reach out and touch that bartender? Certainly not the most conservative Christians. They'd never walk into a bar.*

Many Times Thereafter

Every time I went back, which I did often, the bartender would introduce me to the others at the bar: "This guy with the beard is trying to follow Jesus this year." As a result I had many wonderful opportunities to talk about my journey with all sorts of people. I discovered that most people at the bar were interested in Jesus, but they were not interested in the church or religion. Even though I'm a pastor, that didn't seem to matter. What mattered was my personal journey in trying to follow Jesus' teachings.

Of course, I never took a Bible to the bar. I simply told my story and what I was learning about Jesus. People were intensely interested in both. Often I'd begin by telling my own story and then people would chime in with all sorts of questions about the Bible: Is Jesus the only way to heaven? What about people who've never heard of Jesus? What about Jews? What about Muslims? Isn't the Bible full of mistakes? How can you trust the Bible? How did we get the Bible? Did Jesus really rise from the dead? And the list goes on. I was delighted to be part of a bar community that was interested in Jesus and his teachings.

One of the men that I often met at the bar even came up with a wonderful idea. He told me, "When you call me on the phone to meet you at the bar, say that you're going to meet me at the library." When we passed each other during the day, we often said to each other, "You been to the library lately?" When I saw his wife I'd say to her, "Tell your husband I need to meet him at the library."

Of course, it's not all that inappropriate. The library is the place where you go to read books, and the bar is where I go to talk about the most important book in the world—the Bible. I've discovered that having a beer in my hand disarms people. They're much more likely to listen to what I have to say about the Bible if I'm sipping beer while I'm talking.

166

Another Time

One day I went down to the beach bar and didn't recognize anyone up at the bar. Then I saw a friend, Fred, sitting at one of the tables nearby. He was sitting with two middle-aged women. I walked up to them.

"This is the guy I was telling you about," he said. "He's a preacher."

This is a great way to be introduced. Usually I like people to get to know me first, and then eventually I'll tell them what I do. But not with Fred. It's his opening line.

"These are two of my friends from Houston. This is Shirley."

"I'm pleased to meet you," I said. Shirley was sitting with her feet up on another chair trying to get some sun. She had short blond hair.

"And this is Megan."

"Pleased to meet you."

"I'm a nonbeliever," Shirley said.

I thought that was a strange way to begin a conversation, but since I was introduced as a preacher, she wanted to make sure I knew where she stood.

"That's fine," I said.

"I'm a believer," Megan said. "I don't go to church, but I'm a spiritual person."

"Sit down and join us," Fred said.

"I think I will."

"You want a beer?" Fred said, pulling out his card.

"Sure, but I can pay for it."

"A preacher shouldn't have to pay for his beer," he said.

So he went up to the bar to order me a beer. Before he got back, Shirley launched into a discussion about why she was not a believer.

"So when you preach what do you say?" Shirley said.

"Well, I try to teach from the stories in the Bible."

"That's a bunch of freaking nonsense," she said. "Those stories are nothing more than fairy tales."

I was going to ask her which story she thought was "freaking nonsense," but before I could, she continued, "I think the idea of God and religion is a freaking crutch that people use to get through life. And I don't need that kind of a crutch."

By this time Fred had returned and handed me a beer. I began to realize that I probably wouldn't get a word in with Shirley.

I took a sip of beer.

"So who comes to hear you teach?" Shirley said.

"We have Catholics, Protestants, and some nonbelievers," I said.

"You don't have any nonbelievers. Nonbelievers would never show up to hear something about God and the Bible. I'd never show up to something like that."

"Technically, you're correct. The true nonbelievers would never show up to talk about God or religion. What I meant was that there are people who show up who are 'believers' and there are some people who come filled with questions, doubts, and would not be considered as 'believers.'"

"I'm telling you that the real nonbeliever would never show up to hear you teach."

"Technically, you're correct."

I paused to take a sip of my beer, and by the time I'd swallowed, she continued, "Prove to me that there's a God and I'll believe you."

I decided to argue with her from a philosophical point of view. I was planning on telling her that for every result there must be a cause. So if the cosmos came into existence through a Big Bang, who caused the Big Bang? From a philosophical point of view it's reasonable to believe that there is some sort of a cause behind the universe—either God or some force.

I said, "Well, from a philosophical point of view there are some good arguments for the existence of God—"

"I couldn't care less about philosophy," she said.

This was the end of my philosophical argument.

"You can't prove there's a God," she said.

At this point Fred jumped into the conversation. "Well, isn't the whole issue of believing a matter of the heart?"

"I think it is," Megan said.

This was the first time Megan had spoken. She was smoking a cigarette and sipping a drink.

"So if you don't believe in God, how do you find tranquility in your life?" Fred said.

"I don't need tranquility in my life," Shirley said.

Even though Fred and Megan entered the conversation, Shirley was bent on talking directly to me. "So since you believe in God, tell me how come this God allows someone to sexually abuse a kid and then ask for forgiveness and God will forgive him?"

"I don't believe that God is involved in those kinds of details. I think humans are fully capable of doing all sorts of evil toward each other," I said.

"So your God's not involved in the details of life?"

"Not those kinds of details."

"Well, I'm a nonbeliever, and I think religion is a freaking crutch for people."

At this point Fred began to say something, but Shirley interrupted him. "Look, I'm talking to Ed. Don't bug me."

"That's amazing. This is probably one of the few conversations you've ever had with a man in your entire life," Fred said, laughing.

"F— you," she said. Then she turned to me and said, "Excuse me."

"Do you have a religious background?" I asked Shirley.

"Yeah, I grew up in the church, but I don't need them

anymore. The whole thing is a freaking crutch for those who can't get through life without it. I don't need it. I'm here. But when I'm dead and gone, that's it."

"I hope you're right."

"I am! Now I'm going to sit back, doze off, and get some sun."

"Help yourself."

We shook hands, and she leaned back to get some sun.

"So tell me how you became a preacher," Megan asked.

"Well, my dad was a minister," I began, wondering how you really explain something like this. "So I decided that the last thing in the world I wanted to be was a minister. So I started college as a pre-med major. But halfway through, I felt called to devote my life to being a minister."

"That's interesting," she said.

"So tell me about your life."

She launched into an extended story of college, hitchhiking all over the country, living in a hippie commune, doing drugs, getting married, getting divorced, having a baby, moving back home. About halfway through she began to cry and sob. I'm not sure if our conversation touched something deep within her soul or if she had been drinking too much. I suspected the latter.

After about an hour, I told them I needed to go. As I walked out of the bar I thought: Fred, Shirley, and Megan will probably never show up in church to hear me speak. I *know* Shirley would never do that. But we did have a wonderful conversation about God and religion. And we had that conversation in a bar! This is probably the only place where such a conversation could have taken place.

Potluck

For the first four months of my journey in living like Jesus, I had a Tuesday night potluck where more than forty people would come, bring a dish, eat together, and then I'd have an open question-and-answer session.

The first potluck was interesting. Everyone came in with their dishes and put them on the table. Then someone said, "We have no wine. We can't have a potluck without wine." So several people went back home and brought back several bottles of wine. Now we were ready to officially begin. Food, salads, desserts, and wine.

Now I didn't drink wine at the potlucks because even one glass of wine would make me slightly dizzy and sometimes I'd slur my words. Not that I'd be drunk, but my tongue is already weak from this disease and a little bit of wine doesn't help my speaking ability. But everyone else drank, and I think that helps when we get to the question-and-answer session.

Sometimes I'd begin with a brief teaching from the Bible. Sometimes I'd begin with a few thoughts from the Apostles Creed. Sometimes I'd just jump in and open it up for questions.

We talked about everything. Is Jesus the only way to heaven? What about people who've never heard of him? What about praying to the Virgin Mary? What about praying to the saints? How do we know that the Bible has all the right books in it? Aren't there contradictions in the Bible? Why are there so many different kinds of Christians? What does it mean for wives to submit to their husbands? What does it mean to be baptized with the Holy Spirit? What does it mean to speak in tongues? Why do we believe in the Trinity? Is the God of the Old Testament the same as the God of the New Testament? Why did God ask the Jews to kill all of the people in the land of Canaan? And so on.

We had Protestants there. We had Catholics. We had Orthodox people. We had agnostics. We had Jews. We even had one atheist. And it made for a wonderful mix. Sometimes I felt as though I wasn't really leading the group; I was simply facilitating a discussion where everyone felt free to throw in their opinion. For a number of people, this was the only time they'd ever been exposed to the Bible. They had never gone to church and never would. But they came to the potlucks.

I think it's because of the food and the wine.

Back in Grand Rapids

So, back in Grand Rapids, my youth-pastor friend and I sat in the bar for a long time, eating and drinking. We talked about my year of following Jesus and about his seminary classes. But no one asked us about Jesus. It was like the first time I went to the bar in Florida—we talked about everything except Jesus. I've often wondered what Jesus talked about when he ate with "tax collectors and sinners." Did they argue about the kingdom? Did they argue about the Torah? Or did they just talk about everyday life?

Jesus had just called Matthew to be one of his disciples. But Matthew had a problem—he was a tax collector. Tax collectors were Jews hired by the Roman government to collect taxes from other Jews. Often they'd overcharge, and as a result, they became very rich. They were hated by the Jewish population. They were considered traitors because of their cooperation with the Roman government. If you were making a list of the top one hundred prospects for Jesus' disciples, Matthew would not have been on the list. The fact that Jesus chose him is totally amazing.

After Matthew was chosen he had a dinner at his house, and many tax collectors and sinners came. The religious establishment, as usual, was upset. "Why does your teacher eat with tax collectors and sinners?"—the underlying implication being that if Jesus was really a rabbi and a religious teacher, then he would never have eaten with that kind of people. They were greedy. They were corrupt. They were traitors. They were sinners. Religious leaders just didn't eat with those people. But Jesus did. As Jesus explained, "It is not the healthy who need a doctor, but the sick."

At one of the Bible studies we talked about whether Jesus was the only way to heaven. He himself said, "I am the Way, the truth and the life, no one comes to the Father except through me."

"So what do you think Jesus meant by this?" I said.

"Well, it's obvious," said one person. "He said he was the only way to heaven!"

"I don't agree with that," said someone else.

"What don't you agree with?" I said.

"I don't agree with the fact that Jesus is the only way."

"So are there other ways?" another person asked.

The person who objected to the idea that Jesus was the only way was a devoted Catholic.

"I think if you're sincere," he said, "God will accept you."

"What about Jews?" someone asked.

"I think if they're sincere about their faith, God will let them into heaven."

"What about Muslims?" someone else asked.

"I think if they're sincere about their faith, God will let them into heaven."

The exchange went on for some time. Whenever someone brought up another person or another group, the devoted Catholic man would answer the same way, "I think if they're sincere about their faith ..."

Finally I said, "You're a Catholic—and you're letting everybody into heaven!"

We all laughed. Then one of the men stood up and said, "I'm getting a beer!"

I know that such a conversation may be offensive to some in the religious establishment, but following Jesus requires it. Unfortunately, some in the modern evangelical church do everything they can to discourage people from partying with "tax collectors and sinners," not that they'd set out to discourage them deliberately, but by promoting programs that essentially discourage people from building relationships with those who do not know the Lord. We've developed our own subculture within the larger culture. We have our own churches, our own small groups, our own Christian schools, our own universities, our own publishing houses, our own magazines, our own radio and television stations, our own musical artists, our own film studios, and our own newspapers. I'm not denying the value of these things, but I am saying that they discourage people from being out in "the real world." And the real world is sick and it needs a doctor. Jesus says, "That's why I came. I came for the real world—not for the religious establishment."

In the evangelical church we focus on attending services, teaching Sunday school, becoming an elder or deacon, singing in the choir, getting involved in a small group, and exercising our spiritual gifts for the benefit of the body. Almost everything we do is focused on ourselves. And all of this is good. But God says, through the prophet Hosea, that this is not enough. What God wants more than anything else is that we show mercy to those who desperately need it.

Throughout this year, as I've tried to eat and drink with those who were outside the church, something interesting has happened. I'm beginning to feel more comfortable with those who *don't* know the Lord than I am with those who *do* know the Lord. Those who don't know the Lord are much less judgmental. They are open to new ideas.

I'm also learning that I don't need to be the spokesperson for God. Truth is truth. God is truth. And he really doesn't need me to defend his reputation.

The Temptation

> Jesus, full of the Holy Spirit, returned from the Jordan and was led by the Spirit into the desert, where for forty days he was tempted by the devil. He ate nothing during those days, and at the end of them he was hungry.

Luke 4:1–2

Matthew's account of the temptation states that after fasting forty days and forty nights, Jesus was hungry. That was the time that Satan chose to tempt Jesus. I've decided to do something similar.

Of course, I can't go out to the desert, unless I travel to Arizona. So I decide that I'll go camping in a remote area where I'm unlikely to bump into people. I've always loved backpacking. There's nothing like putting everything you need in a backpack and walking into the woods. And I love every season. My favorite time of year is in the middle of winter when it's snowing. There's something unbelievable about staying in a tent and having it snow a foot or more. Waking up in the morning and cranking up the stove for that first cup of coffee is exhilarating.

Since I have ALS, however, it will be impossible for me to backpack. My upper body strength has greatly diminished, and there's no way I can carry a backpack. So maybe I can find a remote campground I can drive to and set up my tent for a night or two.

Jesus fasted for forty days and forty nights—which is not something I'm able to do. Years ago, when I was at Liberty University, several religion professors went on forty-day fasts, and they inspired me to try it as well. Of course, I had no intention of going forty days without food, but I wanted to go as long as I could. So on the day I began my fast, I ran a 10K race (a little over six miles) and placed near the top of my age group, having run at a 6.3-minutes-per-mile pace. After the race I didn't eat—I started my fast. Talk about stupid! Beginning your fast with a race is really dumb. But I did it.

About ten days into the fast I got sick. Really sick! So sick that I had to go to the doctor. When I explained to him that I'd been fasting for ten days and had started by running a 10K, he was angry. "With your body type you shouldn't fast more than a day without being under a doctor's supervision. And starting your fast by depleting your body by running a race—*really* stupid!"

Since then I've seldom fasted. I learned my lesson.

But if I am to follow Jesus, I need to fast. So instead of fasting for forty days and forty nights, I decide to fast one day and one night—one-fortieth of what Jesus did. This should be a challenge because the doctors who help me with my ALS recommend that I don't miss any meals at all. Eating good food consistently is important in maintaining my body weight.

So where do I go to be alone in the wilderness? I've hiked many trails, including the North Country Trail in Michigan, and all of them have parking areas where you can begin. I need to find a place where I can park and set up my tent next to my car. After looking through several hiking books, I decide that the best place would be the Nichols Lake Campground. It's remote and doesn't have electricity available for the campers; consequently it's not as popular as many of the other campgrounds in Michigan. Besides, in the month of September, very few people will be there anyway.

Several days ahead I begin going through all of my camping gear. I discover that my WhisperLite stove is missing and so is my French-press coffeepot. So I go to the camping store to purchase new ones. I can do without food, but I can't do without coffee.

When I get home I load the truck.

Sleeping bag.

Tent and stakes.

Two inflatable sleeping pads.

The rosary, the prayer rope, and the Episcopal prayer beads.

Inflatable pillow.

A lighter.

A headlamp.

A knife.

A spoon.

A Bible.

The iPod.

A notebook and pen.

The Crazy Creek chair (a small, lightweight, foldable chair used for backpacking).

A windbreaker and a hat.

The beauty of camping next to the car is that I don't have to worry about stuffing everything into a backpack and carrying it long distances. After throwing all my stuff into the back of the truck, I have lunch and head for the Nichols Lake Campground. It's about an hour's drive. On the way, I stop at one of my favorite coffee shops for a final espresso before "the temptation."

I sit there sipping coffee, excited about what lies ahead. For a number of months I've been thinking about getting out into the wilderness, fasting, and seeing what happens. Now I'm actually doing it.

When I arrive at the campground, I drive around the circle. Only three or four people are there. I stop in front of the bathrooms and ask a person who's walking out, "Who do I see about paying to stay overnight?"

"The guy in the large trailer."

So I go to the trailer, knock on the door, and ask the person inside what I need to do.

"Next to the bathrooms you'll see a box, and above the box are envelopes. Fill out an envelope, put your money in it, and drop it in the box." I pay thirty dollars for two nights.

Then I drive back around the circle and find the campsite farthest away from everyone else. I back the truck in and begin setting up camp for the night. I spread the tent out flat and lay down on top of it to make sure that I won't be sleeping downhill. It feels fine, so I set up the tent. I have some difficulty with the tent poles, for it takes every ounce of my strength to bend them enough to fit the tent. I've lost a good bit of strength since the last time I set it up. I inflate the sleeping pads and put them in the tent, along with the sleeping bag, headlamp, extra clothes, and pillow.

It's a beautiful fall afternoon. The sun is shining. You can see through the trees to the lake. I decide to take the Orthodox prayer rope and walk through the woods to the small beach. I walk out on the dock and sit down on the bench. The beauty of the Nichols Lake Campground is that it's remote. As I sit there looking across the lake, I see no houses, no boats, and no people. Just the beauty of nature. So I pray the Orthodox prayer rope: "Lord Jesus Christ, son of God, have mercy on me, a sinner." I pray through each prayer slowly and deliberately. I focus on my breathing. After praying it a hundred times, I pray through it again. And then I pray through it again. The combination of the words, the repetition, and the beauty of nature around me is profound. It's as if I were in sync with the God who created the universe. Though I've prayed the Orthodox prayer rope many times, this time seems particularly powerful.

I walk back to the truck to get something to drink. I'd like a cup of tea. I take out the bag of stuff I bought at the camping store, and when I open the box with the WhisperLite stove, I'm stunned to find that it's empty. No stove! Apparently, at the camping store, I picked up the box that the display model had come out of—my stove was probably still sitting on the shelf at the store for everyone to see! Initially I get really mad at myself. How in the world could I come all the way up here and not have a stove to heat water with? Why didn't I open the box and check it at the store? Why didn't I check the box before I left the house? But now it's too late.

So I take a deep breath.

"Think like Jesus," I say. "Did he have a camping stove? No! So get over it. It's not all that important. You came to spend time alone and to fast."

So I go back down to the beach and continue praying the Orthodox prayer rope. I pray through it one time. Then I go back down to the dock and pray it again. On the way back to camp, I stop at a remote area and stand there to pray through it a third time. So far I've prayed through the prayer rope five times—the equivalent of praying the prayer five hundred times.

After praying three more times, I get in the tent and organize things for the evening. I know from experience that it's important to organize your tent before it gets dark. I make sure the inflatable air mattresses are lined up, the sleeping bag is smoothed out, the headlamp is in the proper place, the pillow is properly positioned, and the extra clothes are within my reach.

After organizing everything, I get into the sleeping bag just to make sure it's comfortable. As I zip it up, I get terrible cramps in my stomach and leg muscles. This is part of my journey with ALS. From time to time I get these cramps, especially when I'm trying to do something unusual. The tent is a small space, and it forces me to maneuver my body in ways that I don't ordinarily do. The result—terrible cramps. As I lie there in pain, trying to stretch out the muscles, I'm glad I didn't go backpacking. I think: *Maybe I should just pack up and go home. After all, Jesus didn't have ALS.*

At this point I start to argue with myself.

During the temptation Jesus suffered. In the Garden of Gethsemane he suffered. On the cross he suffered. The least you can do is endure some muscle cramps.

But what if I'm awake all night?

Jesus spent all night in prayer. If you're awake all night, you're awake all night. Spend the night in prayer.

So I get back out of the tent. It feels good to stand up again.

By this time it's early evening, and I can smell hamburgers being grilled on an outdoor grill nearby. It's a terrible smell, and I am getting really hungry. So I decide to walk around the circle and pass the people who are cooking. I'm actually hoping they'll invite me to have a bite with them. After all, Jesus told his disciples that when they went out to preach and heal, they should eat whatever is set before them and be grateful. Well, maybe I won't actually eat, but perhaps I could at least heat up some water for tea. I walk around the circle twice and say hello to the people who are cooking.

They don't invite me to join them. Maybe I should pray that they will.

I go back to the beach as the sun is setting. I pray the Orthodox prayer rope twice (that is, two hundred times praying the Jesus Prayer). I walked around the circle many times, praying the Jesus Prayer. By this time I've prayed through the prayer rope nine times and am very tired, so I decide to pray through it one more time to make it ten. I get my Crazy Creek chair, go into the woods where I can be alone, and pray.

As I walk back to camp I'm pleased that I've prayed through the prayer rope ten times—that's one thousand times praying the Jesus Prayer.

By the time I get to camp, however, I realize I've simply been overcome with a competitive spirit. The prayer is supposed to be prayed slowly and unhurriedly. I've done that, but the idea is not to compete with oneself to see how many times you can pray it. Praying the prayer a thousand times appeals to my pride. And this is very un-Jesus-like.

The sun is beginning to set now. So I decide to get in the tent and get ready for a night's sleep. Normally when I backpack I go to bed when it gets dark and wake up when it gets light. Even in the winter, when it gets dark by five o'clock, I still get in bed and go to sleep. And I usually sleep well. The wind blowing through the leaves, the sounds of animals, and the stillness lull me to sleep. I usually don't wake up until morning.

So I take off my clothes and get in the sleeping bag. Again I get muscle cramps. Only this time they're worse than before. I lie awake for thirty minutes. Then for the next hour I'm more than wide awake. I can't go to sleep. It's hot and I'm sweating. I keep slipping off the sleeping pad because the sleeping bag is extra slippery. And every time I move I get a cramp.

The best thing, I think, is to pack up all my belongings and go home.

That's ridiculous! Jesus suffered and you can suffer too.

But Jesus didn't have ALS. This is a serious disease, and it's seriously impacting my ability to sleep.

Yes. But Jesus was the creator of the universe, and he confined himself to a physical body. You think he had problems with that?

Of course he did. He was confining deity to human flesh. He struggled with the limitations of his physical body. But I still think that the best I can do is pack up and go home.

If you do that, you will fail miserably and give in to temptation — the temptation to be comfortable.

But what am I learning from lying awake in a tent?

I lie there for thirty minutes, arguing back and forth about what to do. Finally I give in. I decide to pack everything up and drive home. Even though it's already late and I'll have to pack in the dark, I still decide to do it.

So I get out of the tent, throw the sleeping bag, the sleeping pads, the headlamp, and the extra clothes into the truck. I take down the tent and throw it into the truck as well. I get in and head for home.

On the way I listen to the Gospels on my iPod. But the farther I drive, the more I realize I have probably not done the right thing. I get home around midnight, park the truck, go inside, and get into bed.

I'm so happy to be there!

When I wake up in the morning I decide not to eat until the sun goes down. Even if I didn't stay overnight at the camp, at least I'll fast one day. I spend the morning studying the temptation narrative found in the Gospels.

After Jesus fasted for forty days and forty nights, Satan comes to him and says, "If you are the son of God, tell these stones to become bread."

In the desert in Israel are millions of stones. Jesus was surrounded by them. And the devil tempts him to turn the stones into bread so that he can eat. In other words, Jesus is uncomfortable, he's desperately hungry, and the temptation appeals to his discomfort.

As I think about this first temptation, I realize that I've failed in this area—miserably. I was more interested in my own comfort, and when I had the opportunity to pack up and leave—I did! Good job, Ed. Jesus lasted forty days and forty nights. You lasted eight hours and didn't even stay overnight.

The devil then takes Jesus to the highest point of the Temple and says, "If you are the son of God, throw yourself down."

The devil here is quoting the Hebrew Bible that states that God's angels will take care of Jesus if he throws himself down. They will lift him up in their hands and prevent him from striking his foot against a stone. Jesus replies, "It is also written: do not put the Lord your God to the test." But Jesus doesn't give in to the temptation. He's being tempted to do something reckless and then expect God to bail him out. But he refuses. If he had jumped off the Temple then he'd be putting God to the test.

I think I've failed on the second temptation as well. I was much more interested in my own well-being than I was in obeying God. I didn't jump from the Temple, but I did bail out on my commitment to camp overnight. And besides, I walked all over the camp hoping someone would offer me some food or drink. Instead of letting God bail me out, I tried to bail myself out.

Satan then takes Jesus to a very high mountain and shows him all the kingdoms of the world and the glory associated with them. "All this will I give you, if you will bow down and worship me."

Jesus responds, "Away from me, Satan! For it is written: worship the Lord your God, and serve him only."

I worked for Jerry Falwell for fourteen and a half years. Toward the end of my tenure at Liberty University and Thomas Road Baptist Church, I was interviewed by Calvary Church in Grand Rapids. The day Calvary voted on my candidacy as pastor was the same day that Jerry Falwell took over Jim Bakker's PTL empire near Charlotte, North Carolina. I was in meetings all day long with Jerry Falwell and one other person. Jerry knew that I was considering going to Grand Rapids, but he was hoping I'd get involved in helping him with PTL.

At one point in the conversation, the other person looked at me and said, "If you agree to help Dr. Falwell, by this time tomorrow everybody in America will know who you are."

Early that evening I was with Dr. Falwell when he convened the board of PTL in a telephone conference call. Each board member agreed to resign, and new board members were appointed. When I arrived home that evening, the chairman of the board at Calvary Church called me to announce the good news—the church had voted nearly unanimously to call me as their new pastor.

"I really appreciate it, but I'm not sure that I should come as the pastor of Calvary Church. When you watch the eleven o'clock news tonight, you'll see that Jerry Falwell has taken over PTL. He's asked me to help him manage this new and huge endeavor. This is so bizarre and so unusual that I need time to think about it and pray about it." The chairman of the Calvary board was immensely disappointed, but I really did need time to think and pray.

So I told my wife that I was going up to my office at Liberty Mountain and was planning to stay there until I was sure what God wanted me to do. I loved Jerry Falwell. I appreciated all the opportunities he had given me. He was a friend and a mentor. And I desperately wanted to help him during this critical time. But could I really turn down Calvary's offer?

When I got to my office, I decided to read my Bible reading for that day. I'd been reading through the Bible, and it just so happened that I was up to the gospel of Matthew, chapter 4, the passage about the temptation of Jesus. I read the verse, "Again, the devil took him to a very high mountain and showed him all the kingdoms of the world and their splendor." I remembered what the person had told me earlier in the day, "If you agree to help Dr. Falwell, by this time tomorrow everybody in America will know who you are."

I immediately recognized that my situation was parallel to Jesus'. I was being tempted by the splendor of earthly kingdoms—in my case, television. Of course I'm not saying that Jerry Falwell was the devil nor that there is anything wrong with being known by people all over America. But I am saying that for me, at that moment in my life, I had a choice—to become a pastor and live in relative obscurity or go to PTL and be known by everybody in America.

In the middle of the night I called Dr. Falwell to tell him that I was accepting the pastorate in Grand Rapids. I also called the chairman of the Calvary board and woke him up with the news: "I'm your new pastor!"

So this temptation to worship Satan and enjoy the splendor of earthly kingdoms was used by God at a critical point in my own journey. But what about the Nichols Lake Campground? Did I also fail in this temptation? I think I did! The splendor of earthly kingdoms also includes convenience and comfort. I was more interested in my own personal convenience and my own personal comfort than I was in staying there all night. So I failed in this temptation as well.

Carrying His Cross

If anyone would come after me, he must deny himself and take up his cross daily and follow me.

Luke 9:23

Jesus tells us that to be his follower, we must deny ourselves and take up our cross daily. So how do I obey his instructions? Maybe I should carry a cross around for several days. I know, that's bizarre, but on one occasion, while preaching on this text, I actually carried a huge cross for the entire sermon. It was highly inconvenient. It cramped my style. It hindered my movement. By the time I was through, I was exhausted.

Historically, criminals carried only the top piece of the cross—not the entire thing. So the paintings of Jesus carrying his cross are not historically accurate. And besides, it really was not a cross. It was more like a *T*.

Still, should I carry an actual cross? One of the challenges for me, whether carrying a whole cross or just the top piece, is that the muscles in my upper body are weak because of my ALS. Carrying a cross for even a day would be nearly impossible.

Earlier this year, I was scheduled to do an open question-and-answer period at one of the potlucks. About fifty people attended, several of whom were not believers. We had a wonderful time, eating, laughing, and getting serious about the Bible. Besides good food, there was good wine as well, although, on this occasion, I didn't drink because I wanted to be clearly focused on answering the questions.

As I walked around saying hello, I saw one man who had a

large wooden cross hanging around his neck. It was about six inches long.

"I like your cross," I said.

"Would you like to have it?" he asked.

I really didn't have a desire to *have* the cross, but before I could answer, he had handed it to me and said, "I make these myself, and whenever anyone admires it, I give it to them."

Maybe this is the answer to carrying my cross, I thought. Maybe I could wear this cross as a reminder that every day I am to deny myself and follow Jesus. So the next morning when I got up, I took the cross and said a blessing: "Blessed are you, God, our God, King of the universe, who demonstrated your love through sending your son to be our savior." I then kissed the cross and put it on. I was anxious to see how wearing it would impact me for the next several days.

I've never been one to put Jesus bumper stickers on my car or wear stuff on my lapel that points to Jesus. In fact, when people ask me what I do, I'm even hesitant to say I'm a pastor. I don't like wearing my commitment to Jesus on my sleeve.

When I worked for Jerry Falwell, he wore a "Jesus First" lapel pin on his coat. He gave away millions of them on his television program. On one occasion I accompanied him to Washington, D.C., where we were to meet with the prime minister Menachem Begin of Israel at the Blair House. As we walked up the sidewalk toward the meeting, I said to Dr. Falwell, "Do you think you ought to take off your 'Jesus First' pin? After all, Jews are highly offended about the idea of Jesus." I thought that I was helping him be more sensitive to the prime minister of Israel.

Without missing a beat, Dr. Falwell responded, "If they take me, they take Jesus with me!" Needless to say, he didn't take off the pin. I don't think he ever took it off. I suspect he had a "Jesus First" pin on his pajamas.

But I am not Jerry Falwell, and I don't like doing certain

things, including wearing a cross around my neck, which could be misunderstood or misinterpreted by others.

Today as I left the house, one of my neighbors walked by and said, "Hello." Without thinking, I immediately folded my arms to cover up the cross. I really didn't want her to see me with this big cross hanging around my neck. And from then on, things went from bad to worse. I stopped by the Catholic Church to get some materials. As I walked into the office, the woman who was helping me kept looking at my cross. I didn't know what she was thinking, but I was sure that she knew I wasn't a Catholic. A Catholic would have had a crucifix around his neck, not an empty cross.

At lunch one time, right after I started wearing the cross, I had this strange feeling that everyone in the restaurant was looking at me. That evening we ate at a very nice restaurant, and I wore the cross. Again I felt that everybody was staring at the cross. It was as if the cross had flashing neon lights that said, "Jesus freak! Jesus freak!" For the next several days I continued to struggle with wearing the cross.

Of course, I have this long, wild, random beard, which, in the circles I move in, is exceptionally rare. No one else has a beard like this, and even if they do, it's neatly trimmed. No one else's beard blows sideways in the wind. But I don't mind the beard. I like the idea of being just a little odd.

But the cross?

I'm bothered by wearing it. And I'm bothered that I'm bothered by wearing it. Maybe I should have carried a huge wooden cross around for several days. At least then people would have assumed that I was doing something really unusual. And if they were to ask me what I was doing, I could have told them about my year of trying to live like Jesus.

But no one asks me about the cross around my neck.

In the text where Jesus tells us to take up our cross daily, he also says, "If anyone is ashamed of me and my words, the Son of Man will be ashamed of him when he comes in his glory and in the glory of the Father and of the holy angels." I'm afraid that my little journey in taking up my cross by wearing one around my neck is tantamount to being ashamed of Jesus. I sure hope not.

The Rosary: Two Perspectives

Until recently, I prayed the rosary every day, but I didn't tell anyone I was doing it.

Then one day I got up enough courage to tell one of my good evangelical pastor friends what I was doing. "I've been trying to focus more on prayer," I said, "and one of the things I've done is to pray the words of Scripture."

"Great idea," he said. "Praying Scripture is a powerful way to pray!"

"And one of the ways I've prayed the Scriptures is by praying the Roman Catholic rosary."

He was speechless. After a long pause he said, "Are you crazy? Don't tell anyone in our circle that you're praying the rosary."

On another day I was talking to a neighbor who is Catholic and a graduate of Notre Dame about my yearlong journey of trying to live like Jesus. "One of the things I've been trying to do is to focus more on prayer," I said. "And one of the ways I've been doing that is by praying the rosary."

"Fabulous! I pray the rosary every day. It's one of the most meaningful things I do."

So it all depends on who you're talking with.

Evangelical Protestants—don't mention the rosary.

Roman Catholics—good for you!

October

High Holy Days

October is one of the busiest months in the Jewish calendar. It's called the "High Holy Days" and includes Rosh Hashanah and Yom Kippur. Rosh Hashanah celebrates the beginning of the Jewish calendar year, and Yom Kippur celebrates the Day of Atonement, when God forgives sin. In Hebrew this period is called *yamim noraim* — days of awe.

So I downloaded the schedule of services at the local synagogue and noticed that on the day before Rosh Hashanah, people go to the cemetery and pray the *kaddish* — the mourners' prayer. So I called the rabbi.

"Rabbi David, I'm planning to attend all of the services for the High Holy Days. I noticed that on Sunday afternoon you go to the cemetery and pray. Would you object if I came along?"

"You'd be most welcome to all of the services, as well as the prayer at the cemetery. Part of the cemetery service, however, is for people to visit their own loved ones who are buried there."

"I see. Maybe it would be best for me not to come at all."

"You'd still be welcome."

Sunday Afternoon

Instead of going to the cemetery with the Jewish community, I decide to go to the graves of my mom and dad. I've never been one to visit graves often. I believe that my parents' souls have entered into the presence of our Lord and that the earthly tent they lived in is buried in the ground. In other words, they're not at the cemetery — they're in God's presence.

189

So why bother?

I think I've gone to my mother's grave only once in ten years, and I've never been to my father's grave since he passed away two years ago.

Shortly after my mother died, I happened to be conducting a graveside service at the same cemetery. So afterward I decided to visit my mother's grave—but I couldn't find it! I looked all over that section of the cemetery but never found it. So I left, and it was years before I came back.

The only time I go to a cemetery is when I go back to Northern Ireland. I visit the church cemetery in the little village where my uncles, aunts, grandparents, and great grandparents are buried. I'm not sure why I go there, but maybe I need some sort of connectedness to my past. Maybe it's because I'm an immigrant. We left family and friends in Northern Ireland in 1964.

But this Sunday afternoon I went to my parents' graves. As I stood there, looking down at the plaque that said "Eileen McKnight Dobson and Calvin Coolidge Dobson," along with a Scripture that said "Better by Far," I began to sob. I never expected to cry so uncontrollably. My plan had been to pray the Hebrew prayers and then leave. But I was overcome with emotion.

My father, a pastor, and my mother moved to Grand Rapids after my dad retired. Every Monday I would go by their house and my mother would fix some of my favorite Irish dishes. She'd make wheat bread and soda bread. Sometimes I'd eat almost the entire loaf by myself. She fixed all the foods I'd eaten while growing up.

But as Calvary Church grew and my responsibilities increased, I'd often skip the Monday lunch at my parents' house. I knew my mom was disappointed, but she understood the complexities of pastoral ministry. She understood that your time is really never your own. She never complained.

My mom battled cancer for five years, and I was with her when she entered into the presence of the Lord. As I stood there in the cemetery that day, I longed to be back in that kitchen one more Monday for a lunch with my mom. There was something special about those days, and now I realized how much I missed them.

Shortly after my parents arrived in Grand Rapids, the man who did the daily hospital visitation for our church had a stroke. So the elders asked my dad if he'd be willing to fill in for a while. Soon he was working almost full-time—and he was wonderful at what he did. He'd get up every morning at 4:30 to read the Bible and pray so that he could have a new word for the patients he'd meet that day. He had a delightful sense of Irish humor and a twinkle in his eye. His favorite color was green; go figure. He'd wear three or four different shades of green that didn't match. But he didn't care.

My dad had a profound influence on my life. Growing up in Northern Ireland, where Protestants and Catholics did not get along, my dad taught me the importance of loving everybody— no matter who they are.

At age sixteen, when I went off to my freshman year at college, my dad drove me down to Bob Jones University in South Carolina. When he dropped me off, he said, "Now, son, don't believe a word they tell you here unless you can prove it from the Bible!" I've tried over the years not to believe anything anybody told me unless I can prove it from the Bible.

Not that my dad and I always agreed on everything. One Sunday night we were walking out of the church together while one of the high school bands was practicing in an adjacent room. My dad did not like contemporary music, so he said, "Son, that music is displeasing to God, and you should go tell them to stop."

"Dad, can you prove it from the Bible?"

"Well, no, I can't. But I know it's not pleasing to the Lord."

"Did the Lord appear to you personally and tell you the music was displeasing to him?"

He laughed and we agreed that we would not argue about this subject again.

After my dad's retirement, he also lived for a while in upstate New York to be near my sister. He'd often call me on the telephone: "Son, have I ever told you about the New Living Bible?"

Of course he had! Every time I talked to him he would begin the conversation the same way: "I was reading the New Living Bible today, and it was so wonderful. In fact, let me read to you what I was reading...."

Here we go again, I'd think.

My father was a wonderful reader of the Scriptures, but he read slowly. For these phone conversations, I would always hope he'd only read a paragraph or two, but usually he read a couple of chapters. Then he would begin. With a slow, deliberate Irish accent he would read the Bible as if he were reading it for the first time. Sometimes my mind would wander to all the things I needed to do that seemed much more important at the moment than listening to my dad reading the Bible. But since he was my dad, I always listened.

That day, as I stood there looking down at the grave, I wanted my dad to call me one more time. I wanted to hear him say, "Son, have I ever told you about the New Living Bible?" I wanted him to read one more chapter to me. I wanted to hear his voice one more time.

I stood there quietly for a few moments with tears running down my cheeks.

"Mom, thank you for the profound influence you have had on my life. I'm sorry I didn't spend more time with you, and I'm sorry I skipped so many Monday lunches. Please forgive me. And Dad, thank you for the profound influence you had on my life. I'm sorry I was distracted sometimes when you called me to read the Scriptures. I miss you. Please forgive me."

When I calmed down, I began praying the mourners' prayer,

called the kaddish. I know it's supposed to be said with a group, but I hope God will cut me some slack.

The prayer begins by declaring the greatness of God. Then you take three steps back from the grave, bow to the left, and say, "He who makes peace in the heights ..."; then you bow to the right and say "... may he make peace upon us ..."; then you bow forward and say, "... and upon all Israel." You remain in place for a few moments and then take three steps forward and say, "He who makes peace in the heights, may he make peace upon us, and upon all Israel."

I remained at my parents' grave for a few more moments and then slowly walked back to my truck. That short visit impacted me deeply. Will I go back more often? I don't know. Maybe next year on the day before Rosh Hashanah I will go to their graves again and pray the kaddish.

Rosh Hashanah

The Hebrew word *rosh* means "the head or the beginning." *Hashannah* means "the year." Together, *Rosh Hashanah* means "the beginning or the head of the new year."

Every December 31 the world celebrates the beginning of the New Year. It's an incredible time of excitement and enthusiasm. People fill Times Square. At midnight the ball drops. We shoot off fireworks. We drink too much. It's exciting to anticipate all the prospects of the New Year.

So you'd think that Rosh Hashanah would have the same kind of wild and enthusiastic celebration. But it doesn't. It's completely the opposite. It's a time for personal reflection and for doing acts of repentance.

This period is devoted to a careful examination of who

we are in an attempt to become cognizant of the ways we have failed—failed others, failed our own selves, and failed God. This introspection is meant to lead to regret and remorse for the harm we have done, to attempts at restitution when possible, and to turning away from our past selves to better selves who will act differently in the coming new year.[1]

Even the cantor who leads the synagogue service uses a musical style that reflects the solemnity of the occasion.

Repentance — *Teshuvah*

> The Lord was very angry with your forefathers. Therefore tell the people: This is what the Lord Almighty says: "Return to me," declares the Lord Almighty, "and I will return to you," says the Lord Almighty.
>
> Zechariah 1:2–3

John the Baptist preached and baptized in the Judean desert. "John's clothes were made of camel's hair, and he had a leather belt around his waist. His food was locusts and wild honey" (Matthew 3:4). I'm grateful that I'm trying to live like Jesus—not John the Baptist. I'm not sure I'd look good in camel's hair and leather, and I don't think I'd like eating locusts and wild honey.

But his message was clear: "Repent, for the kingdom of heaven is near" (Matthew 3:2). After John baptized Jesus in the Jordan River, Jesus began his public ministry, and his message was the same as John's: "Repent, for the kingdom of heaven is near" (Matthew 4:17).

Over time Jesus called twelve disciples who followed him all over Galilee and Judea. They listened to his teaching. They watched him perform miracles. They saw him interact with all kinds of people. Then "they went out and preached that people should repent" (Mark 6:12). The message of John the Baptist was picked up by Jesus, and the message of Jesus was picked up by his disciples, and they went from village to village preaching "repentance."

After Paul was converted to the Way, he became a missionary all over the ancient world. When he arrived in the city of Athens he was perplexed because the city was completely devoted to idols. After trying to reason with the philosophers, he preached a sermon that concluded, "In the past God overlooked such ignorance, but now he commands all people everywhere to repent" (Acts 17:30).

The idea of repentance is central to the message and teaching of Jesus and the early apostles. But what is repentance? The Greek verb that is translated "to repent" is *metanoeo*, which literally means "to change one's mind." But neither John the Baptist nor Jesus spoke in Greek. They spoke in either Aramaic or Hebrew. In everyday conversation, I happen to think, the Jews in Jesus' day spoke Aramaic, but when they talked about the Torah and discussed its implications in the synagogue and in public, they spoke Hebrew.

So even though the teachings of John the Baptist and Jesus and his disciples were written in Greek, they were actually spoken in Hebrew. The Hebrew word for repentance, *teshuvah*, means a whole lot more than just "changing your mind." It comes from the Hebrew verb *shuv*, which means "to turn back or to turn around," and has a variety of nuances in the Hebrew Bible. When you study these nuances you get a better understanding of *teshuvah*:

1. Teshuvah *Is a Fundamental Change of Condition*

God created Adam (the Hebrew word for "man") from the dust of the ground (the Hebrew word *adamah* means "red dirt"). God breathed into Adam the breath of life, and Adam became a living being. God then created a wife for Adam—called Eve (the Hebrew word means "living"). God then placed them both in the garden of Eden and told them they were free to eat from any of the trees in the garden except the one. If they ate from that tree they would surely die.

The serpent (representing the devil) came to Eve and tempted her to eat the forbidden fruit. She ate it and gave some to her husband. Their eyes were opened. They realized they were naked. They sewed fig leaves together to cover their nakedness, and they hid from God. (Sewing fig leaves together is not a smart idea. Fig leaves shrivel after they're taken from the tree.)

God walked in the garden and had a conversation with the serpent, the woman, and the man. He pronounced judgment on all three. To Adam he said, "By the sweat of your brow you will eat your food until you *return* to the ground, since from it you were taken; for dust you are and to dust you will *return*" (Genesis 3:19, emphasis added). The Hebrew verb *shuv* is used twice in this text. God declared that since Adam was taken from the dust of the ground, when he died he would return to dust. Adam was a living, breathing, talking, walking human being. He was fully alive! But one day his condition would be dramatically altered. When he died he would go back to the dust.

This is the idea of *shuv* and *teshuvah*. It's not simply "changing your mind." It's a basic and fundamental change in one's condition.

2. Teshuvah *Is Movement in a Specific Direction*

After humans began to multiply on the earth, God saw how evil they had become. In fact, God was grieved that he had created them in the first place. So God decided to wipe out the whole human race through a flood. But Noah found grace in God's eyes. God instructed him to build an ark and bring all of the animals into it. Then it began to rain, and the flood covered the earth for a hundred and fifty days. Noah survived the flood, and the text records, "The water *receded* steadily from the earth. At the end of a hundred and fifty days the water had gone down" (Genesis 8:3, emphasis added). The word translated "receded" here is again the Hebrew verb *shuv*. It has the idea of consistent movement in a certain direction. And so it is with *teshuvah*. It means consistent, steady movement in a certain direction.

3. Teshuvah *Is to Recover What Was Stolen*

God called Abraham to leave his country (modern day Iraq) and travel to the Promised Land, which God promised to give him. God also promised that Abraham's descendents would be as numerous as the stars in the sky and that through Abraham and his descendents all the peoples of the earth would be blessed. When Abraham left, he took his nephew Lot along with him, but the land could not sustain both of their herds, so they parted ways. Lot went to live near the cities of Sodom and Gomorrah while Abraham continued to wander as a nomad. Eventually Lot started living in the city of Sodom, "sitting at the gate."

A coalition of ancient kings decided to attack Sodom and Gomorrah. The armies of Sodom and Gomorrah marched out to meet these kings but were defeated. Lot, who served in the army, was taken captive.

When Abraham heard that his nephew was a prisoner, he ordered 318 trained men to pursue the coalition of ancient kings. Abraham and his trained men defeated them and rescued Lot. "He *recovered* all the goods and brought back his relative Lot and his possessions, together with the women and the other people" (Genesis 14:16, emphasis added). The word translated "recovered" is yet again the Hebrew verb *shuv*. It means that Abraham recovered what was stolen. And this is also part of what *teshuvah* means—to recover what has been stolen and taken away.

4. Teshuvah *Is a Process that Must Be Repeated*

After the children of Israel went into Persian captivity, they returned under the leadership of Ezra and Nehemiah. They rebuilt the walls of Jerusalem, rebuilt the houses, and eventually rebuilt the Temple. Shortly after arriving in Jerusalem, Ezra realized that many of the people had intermarried with the surrounding inhabitants, which had been forbidden by God. So Ezra tore his clothes as a sign of repentance and offered prayers to God. Toward the end of the prayer he made this statement: "Shall *we again* break your commands and intermarry with the peoples who commit such detestable practices?" (Ezra 9:14).

The word translated "again" is *shuv*. The passage is sometimes translated as, "Shall we return to break your commands . . ." Ezra was bemoaning the fact that the people had repeatedly broken God's commands—they kept returning to disobedience. Over and over and over again, they broke God's commands. *Teshuvah* is both an act and a process. It is an act. That is, you have to come to the point where you're willing and ready to change. But it is also a process, so you need to keep doing it over and over again.

5. Teshuvah *Is Returning to God*

Ultimately *teshuvah* is a returning to God. It is the recognition that we have wandered off the right and proper path. It is the recognition that the path we are now on is not the path God intended for us. It is the passionate desire to leave that path and return to God's path.

Jesus said something similar in his teaching: "Enter through the narrow gate. For wide is the gate and broad is the road that leads to destruction, and many enter through it. But small is the gate and narrow the road that leads to life, and only a few find it" (Matthew 7:13–14). Jesus was reminding us that there are two paths: a wide one and a narrow one. And the choice is up to us. We are responsible to do the "entering."

So what is *teshuvah*? It's a whole lot more than "changing your mind." It includes:

a fundamental change in your condition

movement in a specific direction — away from self and toward God

recovering what has been stolen — stolen by selfishness, greed, drugs, alcohol, etc.

an ongoing process — something we must do over and over

a returning to God — the ultimate act of *teshuvah*

Teshuvah is the central and dominant theme of Rosh Hashanah, the ten days of repentance, and Yom Kippur. It's not something to be taken casually — like "changing your mind." I can change my mind instantly. But the process of repentance is a whole lot more than that.

So how will we know if we have done *teshuvah*? Let's go back to the life and teaching of John the Baptist, the forerunner of Jesus, for an answer.

Large crowds used to come out to the Jordan River to hear John's teaching and be baptized. He said, "Produce fruit in keeping with repentance" (Matthew 3:8). He's saying that people must produce "fruit" that corresponds to their acts of repentance. When the people asked, "What should we do then?" John gave them specific answers that characterize the qualities of *teshuvah*.

For instance, John said, "The man who has two tunics should share with him who has none, and the one who has food should do the same." One of the characteristics of repentance is a willingness to share what we have with others. Greed compels us to hold on to what we own. Our repentance compels us to share what we have with others who are in need.

When tax collectors asked John what they should do to show repentance, he replied, "Don't collect any more than you are required to," because, of course, it was their custom to skim money off the top for themselves.

When soldiers asked him what they should do, he replied, "Don't extort money and don't accuse people falsely—be content with your pay." Once again John focused on the issue of greed. The soldiers often demanded money from people, perhaps as a means of extortion, and soldiers were notoriously dissatisfied with their pay.

John the Baptist never told people that there was nothing they could do to repent. In a sense, he was saying that repentance is up to me—not up to God. Even the Talmud advises, "A man should always consider himself evenly balanced, i.e., half sinful and half righteous. If he performs one mitzvah, happy is he, for he has tilted the scales toward righteousness. If he commits one sin, woe unto him, for he has tilted the scales towards sinfulness."[2]

During Rosh Hashanah, according to Jewish custom, God writes the names of the righteous in the Book of Life, and he also writes the names of the wicked in the Book of Death. Those who are neither righteous nor wicked have until Yom Kippur to repent and have God write their names in the Book of Life.

The synagogue service centers around the idea that God is king. The service is accompanied by the blowing of the *shofar*—a ram's-horn trumpet intended to wake people up from their slumber and cause them to reflect on their own personal lives and make improvements. Each service centers around the thirteen attributes of God taken from Exodus 34:6–7. Three major ideas are reflected at Rosh Hashanah:

1. The acceptance of God as king of the universe
2. The acknowledgment that God intervenes in the world to punish the wicked and reward the good
3. The recognition that God revealed himself in the Torah at Mount Sinai and willfully revealed himself again to bring about the end of days.[3]

Monday Evening

Rosh Hashanah begins at sundown on Monday. In Judaism, the day does not begin at midnight as it does for most of the world, but at sundown and continues till sundown the next day. For example, Shabbat begins at sundown on Friday and continues until sundown on Saturday. This is based on the creation story: "And there was evening, and there was morning—the first day" (Genesis 1:5).

So I put on my undershirt with tassels, wear a dark suit and tie, and make my way to the synagogue. As I walk in I put on a *kippah*. During Rosh Hashanah and Yom Kippur, the synagogue has an entirely different *siddur*—prayer book. It's called the *mahzor*. The evening service is held in a small chapel rather than the main sanctuary.

About fifteen or so people have come here for the evening service. Rabbi David stands in front, along with the cantor, who is dressed in a long white robe accompanied with a hat that looks like a crown. I sit in the back row, and I'm a little nervous because I'm not sure how to act. The entire service is in Hebrew with the exception of a few short sections in English:

> *The year gone by has faded with the sunset*
> *as we move always forward into life.*
>
> *This day which borders past and future*
> *summons us to this sanctuary.*
>
> *It summons us to account for the gift of life.*
>
> *This sacred day we join as a congregation*
> *with repentance on our tongues,*
>
> *with resolve in our hearts*
> *that repentance be reflected in our deeds.*
>
> *We seek forgiveness from ourselves, from others and from God.*

In cleansing repentance we seek atonement,
to be at one with ourselves, with others and with God.

Wholeness and holiness we seek
as we enter a new year.

Help us, Lord, to realize the truth
that we are as holy as we allow ourselves to be.[4]

This is how the service begins. I'm impressed that the idea of repentance includes one's "deeds." This seems to be in line with the teachings of Jesus. I'm also impressed with the need to ask others for forgiveness. This too is close to the teachings of Jesus. I am most impressed with the thought that we are "as holy as we allow ourselves to be."

I'm not sure when to stand and sit. So I watch everyone carefully so as not to look so odd. Soon we rise for the call to public worship. The cantor begins in Hebrew, "Praise the Lord, source of blessing." The congregation responds along with the cantor: "Praise the Lord, source of blessing, throughout all time." This is followed by the saying of the Shema.

Then comes the Amida. These are the eighteen blessings used in every synagogue service as well as in personal prayer. On festival days, however, there are seven blessings. The Amida, however, is prayed in silence or near silence. Throughout the room people mutter phrases in Hebrew as they repeat their prayers. It seems strange to me to have everyone standing but praying in silence.

The rabbi's sermon (I doubt if that's what it's called) is in English. I like his sermon a lot. He talks about the idea that we are never really ready for the most important things in our life. I also love his honesty when he says that he actually wasn't ready to give a Rosh Hashanah sermon. And no one seemed to mind. If I had ever stood up at Calvary Church and said, "You know, I really don't have anything to say; I'm not really very well prepared," an elders meeting would have followed the service and the whole congregation would have been displeased.

But not in the synagogue.

Tuesday Morning

The synagogue service begins at 9:00 a.m. What I don't realize is that it will last until almost 1:30 p.m.—more than four hours. With the exception of a few comments in English, the entire service is in Hebrew. My brain hurts by the time the service is over because I try to follow the Hebrew. If the cantor simply spoke in Hebrew, I would understand most of it, but he uses musical notations that I find difficult to follow. When he speaks the words, I catch on, but when he speeds up or chants, I'm completely lost. Fortunately, from time to time, the rabbi interrupts and announces the page numbers—in English.

The highlight of the morning service is the reading from the Torah scrolls, which are kept in a closet on the platform. At a specific point in the service they are brought out for public reading. Before the scrolls are read, they are carried around the synagogue in a procession. As the scrolls pass by, you reach out, touch them, and then kiss your hand. Some of the people wearing prayer shawls reach out and touch one of their tassels to the Torah scroll; then they kiss the tassel. I was amazed at the high view that Jews have of the Torah scrolls. Even though they have Hebrew Bibles at home, as well as the prayer book, which contains many passages from the Hebrew Bible, something about bringing out the Torah scrolls simply ignites the congregation into an enthusiastic response.

Several laypeople come forward and read sections from the Torah. The main reading was about the birth of Isaac in Genesis 21. The story also includes the sending away of Hagar and Ishmael.

Sarah's servant Hagar was the woman through whom Abraham had a son named Ishmael. But Ishmael was not the promised son. Isaac was. Sarah, Abraham's wife, is upset with Ishmael and Hagar and says, "Get rid of that slave woman and her son, for that slave woman's son will never share in the inheritance with my son Isaac" (Genesis 21:10). Perhaps this story is retold to remind us that God is the God of Isaac and the God of Ishmael. He is God of all peoples on earth.

When God appears to Abraham to tell him that he will have a son through Sarah, she is outside the tent, overhears the conversation, and begins to laugh. But God is true to his word and Isaac is born — his name means "laughter." Sarah becomes a central figure at Rosh Hashanah to remind us that we are all filled with faith and doubt at the same time.

In addition to the reading of the Torah, the blasting of the shofar is unique to Rosh Hashanah. "On the first day of the seventh month you are to have a day of rest, a sacred assembly commemorated with trumpet blasts" (Leviticus 23:24). There are several different blasts of the trumpet:

> *tekiah* — a short blast
> *shevarim* — three broken sounds
> *teruah* — many short sounds
> *tekiah gedolah* — one long sound

Before the shofar is sounded, we rise and say the following:

> *In your great mercy, Lord,*
> *bring us nearer to your presence.*
>
> *Help us to break down the barriers*
> *which keep us far from you:*
>
> *falsehood and faithlessness,*
> *callousness and selfishness,*
> *injustice and hardheartedness.*

Our hope is in you,
for you respond in mercy
when we sound the shofar.

At this point several young people come forward. The rabbi announces the specific sounding of the shofar (from the list above) and then the young people do it. At the first blast, several kids in the congregation begin to cry because the sound is so piercing. It's designed to wake people up from their slumber and realize the importance of doing better in the new year than they did in the previous year.

After the service, which seems to last forever, the rabbi invites us to another room where we have dessert and wine. The cantor, who's now dressed in a suit, blesses the wine: "Blessed are you, God, our God, King of the universe, who creates the fruit of the vine."

Having grown up with teetotaling Christians, I find it unusual to have someone bless God—for wine! The cantor also announces that shortly they will take the bread to a nearby body of water and perform *tashlikh*. I notice about a dozen loaves of bread on a table nearby. One of the customs of Rosh Hashanah is to throw bread on the water to remember that God has cast our sins into the deepest sea.

I decide not to go with the group for that ceremony, but I would like to observe the custom. I like the idea of God casting my sin into the sea. So after drinking some wine, I get in my truck and go home to get some bread. I realize, of course, that since I don't often eat bread, I don't have any in the house. So I get several crackers and put them in a plastic bag instead. I then drive down to the Grand River, which flows through downtown Grand Rapids. There's a boat ramp just north with a dock next to it.

When I get there, several fishermen are launching their boats. I'm still dressed in my suit, and my long, partially gray beard blows in the wind. I'm also carrying my Bible. I walk down to the boat ramp and then out to the end of the dock. The fishermen look at me like I'm crazy. I open the Bible and begin reading from the prophet Micah.

> Who is a God like you,
>> who pardons sin and forgives the transgression
>> of the remnant of his inheritance?
> You do not stay angry forever
>> but delight to show mercy.
> You will again have compassion on us;
>> you will tread our sins underfoot
>> and hurl all our iniquities into the depths of the sea.
> You will be true to Jacob,
>> and show mercy to Abraham,
> as you pledged on the oath to our fathers
>> in days long ago.
>
> **Micah 7:18–20**

Then I take the crackers out of my pocket, crush them, and throw them into the river. I stand there until all of the crackers have floated away. Of course, I keep wondering what the fishermen are thinking. It's not every day you see someone dressed in a suit and a tie with a Bible, throwing crackers into a river.

By the time I get home I'm exhausted. I've listened to more Hebrew than I have in a long time. But I don't have much time to rest because I need to get back to the synagogue for the evening service. I think when I get in bed tonight, I'll dream in Hebrew.

Wednesday

Back to the synagogue this morning for the 9:00 a.m. service. When I arrived only about a dozen people were in the sanctuary, but more and more people came in during the service and sat down. By the time it was over the sanctuary was three-quarters full. As I sat there trying to focus on the Hebrew, I was amazed that so many came late. During the service people would get up, walk out, and then come back in. Those of us who grew up in the evangelical church always try to arrive on time, and wherever you sit—you're stuck there for the rest of the service. You don't get up and move around. But not so in the synagogue.

The morning services are similar to the first day of Rosh Hashanah with the exception that the Torah reading is different. Today the main Torah reading was the binding of Isaac. This is the story about God testing Abraham. He tells Abraham to take his son, his only son, Isaac, up on the mountain and offer him as a sacrifice. Abraham obeys. He binds Isaac and puts him on the altar. As he is about to kill Isaac with a knife, the angel of the Lord speaks to Abraham and tells him not to do it. Next to the altar a ram is caught in the bushes, and Abraham sacrifices the ram instead. Some of the rabbis claim that the ram was created in the garden of Eden and then made its way to the place where Abraham offers his son. Along the way it got delayed and almost didn't make it on time.

I've always loved this story. It gives me hope on my journey with ALS. As I walk up the mountain, about to lose everything that is meaningful, God has a ram coming up the other side. Even though I don't see it, God's provision is already on the way. At the right moment, he will reveal it.

One of the most moving parts of the entire service was when the cantor came down from the platform, walked to the back of the auditorium, and then began a slow walk down the center aisle. He took one step and then prayed. He took another step and then prayed. And he did this the entire way down the center aisle until he reached the platform. Here is the prayer he prayed (although he prayed it in Hebrew):

Here I stand, impoverished in merit, trembling in your
presence, pleading on behalf of your people Israel even though
I am unfit and unworthy for the task. Therefore, gracious and
compassionate Lord, awesome God of Abraham, Isaac, and
Jacob, I plead for help as I seek mercy for myself and for those
whom I represent. Charge them not with my sins. May they
not be ashamed of my deeds; and make their deeds cause me no
shame. Accept my prayer as the prayer of one uniquely worthy
and qualified for this task, whose voice is sweet and whose
nature is pleasing to his fellow man. Remove all obstacles and
adversaries. Draw your veil of love over our faults. Transform our
afflictions to joy and gladness, that we may live in peace. May we
always love truth and peace. And may no obstacles confront my
prayer.

Revered, exalted, awesome God, may my prayer reach your
throne, for the sake of all honest, pious, righteous men, and for
the sake of your glory. Praise to you, merciful God who hears
prayer.

The cantor had come down into the congregation to show
that he is not above the congregation. He was one of us. Listening
to the voice of the cantor as he slowly moved forward was very
moving for me. The above translation is actually a paraphrase of
a much longer prayer in Hebrew. In fact, one of the lines carries
the idea, "May my beard be long on me and white enough." In
other words, may I be mature enough to lift my prayers to you,
God. At this point in my journey my beard is quite long. In fact,
some people in the synagogue passed the word around that an
Orthodox Jew had joined them for Rosh Hashanah. Of course
that Orthodox Jew was me. My beard is not quite white enough.
The prayer is fundamentally asking God for the ability to pray.

I go back to the synagogue for the evening prayers. I've now
spent two complete days in the synagogue. By the end of the second day I'm beginning to catch the flow of what's going on. I'm

even beginning to understand more of the Hebrew. And to think that Jews all over the world follow the same liturgy, sing the same prayers, and read the same sections from the Torah. And they do it in Hebrew, which is not only the language of their culture, but the language of the Bible. I could have gone to any synagogue in Jerusalem, Ireland, Europe, Africa, Australia, Canada, North America, or South America, and the service would have been exactly the same. I was in communion with Jews not just in Grand Rapids but all over the world.

After two days in the synagogue, listening to and getting lost in the Hebrew, I finally go home. Frankly, I'm exhausted. My head is spinning. My brain hurts. One of the traditions of Rosh Hashanah is to dip apples in honey. So when I get home I ask my wife to cut up some apples and put some honey in a bowl. I sit down and slowly dip each apple slice in the honey and eat it. The symbolism is that we ask God to give us a sweet new year. Just as the apples in honey taste sweet, so we are asking that life in this new year be sweet as well.

Between Rosh Hashanah and Yom Kippur

The days between Rosh Hashanah and Yom Kippur are known as "the ten days of repentance," when it is our responsibility to seek forgiveness from those we have wronged. I've been working at Cornerstone University for almost six months, and during that time I've made major changes in the life on campus. Some of those changes have not been well received.

Every Tuesday I have lunch with the three key people that I work with: the dean of community life, the dean of student services, and the dean of discipleship. Each of them is vital to the student life at the university. And I've grown to love and respect them.

At the lunch on the Tuesday after Rosh Hashanah, I said to them, "I really appreciate the time we've spent together this year, focusing our efforts on spiritual formation. I'm asking you to forgive me for things I may have said or done that have offended you."

Though they claimed that I hadn't offended them, each of them, in turn, extended their forgiveness.

Still, I know I've offended some of the people at the university. In the process of reorganizing the staff, I made major changes in the responsibilities of the administrative assistants—and I know they weren't happy with me. So I went to the office to ask each of them for their forgiveness, which they graciously extended.

In fact, I had a powerful conversation with one of them. She was deeply moved and greatly encouraged by our conversation. Sometimes I think it's too easy for those of us in leadership to not pay enough attention to how people are receiving our decisions.

From time to time it's important for spiritual leaders to ask the forgiveness of the people around them. I didn't mean to hurt anyone's feelings. I did not mean to offend anyone. I felt I was making the right decisions for the benefit of the university. Nonetheless, I offended some people and now I was asking forgiveness.

By the way, this is a very Jesus thing to do. He said, "If you forgive men when they sin against you, your heavenly Father will also forgive you. But if you do not forgive men their sins, your Father will not forgive your sins" (Matthew 6:14–15).

Yom Kippur

Yom Kippur means "the Day of Atonement." During the Temple period, the high priest would enter the Holiest of Holies (the most sacred place in the Temple where the glory of God resided) and sprinkle blood on the Ark of the Covenant for the forgiveness of the sins of the entire community. Other than on the Day of Atonement, no one can enter the Holiest of Holies. It was also the one day when the high priest would pronounce God's sacred, unpronounceable name. Of course we no longer know how it was pronounced.

After the destruction of the Temple in AD 70, it could no longer be used by the priests to offer sacrifices for the forgiveness of sins. So the rabbis moved the Day of Atonement rituals to the synagogue.

Most of the day is spent in prayer. First, you are forgiven for sins you have committed against God, not those you have committed against others. You must go to those people individually to ask their forgiveness. Leviticus 16:30 says, "Because on this day atonement will be made for you, to cleanse you. Then, before the LORD, you will be cleansed from all your sins." In the Hebrew text, the word order is slightly different: "From all your sins before the face of the Lord you will be cleansed." There are two ways to read the Hebrew. One is to argue that we will be cleansed from all our sins before the Lord—since all of our sins are committed "before the face of the Lord." Then one could argue that we are forgiven of all sins, those against God and against others. The other way to read the text is to limit the cleansing only to those sins that are committed "before the Lord," that is, we are only cleansed of sins we have committed against God. This is how the rabbis interpret the text, and so, leading up to the Day of Atonement are ten days of repentance. On those days you go to those whom you've offended and seek their forgiveness.

Second, on the Day of Atonement you must follow five restrictions:

1. No eating or drinking
2. No bathing
3. No anointing of the body with oil

4. No wearing of leather shoes

5. No sexual relations[5]

This is based on the instructions given in Leviticus 23:32: "It is a sabbath of rest for you, and you must deny yourselves. From the evening of the ninth day of the month until the following evening you are to observe your sabbath." Perhaps the most difficult thing of all is that from sundown to sundown you cannot eat any food or drink any liquid.

The Evening of the Day of Atonement

I eat my last meal and drink my last drink of water before heading off to the synagogue. Of course I have not decided how long I will maintain the fast. Because of my disease it's not advisable for me to miss too many meals. I know this would exempt me from fasting on the Day of Atonement, but I'll at least fast for part of the time.

I also dress up. I wear a dark suit and a tie, and instead of leather shoes, I wear sandals. I feel strange. I hope no one sees me. All dressed up—and wearing sandals. My wife doesn't join me at the synagogue, nor do any of my kids. For better or worse, this is a journey I'm taking on my own.

The evening service begins before sundown. The reason for this is that the first part of this service is called *Kol Nidrei*—a formal service in which all vows are renounced. "Chanted dramatically by the service leader, it proclaims null and void these vows and promises that we may make and fail to fulfill in the coming year."[6] The cantor stands up front, and on either side of him two men hold Torah scrolls. This forms a court of three. The declaration of the annulling of the vows is repeated three times: "All vows and oaths we take, all promises and obligations related to

212

God between this Yom Kippur and the next we hereby publicly retract in the event that we should forget them, and hereby declare our intention to be absolved of them."[7]

Over the years, some people have argued that Jews cannot be trusted—after all they begin the Day of Atonement by annulling all vows and promises. But of course this is not true. The Torah clearly states that everyone should keep the vows they have made to God: "If you make a vow to the LORD your God, do not be slow to pay it, for the LORD your God will certainly demand it of you and you will be guilty of sin" (Deuteronomy 23:21). Still, we sometimes make rash vows to God. The purpose of Kol Nidrei is to relieve us of those vows and the guilt of not fulfilling them. The annulment is "restricted to those vows which involve one's relationship with his conscience or with God, involving no other persons or their interests."[8]

Following this brief and dramatic introduction, the evening service formally begins. During this service and the ones tomorrow will be several opportunities for people to confess their sins. The first is an abbreviated listing of sins. In the Hebrew language, which is used in confession, it forms an acrostic. The first sin begins with the first letter of the Hebrew alphabet; the second sin begins with the second letter; the third sin with the third letter, and so on. In English it reads:

> *We abuse, we betray, we are cruel.*
> *We destroy, we embitter, we falsify.*
> *We gossip, we hate, we insult.*
> *We jeer, we kill, we lie.*
> *We mock, we neglect, we oppress.*
> *We pervert, we quarrel, we rebel.*
> *We steal, we transgress, we are unkind.*
> *We are violent, we are wicked, we are xenophobic.*
> *We yield to the evil, we are zealots for bad causes.*

As I stand with the congregation and repeat this prayer in Hebrew, I am deeply moved by how serious everyone is about sin. Note the confession's use of the first person plural—"we." While the Day of Atonement is for our personal confession of sin, that confession cannot be separated from the larger community. We are praying for both personal forgiveness and the forgiveness of our whole community.

This is all very Jesus-like. When teaching his disciples to pray, he told them to say, "Give us today our daily bread. Forgive us our debts, as we also have forgiven our debtors. And lead us not into temptation, but deliver us from the evil one" (Matthew 6:11–13). Note that all the requests in Jesus' prayer are in the first person plural—"us"—like the prayers in the synagogue.

After the more lengthy confession of sin, there is a section called *Hu ya'aneinu*—"may he answer us." It is a very moving section that recalls the history of the Jewish people and how God answered them at various moments in their history.

> *He answered Abraham on Mount Moriah*
> *and his son Isaac, found on the altar.*
> *May he answer us.*
>
> *He answered Jacob, praying at Bethel*
> *and his son Joseph, imprisoned in Egypt.*
> *May he answer us.*

And the list goes on. Each time the congregation responds with "May he answer us." The service concludes with *Yigdal-I him* based on the thirteen principles of faith from Maimonides:

> *There is a Creator who alone created and creates all things.*
> *He is one, unique.*
> *He has no body, no form.*
> *He is eternal.*
> *He alone is to be worshiped.*

The words of the prophets are true.
Moses was the greatest prophet.
The source of the Torah is divine.
The Torah is immutable.
God knows the deeds and thoughts of man.
God rewards and punishes.
The Messiah will come.
God, forever praised, will resurrect the dead.[9]

After the service, I ask to borrow one of the siddurs for the Day of Atonement. I bring it home so that my wife and I can go through the lengthy prayers of confession. She is surprised at the depth of confession as well as the words that are used. "These are unbelievable prayers," she says. "They deal with every area of sin. They'd be a good guide for us Christians."

The Day of Atonement

If you think that Rosh Hashanah requires you to spend a long time in the synagogue, you haven't been to Yom Kippur. This is the day on which Jews spend almost the entire day in the synagogue, praying.

I get up, get dressed, skip breakfast, put on my sandals, and head to the synagogue. When I arrive shortly before 9:00 a.m., the parking lot is already full. I have to park at the far end and walk a considerable distance to the front door. A sheriff's deputy is standing at the door—in uniform and armed. At first I'm taken aback, but then I realize how many people in the world would love to harm the Jews—and what better time to do it than on the Day of Atonement.

The sanctuary is already filled. I've never seen so many people at the synagogue, not even during Rosh Hashanah. Every Jew associated with the synagogue seems to be here. I notice several people wearing long white garments. This garment, called a *kittel*, is a burial shroud used at funerals. "On Yom Kippur, we are meant to feel the touch of death, for death cuts through all the defenses and illusions we have carefully created around our own mortality."[10]

I sit down on the back row. I realize I haven't taken a shower or put on deodorant, so I smell. I'm also starved. My stomach is rumbling and complaining. But I realize that everyone in the crowded synagogue is in the same situation.

The service, which begins at 9:00 and goes through midafternoon, is actually three services, but I'm not sure when one ends and the next begins.

The Torah reading is from Leviticus 16—the detailed story of the Day of Atonement. It is divided into six sections, and a different person reads each section. The other reading is from the prophet Isaiah, and I am quite taken aback by it:

> " 'Why have we fasted,' they say,
>   'and you have not seen it?
> Why have we humbled ourselves,
>   and you have not noticed?'
> "Yet on the day of your fasting, you do as you please
>   and exploit all your workers.
> Your fasting ends in quarreling and strife,
>   and in striking each other with wicked fists....
> "Is not this the kind of fasting I have chosen:
> to loose the chains of injustice
>   and untie the cords of the yoke,
> to set the oppressed free
>   and break every yoke?"

Isaiah 58:3–4, 6

It's interesting to me that on this day of total fasting, the prophet reminds us that there's something more important—namely, loosing the chains of injustice:

> Fasting on Yom Kippur is a turning from material to spiritual concerns. Judaism is not an ascetic religion. It does not sustain the body: whether it wishes to sanctify the body.... Fasting should help us to concentrate on the concerns of the Spirit, so that we might understand the proper role of the material in our lives during the rest of the year.[11]

We stand several times to confess our sins, using both the abbreviated confession of sins and the extended confession. During the morning service the abbreviated confession is sung to a beautiful and mournful melody. Several times during the extended confession, we say the following words in Hebrew: "For all these sins, forgiving God, forgive us, pardon us, grant us atonement."

We also sing a Hebrew hymn entitled "Avinu Malkeinu," which means "Our Father, Our King." This same hymn is sung on Rosh Hashanah, but on Yom Kippur the words are slightly different. On Yom Kippur the emphasis is on the confession of our sin and the forgiveness of God. The opening line is "Our Father, our King, we have sinned against you ..."

The second service contains an extended section on martyrs and details the story of famous Jewish sages who were killed by the Romans during the reign of Hadrian:

> Rabbi Akiba also chose to continue teaching in spite of the decree. When they led him to the executioner, it was time for reciting the Shema. While iron combs scraped away his skin as he recited "Shema Israel," freely accepting the yoke of God's kingship. "Even now?" his disciples asked. His reply: "All my life I have been troubled by a verse: love the Lord your God with all your heart and with all your soul, which means even if he takes

your life. I often wondered if I would ever be able to fulfill that obligation. And now I can." He left the world uttering, "The Lord is one."[12]

The third service, the shortest of the day, includes the reading of the prophet Jonah. I'm particularly excited to hear the entire book read in Hebrew. It was one of the first books I translated when I studied Hebrew many years ago. The book of Jonah records the ultimate state of repentance — when an entire city turns to God. If God can forgive the wicked city of Nineveh, then he can also forgive us. The prophet Jonah is read on this occasion for at least three reasons:

1. It's an example of a whole city, with no particular relationship to God, that repents and is forgiven. What better example of successful repentance and its consequence can be found!

2. It's a message to us that God cares compassionately for all living things and prefers repentance to destruction. God's compassion is meant to be a model for us to copy.

3. Finally, it shows us that we, like Jonah, cannot flee the service of God.[13]

Between the afternoon and evening services, I go home to take a shower and eat. I'm taking a medical exemption from fasting until the sun goes down.

By the time I arrive at evening service, I'm wondering how Jews make a living during this month. I've spent more time in the synagogue, listened to more Hebrew, and prayed more prayers than in any other two weeks of my life. Being Jewish is a serious undertaking!

The theme of the evening service focuses on the idea of gates. This may have been inspired originally by the closing of the gates of the Temple on the Day of Atonement, the idea being that the gates are soon closing and time is running out.

Awesome God, let us live; forgive.
The gates are closing.

Our merits few, we look to you.
The gates are closing.

Save us from foes; your power just, in you we trust.
The gates are closing.

Our ancestors great, our merits few, our lives renew.
The gates are closing.

In spite of sin, again help us begin.
The gates are closing.

Your flock embrace, with love and grace.
The gates are closing.

In great compassion, forgiveness fashion.
The gates are closing.

Let joy, not strife, embrace our life.
The gates are closing.

Redemption bring, that we may sing,
though the gates are closing. . . .[14]

Later on in the service we repeat:

Open for us the gates, even as they are closing.
The day is waning, the sun is low.
The hour is late, a year has slipped away.
Let us enter the gates at last.
Lord, have compassion. Pardon, forgive, take pity.
Grant us atonement. Help us to conquer our iniquity and sin.[15]

The gates are starting to close on my own year of living like Jesus. The year has slipped away, and I only have two months left. I feel like the gates are closing too early.

The gates are also closing on my earthly life. Even though I have a slow-growing form of this disease, it will eventually get me. And it will get me sooner than later. So I have this deep sense in my soul that the gates are truly closing. I want to keep them open as long as possible. Although I do want to enter the gates at last, I want to delay it as long as possible. I can't believe that this year and my life have slipped away so quickly.

But the truth is, I don't want to think about it.

November

New Life

At the beginning of November, one of the most important events of the entire year occurred, and it had nothing to do with my year of living like Jesus. My daughter gave birth to a beautiful baby girl. On November 2 (a Sunday) she called us. "My water just broke. We'll call you later."

That was it. Just two sentences. So the rest of the day I prayed constantly, "Jesus, son of David, have mercy on Heather." I repeated the prayer hundreds of times as I thought about her going through labor. Of course I wanted her to be healthy. Of course I wanted the baby to be healthy. Of course I wanted her husband to be a good support during the labor process. But most of all, I wanted God to have mercy on her.

We waited all afternoon—no call. We waited all evening—no call. We went to bed—no call. Throughout the night I would wake up and pray the same prayer.

Finally we got a call on Monday morning. "We're at the hospital, and Heather's going to have a C-section," my son-in-law said.

Originally they'd planned to have the baby at home, but after almost twenty-four hours of labor, they decided to go to the hospital. My wife and I rushed to the hospital, and shortly after we arrived, the baby was born.

And what a beautiful baby!

We spent a good part of Monday at the hospital with our daughter and son-in-law. We all got to hold the baby. Of course, because of my disease, I can't physically pick up a baby or hold one in my arms, so I sat in a chair as they put the baby on my lap.

As I sat there I realized how quickly life had passed.

It seemed like yesterday that I was a kid growing up in Belfast. It seemed like yesterday that we got on the boat and made our way to America. It seemed like yesterday that I fell in love with Lorna and we got married. It seemed like yesterday that our first son was born. It seemed like yesterday that our daughter, who now has a baby of her own, was born. It seemed like yesterday that our youngest son was born. It seemed like yesterday when we moved to Grand Rapids.

As I held this baby in my arms, I could see that the Lord was opening the gates for me even as they were closing.

I've Heard This Story Before

I was sitting at home one afternoon when the doorbell rang. A poorly dressed, middle-aged African American man stood on the front porch, holding a crumpled paper.

"Can I help you?" I asked.

"I hope so," he said. "I'm a Vietnam veteran, and I have an appointment in Lansing, but I don't have enough money to pay for the bus ticket to get there."

He then handed me the piece of paper.

"This is my appointment at the Veterans Administration in Lansing. I have some medical issues, and I need to get there in order to get some help."

I looked at the guy. I'd heard this story before. Was it the same guy? I wasn't sure. But the story was sure the same. The crumpled piece of paper looked the same, and he needed money to get to Lansing. So I thought, *Do I help him or not?* The more I stared at him, the more I realized it was indeed the same person who'd asked me for bus money back in August. Maybe he thought someone else would answer the door this time and help him. But he got me — the same guy who'd helped him before.

At first I thought that helping him a second time would be the worst thing in the world to do. Whatever he used the money for before (most likely alcohol), he'd use the money this time for the same thing. If I gave it to him I'd be enabling him to continue his bad behavior.

But the problem is that this is a very un-Jesus-like way to think. Jesus says, "Give to the one who asks you, and do not turn away from the one who wants to borrow from you" (Matthew 5:42). Jesus didn't say give once to the one who asks you and if he asks you again—forget it. This man was asking, and the only Jesus-like response was to give him more money.

So I reached into my pocket and gave him everything I had—a twenty-dollar bill.

"Thank you very much," he said. "God bless you!" Then he left.

Back in my living room, I realized I'd been had. He'd fed me that story once before and I gave him money. Now, three months later, he feeds me the same story, and I give him money again. He must think I have Alzheimer's—or that I'm really dumb.

Had he asked me for forgiveness instead of cash, I would have known what to do. Peter once asked Jesus, "Lord, how many times shall I forgive my brother when he sins against me? Up to seven times?" Jesus replied, "I tell you, not seven times, but seventy-seven times" (Matthew 18:21–22). You see, Peter thought he was being generous by being willing to forgive his brother seven times. But Jesus wants us to forgive people up to seventy-seven times, or, as it says in some translations, "seventy *times* seven." In either case, Jesus is saying that we should keep on forgiving people no matter what they have done to us.

So if that is true for forgiveness, shouldn't it also be true for giving money? I hope so. I only gave to this man twice. Maybe he'll come back next month and next month and next month.

What will I do? I'll keep giving him money until he comes seventy times seven times.

The Jesus Party

> Jesus said to his host, "When you give a luncheon or dinner, do not invite your friends, your brothers or relatives, or your rich neighbors; if you do, they may invite you back and so you will be repaid. But when you give a banquet, invite the poor, the crippled, the lame, the blind, and you will be blessed. Although they cannot repay you, you will be repaid at the resurrection of the righteous."
>
> **Luke 14:12–14**

One evening we were eating dinner with the couple who lives upstairs in our house. As we talked, we decided that we should have a party and invite the poor, the crippled, the lame, the blind, though we also decided to take a few days to think about the idea. Several nights later, we met again for dinner to talk about our party—we called it "the Jesus party."

I was quite excited about inviting the poor, the crippled, the lame, and the blind. I even had some specific people in mind to invite to the Jesus party.

But then my wife, Lorna, spoke up: "I'm not sure it's a good idea. It smacks of tokenism—and I don't think it's what Jesus had in mind. Did he mean we should invite these people specifically? Or did he simply want us to be compassionate toward everyone who is less fortunate than we are?"

"Wow! I never thought of that," I said, "but you're right. If the people we invited to the Jesus party asked me why they were invited, what would I tell them? 'Oh, you were invited because you're poor or crippled or lame or blind.' That would contradict the whole spirit of what Jesus wants us to do, wouldn't it?"

So that was the beginning and the end of the Jesus party.

Still, I managed to follow this instruction—at least in part. Two men with ALS from Lansing wanted to have lunch with me. One uses a walker and the other is in a wheelchair. So they drove over in their handicapped van, picked me up, and we went to a restaurant. It was quite an ordeal.

First, it took quite a while for everyone to get out of the van —at least ten minutes. Second, it took us awhile to maneuver through the restaurant to our seats. They had to move chairs out of the way so the man in the wheelchair could get through. This restaurant was clearly not accustomed to handicapped people.

The man in the wheelchair has full use of both hands, but since I cannot eat with my right hand, I eat with my left, and the man with the walker has difficulty with both. I can walk without assistance, but the other two cannot. After we sat down I said, "Between the three of us there's one good person!" They all laughed.

It even took a while to eat because two of us have difficulty. By the time we finished our meal, everyone in the restaurant was gone—except us. The man with the walker needed to go to the bathroom. "Need any help?" I asked. Of course I was hoping he'd say no because helping someone in the bathroom is not high on my list of priorities. Fortunately he declined my offer.

After the meal, they dropped me off at home. I went in and collapsed on the living room couch, exhausted. I think what I struggled with most was the fact that it took so much time to do everything. It wasn't a quick lunch. It wasn't an easy lunch. But it was enjoyable. We had wonderful conversations about our journeys and about the disease. I'm just glad that all three of us are still capable of going out to a restaurant.

I think Jesus wants us to focus on those who are crippled and lame because it requires significant effort on our part. I think he wants us to focus on the crippled and lame because it forces us to slow down and help them. I think he wants us to focus on the crippled and lame because when we do, we discover what truly matters in life — and it's not our ability to walk and move. These men remind me that what really matters in life is our relationship with God and the time and love we invest in others.

The Election

It's early November and I'm sick and tired of all the political advertisements. In fact, when they come on the television I mute them. I'm tired of the commercials put out by those running for national office as well as those running for local and state offices. And opposing candidates often run their commercials back to back.

One of the commercials is by the chief justice of the Michigan State Supreme Court. When you watch it, you would think that his opponent was the most incompetent, vacillating person ever to walk the face of the earth. His opponent's commercials are just as bad about the chief justice, showing a video of him falling asleep during a major hearing and then ruling against the family in a serious accident case. The implication is that the chief justice doesn't really care about the real needs of Michigan families. And then I think of all of the money spent on these commercials. It's ridiculous!

So I can't wait for the election to be over and to be free of all these advertisements. By the way, have you ever noticed that when one candidate runs a commercial against the other one, they use the worst-looking picture of that candidate they can find?

Growing up in Ireland, I remember my family watching programs about the American elections. It all seemed so bizarre to us. The parties had these massive conventions with balloons and people dressed in funny hats. They cheered and yelled and did all sorts of crazy things. To us it looked slightly better than a circus — but only slightly. But now I'm an American citizen and I need to vote.

Or do I?

Why Bother Voting?

> Pilate then went back inside the palace, summoned Jesus and asked him, "Are you the king of the Jews?"
>
> "Is that your own idea," Jesus asked, "or did others talk to you about me?"
>
> "Am I a Jew?" Pilate replied. "It was your people and your chief priests who handed you over to me. What is it you have done?"
>
> Jesus said, "My kingdom is not of this world. If it were, my servants would fight to prevent my arrest by the Jews. But now my kingdom is from another place."
>
> **John 18:33–36**

This is the record of Jesus' trial before the Roman governor named Pilate, who had the power to release Jesus or to have him crucified. Pilate had authority, after all, because he represented the Roman empire. But Jesus made it clear that his own kingdom, unlike the kingdom of Caesar, was not of this world. He said that it was from another place.

Underneath the story is a clash between two kingdoms. The kingdom of Caesar versus the kingdom of God. The kingdom of Pilate versus the kingdom of Jesus. An earthly kingdom versus a heavenly kingdom. As I reflect on this passage, I'm reminded that the kingdom of Jesus is "not of this world." It's a kingdom where there is "neither Jew nor Gentile, slave nor free, male nor female" (Galatians 3:28). The kingdom that Jesus represents is a kingdom that transcends religious differences, social and economic differences, and gender differences. We are "all one in Christ Jesus" (Galatians 3:28).

This was a completely foreign idea to someone like Pilate. The only thing Pilate knew was the earthly kingdom. He had been appointed by Caesar as a governor in Israel and had all the power and might of the Roman empire behind him. But Jesus came along and seemed to blatantly ignore Pilate and his kingdom. Jesus was busy building an entirely different kingdom, the kingdom of which I am a part of today and the kingdom to which I've committed this whole year.

So should I even bother to vote? If Jesus' kingdom is not of this world, do the kingdoms of this world even matter? Should we be so passionate about Jesus' kingdom that we completely ignore the earthly kingdom in which we live?

So I'm tempted not to vote. Why? Because my commitment is to the building of a spiritual and heavenly kingdom. By voting, I invest in a kingdom that ultimately doesn't matter. Or does it?

Dealing with Caesar

> Then the Pharisees went out and laid plans to trap him in his words. They sent their disciples to him along with the Herodians. "Teacher," they said, "we know you are a man of integrity and that you teach the way of God in accordance with the truth. You aren't swayed by men, because you pay no attention to who they are. Tell us then, what is your opinion? Is it right to pay taxes to Caesar or not?"
>
> But Jesus, knowing their evil intent, said, "You hypocrites, why are you trying to trap me? Show me the coin used for paying the tax." They brought him a denarius, and he asked them, "Whose portrait is this? And whose inscription?"
>
> "Caesar's," they replied. Then he said to them, "Give to Caesar what is Caesar's, and to God what is God's."
>
> When they heard this, they were amazed. So they left him and went away.
>
> Matthew 22:15–22

The Pharisees (a group of well-respected men who had committed their lives to obeying all of the commands in the Torah) and the Herodians (Jews who cooperated with and were involved with the Roman government—they were more Greco-Roman than Jewish) came to Jesus and asked him, "Is it right to pay taxes to Caesar or not?"

No matter what answer Jesus gave, he would offend someone. If he answered yes, then he would offend the Jews who hated the Roman government and were willing to do anything they could to resist its power, including not paying taxes. If he said no, then he would offend the power and might of the Roman government. It would be an act of treason and could lead to his execution. So Jesus was in a bind.

So Jesus called for a coin and asked, "Whose portrait is this? And whose inscription?" The answer to the first question was the Roman Emperor Augustus Tiberius. The answer to the second was "Augustus Tiberius, son of the Divine Augustus." The inscription clearly defined Caesar as the son of God.

From a Jewish point of view, you should not even handle a coin like this. To use such a coin would have been a violation of one of God's commands: "You shall not make for yourself an idol in the form of anything in heaven above or in the earth beneath or in the waters below" (Exodus 20:4). So should Jews pay taxes to Caesar?

The first part of Jesus' answer is "Give to Caesar what is Caesar's." Even though the Romans believed that Caesar was a god, and even though the coin declared him to be so, and even though this was a violation of one of God's commands, you still had an obligation to pay the tax.

Then Jesus added some interesting words: "... and to God what is God's." According to the creation account, humans were created in the image of God: "So God created man in his own image, in the image of God he created him; male and female he created them" (Genesis 1:27). Since the Roman coin bore the image of Caesar, Jesus said, "Give to Caesar what is Caesar's," but since we human beings reflect the image of God, not the image of

Caesar, it is our responsibility to give our whole life back to God. As important as it is to give to Caesar what is due to Caesar, it is insignificant compared to giving God what is due God.

So what about voting in this election?

My dad was born in Detroit, the oldest son of Irish immigrants. His mother died when he was a few months old. His father met another Irish girl in Detroit, and they got married. They were so homesick for Ireland that they decided to take the family back there. Years later when my dad decided to come and visit the place where he was born, he discovered that he was actually an American citizen since he'd been born in the United States. When he was going through the process of establishing his citizenship, one of the questions he was asked was, "Have you ever voted in the British election?" Since he hadn't, he was eligible to claim his American citizenship. Maybe I should be like my dad. Forget voting.

Should I vote or not? If paying taxes to Caesar is important, then voting in an election is important—but not all that important! The real issue is what I am giving to God. My obligation to God is so much more important than my obligation to Caesar.

So if I decide to vote, I know that my vote is not all that important. In fact, I have little faith in either party and either candidate because my ultimate hope is not in Caesar, even if Caesar is the United States of America. My ultimate hope is in God, in whose image I have been created and for whose glory I now exist.

Far too many of my conservative friends seem to place more hope in government than they should. For years, at every election cycle, I've heard, "This is the most important election in America's history. We need to make sure that we vote the right person in because the whole future of our country depends on him." Other people say, "We need to vote the right person in because they will have the ability to appoint Supreme Court justices and ultimately they will determine for generations to come what kind of country we have." Of course, there is some truth in these statements—and Jesus does seem to imply that we have some obligations to Caesar.

But compared to our obligations to God, our obligations to Caesar are relatively insignificant.

So I've decided to vote.

But *how* should I vote? I'm a registered Republican. Ever since I became a U.S. citizen, I've voted along party lines. Back in my days with the Moral Majority I had no other choice but to vote Republican. After all, Republicans were the only ones who had a party platform that protected human life beginning at conception. Republicans were also pro-family, pro-Israel, pro-limited government, and pro-business. For most of my life, these issues have seemed important to me.

So do I just vote along party lines again? Or do I consider other options?

Since I've been reading through the Gospels and trying to live like Jesus, I decided to let the Gospels and the teaching of Jesus guide me in deciding who to vote for. The candidate and the party that best reflect the teachings of Jesus will get my vote.

For diehard Republicans, that choice is easy. The Republican Party best represents the essential teachings of Jesus. Right?

Unlike past elections, this time I decided to read the platforms of the Republican Party, the Democratic Party, and the Green Party. Jerry Falwell used to say, "Jesus was neither a Republican nor a Democrat—and he sure wasn't a Democrat!" I spent several days reading and studying each of these platforms, and I came to the conclusion that none of them reflect Jesus' teachings—although in my opinion the Green Party platform came a little closer than either the Republican or Democratic platforms.

So instead of looking at the party platforms, I examined each of the presidential candidates to determine which one seemed closest to Jesus' teachings. Up front I eliminated the Green Party candidate because that person did not share my values. So I then focused on Senators Obama and McCain. Which of these candidates best reflected the teachings of Jesus? Now, I was not asking which of them was the most "Christian." For me, whether they were "Christian" was fundamentally irrelevant. I wanted to know which of them in background, experience, and policies most closely reflected the teachings of Jesus.

But which teachings of Jesus should guide my choice? This is an important question. Most of my conservative friends believe the issue of abortion is the defining issue. If a candidate is pro-choice (allowing abortion), then that is the determining factor in not voting for them. If a candidate is pro-life (limiting abortion), then that is the determining factor in voting for them. Jerry Falwell used to say, "If someone's running for dogcatcher and they're pro-life, I'll vote for them." In other words, the protection of human life before birth is the ultimate issue for many people in deciding who to vote for.

Fortunately or unfortunately, Jesus never mentions the issue of abortion.

The Issues

I decided to focus on three major areas of Jesus' teaching:

1. Treatment of the poor, the marginalized, and the oppressed
2. Treatment of one's enemies
3. Commitment to peacemaking

There are probably many more areas I should have examined but I limited myself to those three.

1. Treatment of the Poor, the Marginalized, and the Oppressed

> Then the righteous will answer him, "Lord, when did we see you hungry and feed you, or thirsty and give you something to drink? When did we see you a stranger and invite you in, or needing clothes and clothe you? When did we see you sick or in prison and go to visit you?"
>
> The King will reply, "I tell you the truth, whatever you did for one of the least of these brothers of mine, you did for me."
>
> **Matthew 25:37–40**

This is the famous story that Jesus tells about the end of the world, when the sheep and goats stand before God in the final judgment. The sheep are invited into the kingdom because they fed the hungry, gave drink to the thirsty, took in strangers, clothed the naked, visited the sick, and visited those in prison. The goats, on the other hand, are sent to eternal punishment because they did not do those things. Jesus makes it clear that whatever you do to the "least of these" you do for him.

Jesus was the friend of the hungry, the thirsty, the stranger, the naked, the sick, and those in prison. That is not to say that he never associated with the rich and powerful. He did. As the punk band Fire Engine Red states in one of their songs, Jesus was a friend of "the poor and needy and the rich and greedy." But Jesus was clearly predisposed toward the poor.

This predisposition toward the poor was not new with Jesus. It is one of the major themes of the Hebrew Scriptures and especially the prophets:

> When you spread out your hands in prayer,
>   I will hide my eyes from you;
> even if you offer many prayers,
>   I will not listen.
> Your hands are full of blood;
>   wash and make yourselves clean.

233

Take your evil deeds
   out of my sight!
Stop doing wrong,
   learn to do right!
Seek justice,
   encourage the oppressed.
Defend the cause of the fatherless,
   plead the case of the widow.

Isaiah 1:15–17

This is what the LORD Almighty says: "Administer true
justice; show mercy and compassion to one another. Do
not oppress the widow or the fatherless, the alien or the
poor. In your hearts do not think evil of each other."

Zechariah 7:9–10

The Hebrew Scriptures are filled with these kinds of quota-
tions. God is on the side of the poor. God is on the side of the
oppressed. God is on the side of the marginalized. He is on the
side of the widow, the orphan, the fatherless. In the story of the
sheep and goats, Jesus is simply repeating the heart of God. And
this is one of the major themes of Jesus' teaching.

So which candidate, Senator Obama or Senator McCain, is on
the side of the poor, the oppressed, and the marginalized? In my
opinion, Senator Obama has done more for those people. After
graduating from college, he was a community organizer in Chicago. He did this for almost five years. Many of my conservative
friends have made fun of his community organizing and have
argued that that is no preparation for becoming president.

I believe the opposite. It is the perfect preparation for becoming president. For five years he was involved in the lives of the
poor, the oppressed, and the marginalized. Having grown up in
poverty himself, he understood the struggles of those who tend to
be ignored by the broader culture. I know many of my conserva-

tive friends argue that Senator Obama is only interested in more social programs.

I argue, so what? As I wrestle with the teachings of Jesus, the choice does not seem to be capitalism versus socialism. The choice seems to be: Who best reflects the teachings of Jesus with regard to the poor?

2. Treatment of One's Enemies

> You have heard that it was said, "Love your neighbor and hate your enemy." But I tell you: Love your enemies and pray for those who persecute you, that you may be sons of your Father in heaven.
>
> **Matthew 5:43–45**

Love your enemies! What a ridiculous concept from a political point of view! It's naive. It's stupid. It's the antithesis of normal political engagement with one's enemies. And there are serious enemies. My oldest son went to school in Israel for almost three years, during a wave of suicide bombings in Jerusalem. A bus was blown up a few blocks from where he lived. A café several blocks away was also blown up.

I was there with him about a week after the café was bombed. We went down there for a cup of coffee. As we walked up to the door, a security guard with a gun was checking backpacks and pocketbooks. My first thought was, where's the safest place to sit if a suicide bomber walks in? Facing the door? By one of the pillars? Toward the back? Close to an exit so I can get out? In the middle surrounded by people?

Many people in the world are bent on the destruction of Jewish people and the Americans. We have real enemies out there.

But Jesus tells us, "Love your enemies and pray for them." Our natural instinct is to destroy our enemies before they destroy us. But Jesus says—love them and pray for them. So as I wrestle with the teachings of Jesus, I ask myself, which candidate, Senator

Obama or Senator McCain, is most likely to love their enemies and pray for them?

Again I conclude, Senator Obama. He made it clear during the campaign that he would talk to anyone and everyone—including our enemies. Of course he got a lot of heat for making such statements, but I'm encouraged that he was at least willing to talk with them and hopefully pray for them.

3. Commitment to Peacemaking

> Blessed are the peacemakers, for they will be called children of God.
>
> **Matthew 5:9 TNIV**

Jesus was the ultimate peacemaker. Peace (*shalom* in Hebrew) is wholeness or completeness with God, others, creation, and yourself. God desires that each of us experience shalom. And Jesus came to offer shalom. The apostle Paul recognized this when he wrote to the church in Rome, "Therefore, since we have been justified through faith, we have peace with God through our Lord Jesus Christ" (Romans 5:1). In other words, through faith in Jesus we have been accepted by God ("justified") and we have shalom. Jesus himself said, "Peace I leave with you; my peace I give you" (John 14:27).

One of the ways we reflect the fact that we are "children of God" is by attempting to make peace. A number of years ago, President Clinton sent Senator George Mitchell to Northern Ireland to try to broker a peace agreement. When I first heard of President Clinton's initiative I thought, "Now that's a dumb idea. No way will Catholics and Protestants ever get together in Northern Ireland."

Although my family emigrated shortly before "the Troubles" broke out, we traveled back to Northern Ireland many times during that tough and difficult time. I had good friends and relatives killed in the Troubles. Senator Mitchell met with all of the parties, and on Good Friday of that year, while we commemorated the sufferings of Jesus, the various parties in Ireland forged a peace agreement. And what a difference it has made! Although there are still problems to resolve, the situation is now much better than it was. Three cheers for President Clinton! Three cheers for Senator George Mitchell! And three cheers for those who got together and agreed that the future would be peace — not war.

Whether in Northern Ireland, in the Middle East, in other difficult places in the world, or here at home, Senator Obama, in my opinion, is much more likely to bring people together and to advocate the cause of shalom. We have deep divisions in our country: between rich and poor, between Democrats and Republicans, between blacks and whites, between gays and straights, between pro-choice and pro-life, and many others. I think Senator Obama is much more likely to cross those divides and bring people together. (I like the fact that he invited Reverend Rick Warren to pray at the inauguration even though he caught flak from some in the gay community who felt that Warren's support of the marriage amendment in California should prohibit him from praying at such a public event.)

So I am leaning toward voting for Senator Obama. I know this will offend many of my conservative friends. Their attitude is that Senator Obama is pro-choice and, therefore, is for the killing of babies. And since life is the ultimate issue, there is no way under heaven that they will ever vote for someone like him. And they make a fair argument. They argue that the issue of life is the most important and fundamental issue of all. Failure to protect human life before birth is far more important than how we treat the poor, the oppressed, and the marginalized, or how we treat our enemies or how committed we are to making peace. So what about the issue of life?

Protection of the Unborn

> And if anyone causes one of these little ones who believe in me to sin, it would be better for him to be thrown into the sea with a large millstone tied around his neck.
>
> **Mark 9:42**

I'm still troubled because Senator Obama is pro-choice; that is, he believes abortion should be a choice between a woman and her doctor. He favors the current law that allows for abortion. He also said in his campaign that if one of his daughters got pregnant, he would consider encouraging her to have an abortion.

The King James Version, which I read growing up, states that if anyone "offends" one of these little ones, then a millstone should be tied around their neck and they should be thrown into the sea. I've been in many church services where the pastor dealt with this passage in the following way: "The Bible says that if you offend one of these little ones you should be thrown into the sea with a millstone tied around your neck. And since *Roe v. Wade*, we have offended many thousands of these little ones. Jesus was on the side of life. Jesus is for the little ones."

These kinds of statements always produce high drama. The pastor's words are met with thunderous applause. Down south, where people are more expressive, he would be greeted with rousing "amens."

But the problem with this interpretation is that it's simply not what Jesus had in mind. He was talking about causing "one of these little ones who believe in me to sin." It has nothing to do with the issue of abortion. It has nothing to do with protecting human life before birth. And even if you stretch the text to include abortion, then the next question becomes, "So if a woman has an abortion, or if a doctor performs one, should they actually have millstones tied around their necks and be thrown into the sea?"

For you created my inmost being;
  you knit me together in my mother's womb.
I praise you because I am fearfully and wonderfully made;
  your works are wonderful,
  I know that full well.
My frame was not hidden from you
  when I was made in the secret place.
When I was woven together in the depths of the earth,
  your eyes saw my unformed body.
All the days ordained for me
  were written in your book
  before one of them came to be.

Psalm 139:13–16

This psalm contains the most concise articulation of the beginning of human life in the entire Bible. It states that our frame was not hidden from God when we were "made in the secret place." This most likely refers to conception. It goes on to say that God saw all my unformed body before it took shape. Even before we were born, God ordained the number of days we should live. The psalm affirms that God is active from the moment of conception to the moment of death. Therefore, it is important that we protect human life from conception to death.

But this is not the only passage that deals with the issue of abortion. Some theologians have argued that life does not begin at conception. Rather it begins when a baby is able to survive outside the womb by breathing on its own. They argue this from the creation account. "The Lord God formed the man from the dust of the ground and breathed into his nostrils the breath of life, and the man became a living being" (Genesis 2:7). God created the first man (in Hebrew, *adam*) from the dust of the ground (in Hebrew, *adama*). But the man did not become a living being until God breathed into his nostrils the breath of life. These theologians argue that what happened to the first man is what happens to every human being—they are not a full living being until they are able to breathe outside the womb.

While this is an interesting perspective, I don't personally accept it. After all, there's a significant difference between God personally creating the first human being and a husband and wife creating every other human being after that. The breath that gave life to Adam was a unique one-of-a-kind creative experience. It has not been duplicated since then.

One more passage deals with the issue of the pre-born. I have probably heard a hundred different sermons on the subject of abortion, but I've never heard anyone deal with this text.

> If men who are fighting hit a pregnant woman and she gives birth prematurely but there is no serious injury, the offender must be fined whatever the woman's husband demands and the court allows. But if there is serious injury, you are to take life for life, eye for eye, tooth for tooth, hand for hand, foot for foot, burn for burn, wound for wound, bruise for bruise.
>
> **Exodus 21:22–25**

In this case, two men are fighting and, as it appears from the text, they intend to kill each other. In the process, they hit a pregnant woman who "gives birth prematurely." The Hebrew verb should actually be translated "miscarries." It's not a situation where the woman gives birth and the baby lives. Rather, the woman miscarries and the baby dies. If the woman herself dies, then the penalty is "life for life." This is in keeping with the Torah. "Anyone who strikes a man and kills him shall surely be put to death" (Exodus 21:12). When you deliberately kill someone, the penalty is that you yourself will be killed. If the pregnant woman survives, then her husband and the court assess a fine. If the pregnant woman dies, then the man who hit her must also be put to death.

According to the sages, "Causing the death of a fetus is not a capital offense, but the person responsible must pay damages. These damages are assessed by the Court in response to a claim made by the father."[1] *The Chumash* is a compilation of opinions about the text from Jewish sources. It appears from this text that the woman is more valuable than the baby. It is more serious to kill the woman than it is to kill the baby. Even though there is a fine for killing the baby, it does not appear to be as significant as the fine for hurting or killing the woman.

This is a troubling text, so I called Rabbi David to ask him about it.

"Rabbi, this is Ed. I have two simple questions. First, I've been studying the text where two men are fighting and they hit a pregnant woman and she miscarries. I was wondering what your take is on this text. Second, in a larger context, I was wondering what the Jewish perspective is on the beginning of human life. When does it actually begin?"

As soon as I asked these questions, David began to laugh. "Simple questions? You're asking difficult and complicated questions about when life begins!"

"Yeah. I probably shouldn't have used the word *simple*."

"The text you're referring to deals with penalties for taking a human life. If you take a human life, then the penalty is capital punishment. The penalty for taking the life of an unborn baby, however, is not a capital offense. It's something less than that. One of the implications of this text is that the taking of the life of an unborn baby is not murder."

"So what does that mean for the issue of abortion?"

"It means that under certain circumstances abortion would be okay. For example, if the health of the mother, either physically or mentally, is in jeopardy then it would be appropriate to have an abortion. The life of the mother has greater value than the life of the baby. This raises the question of what we mean when we talk about physical and mental issues. If a pregnant woman is suicidal and on the verge of committing suicide because of her pregnancy, then it would be appropriate to take the baby in order to save the mother's life. On the other hand, if a pregnant woman already has several children and really doesn't want another one or cannot afford it, this would not be an appropriate basis on which to have an abortion."

"So where do Jews stand on the issue of abortion?"

"Most Jews would be pro-choice because we believe that there are certain circumstances under which abortion is legitimate. This is a much different position than evangelical Christians or Catholics."

"So when does life begin?"

"I recently gave a lecture at one of the local hospitals on that question. I argued that life begins at conception but personhood begins at birth. Many Jews, however, argue that life begins when the baby can live independent of the mother."

This was a completely different perspective than I'd ever heard. But it comes directly from the Bible. Life may begin at conception. Abortion is legitimate under certain circumstances. Consequently, Jewish people are in favor of keeping abortion legal because there are certain circumstances under which it would be acceptable.

So there are really three positions when it comes to protecting pre-born human life.

1. The traditional Catholic position: Life begins at conception and should always be protected.

2. The general evangelical position: Life begins at conception and, with the exception of the life of the mother, rape, and incest, ought to be protected.

3. The Jewish position: Life may begin at conception but the physical and mental health of the mother takes precedence over the life of the baby.

I was friends with a longtime pastor of one of the large African American churches in our community. One day in his office we were talking about politics: Republican versus Democrat.

"You know," he said, "I am pro-life. I believe in protecting the unborn. But I have been around a long time and have watched many of our young women get pregnant and give birth. I have watched their kids grow up—especially the boys. And I see them getting into gangs, doing drugs, and ending up in prison. And I have to tell you, sometimes I think it would be better had they been aborted. It would've been better for everyone had they not been born."

My daughter taught in a public urban school in Virginia for three years. She is pro-life. Many of the young women she taught got pregnant. Some of them had abortions. Some did not.

"I tell you, Dad," she said to me one time, "the young girls who've had abortions would have had the abortions whether they were legal or not. I'm just glad it was legal and could be done by physicians in a medical facility."

So maybe the issue of abortion is not as black-and-white as some conservatives think. It's a complicated question.

So where do I stand? I still believe that human life begins at conception and that being pro-life is being for life from conception to the grave. So what are the implications of this statement? Simply put, I am for life. As a follower of Jesus, I am for protecting life before birth *and* after birth. After all, Psalm 139 clearly states that God is involved in our lives from the beginning of life to the end of life.

But here's an important point: being pro-life not only means I'm interested in protecting the unborn. It also means I'm interested in protecting those who have already been born.

Being pro-life means being concerned about those who are dying of HIV/AIDS.

Being pro-life means being concerned about those who are living in poverty.

Being pro-life means being concerned about those who lack adequate health care—especially children.

Being pro-life means being concerned about those in our communities who are into gangs and drugs and will ultimately end up in prison.

Being pro-life means being concerned about those innocent civilians who are being killed in Afghanistan, Iraq, the Gaza Strip, Israel, and places all over the world.

Being pro-life means being concerned about those who are experiencing genocide in countries around the world.

Being pro-life means being all of these and a whole lot more.

I am concerned about those within the conservative movement whose only concern is with the unborn. I agree with them. I stand with them. I support them. But I want to know why in the world they seem not to care about those who are *already* born.

So I plan to vote for Senator Obama. Even though I disagree with him on the issue of abortion, being pro-life is a whole lot more than being concerned about abortion alone!

Election Day

I drove a few blocks from our house to the polling place. I parked my car in the parking lot and walked up to the building. It was about 10:00 a.m. and the sun was shining. As I walked up to the building, I noticed that there were more than three hundred African Americans standing in line. Not a single white person!

I wasn't excited about standing in line. As I made my way to the back of the line, one of the election officials said, "Which precinct are you in?" I then realized that two precincts vote at this particular place, and my precinct had a very short line. Amen and amen.

Inside, my heart was beating really fast. For the first time in my life, I was going to vote for a Democrat, and I wasn't sure how I felt about it. I knew that my vote for Senator Obama would be profoundly misunderstood by my conservative friends. I knew that I'd catch heaven (then make a U-turn) for my vote. But I made a commitment to try to live out Jesus' teachings, and to the best of my knowledge I was making a vote in keeping with that.

Foolish? Maybe. Off-base? Maybe. Dumb? Maybe. But I had to do it.

Several of the African American women working at the polling booth hugged and kissed me. They were members of the Messiah Missionary Baptist Church where my wife and I occasionally attend. For the last three years I've preached more often in black churches than in white churches, and I had a deep sense of pride that an African American was one of the major candidates for president. I remember going to college in the 1960s when there were separate water fountains for white and black people. The college I attended, Bob Jones University, would not admit blacks. (The school recently apologized for their racist attitudes. Amen.)

Once I went with eleven African American pastors from our community for a week in Atlanta. One of them told me, "Before we flew out of Grand Rapids, I took my Sunday offerings to deposit at the bank. I was wearing a sweat suit. The clerk looked at me and said, 'Where'd you get this money?' I said, 'These are the offerings from my church.' The clerk said, 'How do I know it's not drug money?'"

The pastor insisted that it was the offerings from his church, but the clerk continued to question him about drug money. Finally he asked to see the manager. The manager came out and immediately began defending the clerk.

"Look," the pastor told the manager, "I'm not only a pastor,

I'm also chairman of the Grand Rapids Public School board. And we deposit millions of dollars in your bank. And if this is the way you treat black people, then I'm going to make a recommendation that we move all of our money to another bank."

At this point the manager became apologetic.

I listened to this incredible story and then asked, "Is this normal if you're black? Or is it the exception?"

All of the black pastors said it was normal daily behavior in Grand Rapids. I couldn't believe it. I've learned over the last few years that racism is alive and well in Michigan and around the country. It may be subtle, but it's real.

So as I looked at all of these African Americans lining up to vote, I was hoping Senator Obama would win because it had been a long and wearisome journey for blacks, though that was really not why I was voting for him.

Finally it was time for me to vote. I clearly marked my ballot and voted for Senator Obama. I also voted for some Republicans as well as some members of the Green Party.

I did not vote for Senator Obama because he would be the first African American president. I was fully aware that we were in the midst of a terrible crisis. The first forty-three presidents were white males, and one could argue that having a black male might make a difference. But that's not why I voted for him.

I did not vote for Senator Obama because he promised to bring change. I agree that we are desperately in need of change. We need to change the way we do politics in this country, and we need to change the way we relate to other countries around the world. We need change. But that's not why I voted the way I did.

I did not vote for Senator Obama because he promised to bring hope. We need hope! But that's not why I voted for him.

Nor did I vote for Senator Obama because I was disappointed in Senator McCain. Senator McCain is a war hero, a bright and engaging person. I was not disillusioned with him.

I voted for Senator Obama because I felt that he, more than any other candidate, best represented the teachings of Jesus.

The Next Sunday

The Sunday after the election I attended the Messiah Missionary Baptist Church. The pastor opened the service by saying, "We have been praying for change, and God has answered our prayers."

There was thunderous applause and amens from every part of the sanctuary.

"We thank God that Senator Obama has been elected president of the United States."

Again, thunderous applause and amens. When the place was quiet again, he continued: "But I want to remind you that our hope is not in President-Elect Obama or in the political system. Our hope is in the Lord. Let's not forget it!"

Less applause, but more amens.

I was grateful to be among people who appreciated the person I voted for.

The End of the Month

At the end of the month, I went to a cocktail party in one of the homes in Florida. More than sixty people were there, almost all of them with the Coast Guard auxiliary. The Coast Guard auxiliary patrols the entire Florida Keys and then reports suspicious activity to the Coast Guard who, in turn, investigate. Almost all of them were wearing Coast Guard auxiliary uniforms, which looked a lot like regular Coast Guard or Air Force uniforms. I felt really out of place. I was wearing sandals, shorts, and a golf shirt. It was obvious that I didn't belong.

The food was wonderful. Lots of cheeses, fresh vegetables for dipping, small pieces of fish with an accompanying dip, small lamb chops, lots of desserts, and an open bar. The liquor flowed throughout the evening. I went around meeting new people and getting reacquainted with people I already knew. Toward the end of the evening I was talking with a Jewish friend whom I'd seen at Shabbat and Passover services. We had talked on several occasions in the past. After some small talk I began telling him about my journey this year.

"I made a commitment for one year to try and live like Jesus," I said. "I eat kosher. I observe Shabbat. I attended the synagogue at various festivals and feasts."

"That's a hell of a lot better than I did!" he responded and began laughing. Then he launched into an extended dissertation about the Bible. "The Bible talks about the universal flood," he said, "but that's a ridiculous idea. Obviously there was some sort of flood, but it was really only local. The stories of the Bible were never intended to be taken literally. But they all have a message for us today. And we can learn from the stories of the Bible."

Even though I believe that there *was* a universal flood and am inclined to take all the stories of the Bible as literally as possible, I wasn't about to argue with him. Besides, I noticed that he had meat and cheese at the same meal—not kosher. But I did agree with his last statement—the stories of the Bible have a compelling message for us today. And I am trying, as I read the Gospels, to remember that all of Jesus' stories have a compelling message for me.

December

Looking Back

This is my last month of trying to live like Jesus. Although I plan to keep living like Jesus in the New Year, this marks the approaching end of my one-year commitment. In some ways I feel as though I am just beginning. There's so much more I need to do to follow Jesus' teaching. I'm making a list of all the things I didn't have a chance to do, and it's becoming rather long.

Throughout the year I kept a journal on my computer. I also filled a notebook with handwritten notes about my reading of the Gospels. If I had included everything that was written in the notebook, this book would be two or three times the length it is. In my notebook I listed the things I wanted to do during this year of living like Jesus, most of which I did, but some of which I didn't do. Maybe I will get to them eventually, but as of the writing of this book, they remain undone. The list includes the following:

Visiting Those in Prison

In the gospel of Matthew, Jesus tells a story about the separation of the sheep and the goats. The sheep are invited into the kingdom and the goats are thrown out of the kingdom. The distinguishing feature is that the sheep fed the hungry, gave drink to the thirsty, invited in strangers, clothed the naked, and visited the sick and those in prison. I had planned to visit someone in prison. Even though I have visited many prisons in the past, I wanted to do it again.

I mostly wanted to visit someone very special. He had grown up in our church, got married, had a baby, and things were going well. Then he and his wife got divorced. After the divorce, he really struggled. One Saturday night he called me at home.

"If you commit suicide can you go to heaven?" he asked.

"First," I said, "let me give you the number for the local suicide hotline. Any time you feel you're sinking into darkness and are considering suicide, call this number."

"Yeah, I have the phone number. But I want to know if you commit suicide do you go to heaven?"

"Since you asked a direct question I'll give you a direct answer. Yes, I believe that even when you commit suicide you go to heaven."

"How do you know?"

"The Bible says that nothing can separate us from God's love. That would include suicide. But I think that God will hold the person accountable for making such a bad choice."

"That makes sense."

"Do me a favor. Please call the suicide hotline."

"I will."

He hung up, and I spent a few moments praying for him.

A few days later, the man barged in on his ex-wife and her new boyfriend. He killed her boyfriend. I visited him several times while he awaited trial in Grand Rapids. My heart went out to him. I thought many times, "I wish he'd committed suicide. That would've been much better than what he now faces."

So he is one person I specifically wanted to visit during this year of living like Jesus. He was convicted of murder and sentenced to life in prison without parole. He's now in a federal prison a long way from Grand Rapids. I even got his parents' phone number out, but I never called them. I wanted to arrange a visit. I'm not sure why I didn't. But I didn't.

Giving Away All I Have

One day Jesus saw the rich giving all their gifts to the Temple treasury. A widow came by and gave two copper coins. Jesus said, "I tell you the truth, this poor widow has put in more than all the others. All these people gave their gifts out of their wealth; but she out of her poverty put in all she had to live on" (Luke 21:3–4). So I added that story to my list of things to do.

Of course, I wasn't willing to give everything away—my house, my cars, my savings, and my retirement. But I thought that at least Lorna and I could give away one or two weeks' salary. Then we'd have to trust God to meet our needs. But I never did it. Why? I never talked to my wife. I knew that if we were going to do something this radical, I'd need her support. She takes care of the checkbook. She takes care of the house. She takes care of all the bills. It would be easy for me to say, "Let's give up our salary for several weeks." But she is the one who knows our finances much better than I do.

Turning My Possessions over to My Wife

Jesus said, "Foxes have holes and birds of the air have nests, but the Son of Man has no place to lay his head" (Matthew 8:20). Jesus was essentially homeless. Even animals and birds have places they call home. But Jesus had no such place. Even though he created the world, he possessed almost nothing while he was in the world. So I thought I might call my lawyer and ask him if I could legally turn all my possessions over to my wife. I know he could change the title on my house, cars, and bank accounts, but I was trying to avoid the hassle of going through all that. So I thought that maybe I could sign a legal document and do the same thing. But I never did. I think I hesitated because I did not want my wife to feel all the responsibility for everything we owned.

Honoring the Sabbath

In my early conversations with the rabbi about the Sabbath, I told him that I wanted to observe the Sabbath strictly every week. He then asked me a series of questions, which is a very Jewish thing to do.

"Are you going to drive?"

"Are you going to use electricity?"

"Are you going to cook?"

"Are you going to write or watch television?"

He suggested that I not try to observe Shabbat every week. He thought it would be too much physical effort. And he was right. I did observe Friday night strictly, as well as Saturday. But never during the entire year did I observe a strict twenty-four-hour Sabbath. I hope God gives me credit for at least trying.

"Try observing Shabbat once a month or once every other month," he said. "Eventually, when you get the hang of it, you'll begin to really enjoy it."

I remember he also told me that if every Jew in the world observed a strict Sabbath, the Messiah would come. Why couldn't I observe a strict Sabbath? There was always some compelling reason: the kids' soccer game, a wedding, a funeral, and so on. Something always interfered.

Reading the Gospels

I read through the Gospels thirty-five times, not fifty-two. For the first part of my journey, I was quite proud of the fact that I read the Gospels four times every month. But I've been humbled. Once I started to work at Cornerstone, it was nearly impossible for me to keep up that kind of schedule. I did the best I could, but it wasn't good enough.

Walking

Jesus and his disciples walked. That was their main way of getting from place to place. So when I started the year, I wanted to spend at least two weeks walking everywhere, but I kept procrastinating. During the summer, I looked at my schedule to figure out when I could do it. Unfortunately (or fortunately), I had obligations every week that required me to be places and involved in situations that were many miles away. Sometimes it required being out of state. So I never did spend two weeks walking everywhere.

Wearing White Clothes

When Jesus appeared on the Mount of Transfiguration, his clothes were whiter than anyone could bleach them. So I thought, if Jesus had white clothes, then maybe, if I want to dress like him, I should wear white as well. So I bought a white shirt and began looking for white pants. I never found pants to match the shirt, but I did wear the shirt for four straight days. And miracle of miracles, I never spilled any food on it.

I remember in A. J. Jacobs' book that he wore all white. Where did he get the pants?

What Comes Next?

Now that my year of living like Jesus is almost over, I'm thinking about what comes next. For instance, I'm looking forward to eating non-kosher food again and have started to list all the things I want to eat.

> bacon
>
> chicken quesadillas
>
> bacon
>
> shrimp
>
> an Irish breakfast (sausage, bacon, fried eggs, fried tomatoes, fried soda bread)
>
> crabcakes
>
> bacon

I will also be glad to shave my beard—I think. The beauty of growing a beard is in not having to shave. In my case this is actually a blessing because I have trouble with my fine motor skills and I'm afraid that if I were to shave with a razor I'd cut myself.

I'm also tired of wearing the undershirt with the tassels. Even though I don't wear it all the time, it's a nuisance.

And I'm looking forward to reading something other than the Gospels.

A Trip to Florida

We plan to spend two months in Florida this winter. We'll be there from the middle of January to the middle of March. So I decided that I should drive a car down to Florida during December, leave it there, and fly home. That way we'll have an automobile when we get to Florida next month.

So I leave Grand Rapids and drive to southern Florida by myself.

I love being on the road. I decided to listen to the Gospels on the drive down. I listened to them two and a half times by the time I got to Florida.

I also limited myself to driving the speed limit—something that really drives me nuts. I realized that Jesus would have obeyed the traffics laws and so must I. This is especially difficult because I'm driving a two-year-old Corvette. Hundreds of people passed me on the highway and looked at me funny. I smiled back and muttered feebly, "I'm driving like Jesus!"

On my second day of driving, my cell phone rang. I answered it. It was my good friend at the *Grand Rapids Press*, Charley, the religion editor. Over the years he has been very fair to me and to everyone else in the religious community. I really like him.

"Hi, Ed. This a good time to talk?"

"I'm in the car driving to Florida, so it's a really good time to talk."

"I want to do an article on your year of living like Jesus and run it in the paper on December 25. I'd like to spend a day or two following you around. I'd also like to bring a photographer. Would that be okay?"

I really didn't want anyone to do an article about my journey. I'm not sure why. Maybe I knew it would be misunderstood and would open me up to all sorts of criticism. Then again, I've never shied away from criticism. I've been the pastor of a large church, and the more people you have, the more critics you have. Still, I didn't have the heart to tell Charley that I didn't want him to do the article.

"When I get back to Grand Rapids next week, call me again, and we can work out the details," I said.

"Thanks Ed. I'll call you."

In Florida I stayed on a friend's boat for several days. It was anchored in a large marina. By this time my beard was at least six inches long. When the wind blew, my beard stuck out sideways. I didn't look very trustworthy.

Later, some friends of mine were at a cocktail party adjacent to the marina and were talking with a couple who had a boat near the one I stayed on.

"I've noticed that the people who own the boat near us have a lot of unusual characters staying on their boat," the woman said.

"What do you mean?" my friend said.

"Well, before Christmas they had some guy with a really long beard staying on the boat. The dock master and the security guard were very concerned about him. They were afraid he might steal stuff from other boats. Of course, I told them not to worry; the guy with the beard is actually a pastor."

Only in America! If I were living in the Middle East, a long beard with gray hairs in it would be a sign of maturity, dignity, and respect. If I were living in Jesus' day, the same would be true.

But not here in America. Nearly everyone wants to judge you by outward appearance. And anyone who has a long beard is either homeless, a thief, or the kind of person you would never want to hang out with.

Maybe I'll keep the beard just to set people off!

Homeless

> Foxes have holes and birds of the air have nests, but the Son of Man has no place to lay his head.
>
> **Matthew 8:20**

Jesus was essentially homeless. But not homeless in the modern sense. Rather, he was dependent on the generosity and kindness of others. We know that a group of women followed him around, taking care of his daily needs. But he didn't have a permanent home. Even foxes and birds have homes but not Jesus. How in the world do I follow that? Do I give away my home? Do I walk around like a homeless person? I certainly looked like one in my beard, it seems.

The community in Florida is a wonderful, family-friendly environment. It has three golf courses, hundreds of homes and condos, and a bunch of restaurants. You need to be a member of the community or a guest of a member, however, to get in the front gate. Once you are in, it's a cashless society. That means you need a little plastic card to play golf, drink a beer, or eat at any of the restaurants. Without the card, you're sunk!

So I arrived at the community in early December and decided that I'd try to exist as long as I could without the card. I stayed with some friends but couldn't buy food at the restaurants or play golf without the card. I was totally dependent on the kindness and generosity of others. Fortunately, the people of the community are kind and generous. The people I stayed with even invited me to a movie one Sunday night.

Now, I am not much into movies. I see maybe two or three a year.

"You'll really enjoy the movie. It stars Jim Carrey, and he's hilarious," they say. "And before the movie there's a buffet."

"Count me in!" I say.

I can tolerate a movie for the sake of food.

I spent the entire week living like this. When I got up each morning I didn't know where I'd eat lunch or dinner. Usually at the last minute someone would call me and invite me to join them. I even got invited to play golf.

Several times, however, I went down to the beach bar to have a beer. I'd wait around, hoping someone I knew would show up and treat me to a beer. But no one did. I realized that when I try to work it out for myself to get a meal or a beer—nothing happens. But if I do nothing—someone always calls.

After a long week I didn't miss a single meal. I was grateful when the week was over, however, and I got a card that allowed me to eat whenever and wherever I wanted. I'm not sure I like the idea of not being in control. I'm not sure I like being at the mercy of others.

I cannot imagine Jesus doing this for the three years of his public ministry. But he did.

Golf on a Sunday

One Sunday afternoon I decided to play nine holes of golf with some friends. I seldom play golf on Sundays. In fact, when I was growing up we'd never have played golf or any other game on a Sunday. It was a day for worship, for studying the Bible, for prayer—and for a nap! Anyone who played a game, including golf, was considered a poor Christian.

But this year I'm following Jesus. He observed the Sabbath (Saturday) but didn't restrict his activities on Sunday. So, since I'm following Jesus, I'm free to play golf on Sunday. Of course this begs the question, "Would Jesus even play golf?" After all, golf was invented 1800 years after Jesus walked on planet Earth. But I'm making the assumption that he would.

So I met my friends for golf.

When I arrived at the golf course, one of the assistant golf pros took my clubs and put them on a cart. One of my friends decided to hit some balls at the driving range, but I didn't waste my energy. I wanted to save all my good shots for the actual course. While he was hitting balls, I sat in the cart with my other friend.

"See that young guy over there with the blond hair?" my friend said.

"Yeah. I see him."

"He's one of the young assistant pros here at the course. When you drove up he said, 'Who's that guy with the beard? Is he the unabomber?'"

We laughed hilariously.

"He really said that?" I said.

"He did! But I told him you're a pastor."

"I'm going to go over to him and say, 'Hi, I'm Ed. I'm the unabomber.'"

"I don't think you should," my friend said. "When I told him you were a pastor he was really embarrassed."

The Sufferings of Jesus

Evangelical Protestants never wear a crucifix—the cross with Jesus on it. Instead, we wear an empty cross to symbolize that

Jesus is no longer on the cross nor in the tomb. Catholics seem to focus on the sufferings of Christ while Protestants seem to focus on the resurrection.

The truth is that both are important. In fact, nearly one third of all the Gospels are devoted to the last week of Jesus' life. Even the prophet Isaiah predicted his suffering: "He was despised and rejected by men, a man of sorrows, and familiar with suffering" (53:3). He was called "the suffering servant."

So in this last month of my year, how do I identify with the sufferings of Jesus?

Every Catholic church I have ever been in displays "the Stations of the Cross." This tradition dates back to the 1300s when the Franciscan fathers established themselves in Jerusalem. They began honoring the specific spots where Christ had suffered. Over time it was developed into fourteen specific stations—beginning with the place where Pilate condemned Jesus to die and continuing to the last station, where Jesus was laid in the tomb.

Since I knew nothing about the Stations of the Cross I went to a local Catholic bookstore and asked for information. I ended up buying five booklets about praying the Stations of the Cross. Even though I've heard that several of the stations are extrabiblical (that is, not included in the Gospels), I decided to go ahead and do it anyway.

My first experience with the Stations of the Cross was at a local Catholic church in Key Largo. As you drive in the driveway, the main sanctuary is straight ahead, a chapel is on the right, and the preschool along with the offices are on the left. The stations are several yards apart and are all outdoors. Each station is built of a large cross—about twice my height.

At the top of each cross is a small enclosed glass case with an old painting depicting that specific station. In the paintings, of course, Jesus and the others look very European—not Middle Eastern. I decided to use one of my booklets that includes an abbreviated liturgy. The introduction states, "The Way of the Cross is a way of prayer. I walk, in spirit, with Jesus on his journey to Calvary and meditate on his suffering and death. Each meditation can be a personal meeting with Jesus and the new discovery of his presence in my life. Each meditation can be deeply personal by recalling specific persons, places and experiences in my own life." The Stations of the Cross, I realized, is a prayer walk that helps me focus on the sufferings of Jesus.

I began with the sign of the cross and then read an opening Scripture about the suffering of Jesus and how we, as his followers, are to take up our cross every day and follow him. Then I read the opening prayer: "Lord Jesus, help me to be open to your closeness and presence as I begin this journey to Calvary with you. Help me to find in your passion and death the strength to take up my cross and follow you." For each station I repeated the following words, "I adore you, Lord Jesus, and I praise you. Because by your holy cross, you have redeemed the world."

I then stop at each of the stations, as follows:

1. Pilate condemns Jesus to die.
2. Jesus accepts his cross.
3. Jesus falls the first time.
4. Jesus meets his mother.
5. Simon helps carry the cross.
6. Veronica wipes the face of Jesus.
7. Jesus falls the second time.
8. Jesus speaks to the women.
9. Jesus falls the third time.
10. Jesus is stripped of his garments.
11. Jesus is nailed to the cross.
12. Jesus dies on the cross.
13. Jesus is taken from the cross.
14. Jesus is laid in the tomb.

I stood at the first station in front of a large cross, looking up at a picture of Jesus standing before Pilate (the picture happened to be crooked). The booklet contains this meditation: "Lord Jesus, often I judge others and fail to be understanding or loving. Help me to see the people in my life through your eyes, not the eyes of a Pontius Pilate."

I stood there for quite a while reflecting on the prayer I'd just prayed. I could hear the wind blowing through the palm trees and the birds chirping, which was a stark contrast to the cross before me.

After each station I prayed the Lord's Prayer, did one Hail Mary and one "Glory be to the Father, and to the Son, and to the Holy Spirit. As it was in the beginning, is now, and ever shall be, world without end. Amen." It took me about forty-five minutes to move through all the stations. As I went from station to station I felt as if I were being carried away with Jesus on his road to suffering.

In most evangelical churches we celebrate Communion every quarter. At Communion we take bread and drink wine and reflect on Jesus' sufferings. In many churches, Communion almost feels tacked on to the regular service. At Calvary Church we would devote the entire service to reflecting on Jesus' sufferings and partaking of Communion. But doing Communion four times a year really ignores the deep sufferings of Jesus. I'm grateful for the Stations of the Cross because they help me better focus on his sufferings.

I think I was most moved by the thirteenth station: Jesus is taken from the cross. The prayer was "Lord Jesus, seeing your body taken from the Cross reminds me how fearful I am of letting go of my own life. I am frightened when I think of being unimportant, useless, helpless. Help me to place my life in your hands." Given the disease I have, I'm not afraid of being dead. But I am afraid of getting dead. The process leading up to death is filled with fear. I am afraid of letting go of my own life.

But as I stood before this cross and realized all that Jesus had done for me, it gave me great hope that the Jesus who suffered on the cross identifies with my own suffering. And the Jesus who identifies with my suffering is with me every step of the way—even leading up to death!

After the last station, I read a passage of Scripture from the gospel of Luke that describes the resurrection of Jesus. Then I prayed the closing prayer: "Lord Jesus, help me to walk with you each day of my life, even to Calvary. The sorrow and joy, the pain and healings, the failures and triumphs of my life are truly small deaths and resurrections that lead me to closeness with you. Give me the faith and trust I need to walk with you always. Amen."

The Interview

Back in Grand Rapids, Charley, the religion editor for the *Press*, kept calling me. Finally I called him back and agreed to do a one-hour interview about my yearlong journey to live like Jesus. He met me at my office at Cornerstone. We talked about the synagogue. We talked about eating kosher. We talked about Rosh Hashanah and Yom Kippur. We talked about picking up hitch-hikers. We talked about drinking beer at the bar. We talked about the beard.

Then he asked me, "What has really surprised you this last year?"

I paused for a few moments to think. "I think the thing that really surprised me is that for the first time in my life I voted for a Democrat for president. I've always been a conservative Republican, but this time I voted for Senator Obama."

"Why?"

"Well, I've been reading through the Gospels every week, and I decided I'd vote for the person who was closest to the essence of

Jesus' teachings. After a lot of consideration, thought, and prayer I felt that Senator Obama was closest to the basic teachings of Jesus."

"In what way do you think Senator Obama reflects Jesus' teachings?"

As soon as I answered him, I knew a lot of my conservative friends would be either mystified or angry. For them the only issue that matters is being pro-life. And besides, they would never vote for a Democrat. And I was grateful that my good friend Jerry Falwell is already in heaven. Were he still alive, I knew he would have called me, and he would not be happy!

But I didn't vote for Senator Obama to make my conservative friends angry. I didn't vote for him just to be different. I voted for him because I felt he was closest to Jesus' teachings. And I stand by that!

Charley also had a photographer with him who took several pictures of me with my long beard. Then, a few days later, the photographer came to my house and took a few more pictures. I hoped and prayed that the article would stir people up to be more committed followers of Jesus. I also knew that my drinking beer at a bar would be controversial among the community at Cornerstone. They are required to sign a lifestyle statement that prohibits the use of alcohol.

Since I'm a volunteer, however, I wasn't asked to sign that statement. But I know that some will be confused by the fact that I drank an occasional beer.

Staff Lunch

Lorna and I decided to have the entire Cornerstone spiritual-formation staff over for a potluck lunch. We asked each person to bring something different. We had a wonderful time. We talked and laughed. We ate and drank (nonalcoholic). The variety of foods was stunning. There were cheese trays. Several people brought chili. There were all sorts of desserts.

After a year of trying to live kosher, I now have the procedure down. First, I look over all the food. Second, I make the decision whether to eat meat or eat cheese. Third, I go back and choose what I will eat.

At this lunch the thing that looked best to me was the chicken chili. As I was about to fill my bowl, my wife said, "I think that might have cheese in it."

So I turned to the person who made it and asked, "Does the chicken chili have cheese in it?" Of course I was hoping that it didn't.

"Sorry," he said, "it has a lot of cheese in it."

So I immediately eliminated that from my diet.

I will be so glad when the end of this month comes.

What Does It Mean to Follow Jesus?

For twelve months I've been trying to live like Jesus. I've read the Gospels over and over. I've tried to obey as many of Jesus' teachings as possible. So what have I learned about what it means to follow Jesus? You would assume I'd have a simple and clear answer, but it's not a simple question.

Early in my ministry I'd have answered it in a very simple way. What does it mean to follow Jesus? It means that you recognize that you're a sinner, that the payment of your sin is death, that Jesus suffered and died and rose again to forgive you, and that by believing and receiving Jesus you become his follower.

I still believe that.

But when you come to the Gospels the whole idea of following

Jesus is much more complicated. Take, for example, some of the people in the Gospels who followed him and some who did not.

"Come, follow me," Jesus said, "and I will make you fishers of men." At once they left their nets and followed him.

Mark 1:17–18

This is the record of Jesus' calling Simon and his brother to follow him. The brothers were casting a net into the lake and Jesus told them, "Come, follow me." The word translated "come" means "come here." It was necessary for them to leave their nets, boat, and occupation to follow Jesus. The second verb, translated "follow me," means "behind me." Being a follower of Jesus means walking behind him. We often assume that as followers of Jesus we are supposed to walk next to him. But the problem with that is that when we get to a fork in the road, we tend to try and negotiate with Jesus: "I know you want me to go to the left, but I want to go to the right. Is there any way that we could reach a negotiated settlement and walk down the middle?" With Jesus, there is no negotiation. We walk behind him. We walk in the dust of the rabbi.

Then the text says that they "left their nets and followed him." The phrase "followed him" contains the idea of being attached to Jesus. Being a disciple of Jesus means attaching ourselves to him so that in the process we can become like him. I'm hoping that as I've poured my life into Jesus and his teaching this past year, I am a little more like him than when I started.

So what does it mean to follow Jesus?

1. It means that we are willing to leave everything behind and come to him.

2. It means that we are willing to walk in his dust and follow him.

3. It means that we attach ourselves to Jesus for the purpose of becoming like him.

I tell you the truth, no one can see the kingdom of God unless he is born again.

John 3:3

Nicodemus was a member of the Jewish ruling council and a Pharisee. He was a well-respected member of the religious establishment. He came to Jesus one evening and said, "Rabbi, we know you are a teacher who has come from God. For no one could perform the miraculous signs you are doing if God were not with them." Had Nicodemus said this to me, I would have said, "Thank you very much." But not Jesus. Jesus responded, "I tell you the truth, no one can see the kingdom of God unless he is born again."

The word translated "again" could also be translated "from above," which I think is the preferred translation. Jesus is saying to this religious leader who is serious about obeying the Torah that the path to God's kingdom is being "born from above." So what does that mean? It is ultimately a mystery. Jesus compared it to the wind. You hear the wind and you feel the wind, but you really don't know where it comes from or where it's going. He said that it's the same way with those who are born of the Spirit (in the Hebrew Bible the word translated "spirit" is the same word that is translated as "wind"). Jesus was saying to this religious leader that obeying the law and keeping the Torah are not enough. In addition, you need to be born from above, or born of the Spirit—and that is, in part, a mystery.

When I first started in ministry I was pastor of a small country church in the mountains of Virginia. One day one of the men in our church came to see me.

"I was wondering if you might go see my dad. He really needs the Lord," he said.

"I'd be delighted." I said.

"But I need to warn you, he hates ministers. He runs the largest moonshine whiskey business in the entire county. He'll probably meet you at the door with a shotgun and tell you to get off his property."

At this point I was upset with myself for agreeing so quickly to go see him. But I was stuck. So I went to see him.

As I stood on the front porch of his home at the foot of the mountains, I prayed, "Please God, don't let him be home." I figured that the best thing to do would be to leave some literature that he could read. But the door opened and his wife greeted me.

"Hi. I'm Ed Dobson. I'm the pastor of the People's Baptist Church."

"Yeah. I think our son goes to your church."

"Yes he does, and he has asked me to come by and talk with you. Could I come in?"

"Of course you can."

She led me through the living room, the kitchen, and out to the back porch. Sitting there was the man I had come to see. He was short and mean looking. I went over to shake his hand but he refused. It was as though he were looking right through me. We talked for a while and then I offered to read some Scripture and pray. I read from the third chapter of John—the story of Nicodemus.

"One of the things that strikes me about this passage," I said, "is the idea that to get to heaven we must be born again."

I waited for a moment to let this sink in. Then I began to talk about what it means to be born again. I presented a simple plan of salvation. I talked about why we need to be born again—because we're all sinners and because Jesus Christ suffered and died so that we could be born again. Then I talked about *when* we needed to be born again—right now. Then I led in a simple prayer. "Dear God, I'm grateful for the opportunity I've had today to share from the Bible. I pray your special blessing on this couple."

Then I paused and asked the wife if she'd like to be born again.

"Yes, I would," she said as she began to cry. I suggested that she pray and ask God to forgive her sins and ask Jesus to take over her life. She did. I struggled with whether or not to ask her husband if he'd like to do the same thing. The entire time I had talked he stared out at the mountains nearby. I didn't think he'd heard a word I'd said. But I asked him.

"Would you like to be born again as well?" I asked.

There was a long silence. I noticed a tear coming down his cheek, and in a few moments he was sobbing uncontrollably. Finally he blurted out, "I sure would!" Then he poured out his heart to God and invited Jesus into his life. The next Sunday he and his wife were in church. I had the privilege of baptizing them in the river.

Then this man asked me to go with him to visit all the people he used to sell moonshine whiskey to. "This man changed my life," he would say, "and he's here to change your life."

That was all he said. The rest was up to me. And given the fact that he was known for being mean, these people listened. Several months later I counted fifty-four people from his family alone in church one Sunday morning.

This was the first time I fully realized that this "Jesus thing" really works. This was the first time I'd seen someone's life radically and permanently changed because they had been "born again."

And because of his words many more became believers.

John 4:41

Jesus went through the region of Samaria and came to a town called Sychar. This story is fascinating because Jesus violated all sorts of cultural taboos when he talked to a woman there. His disciples had gone into the village to buy bread, and Jesus sat down by a well. A Samaritan woman then came to draw water, and Jesus asked her for a drink. The woman was shocked. She knew that Jews had absolutely no dealings with Samaritans, and besides, men didn't talk to women in public.

But here was Jesus, asking her a question, and in the course of the conversation, Jesus offered her "living water" that if she drank of it, she'd never thirst again. The woman immediately asked Jesus to give her that kind of water.

Jesus told her to go call her husband. She responded that she had no husband. Then Jesus reminded her that she had had five husbands and that the man she was living with now was not her husband.

This was not the kind of woman, by the way, that you'd want to be caught talking to in public. She reminds me of a young man who attended our church a number of years ago. He was gay. He had purple hair and earrings and smoked constantly. I went out to eat with him at a local restaurant, back in the days when you could still smoke in restaurants. A number of people there recognized me from our church or from television. This young man and I sat in the smoking section for an hour and a half while he smoked one cigarette after the other—blowing the smoke in my face. I could see people looking at me and wondering, "What in the world is *he* doing talking with a person like *that*!"

Anyway, the woman then responded that Jesus must be a prophet since he knew so much about her. Later, when she went back to the village and told others about her conversation with Jesus, the Samaritans implored him to stay with them for two days. So he stayed with them, and many became believers because of Jesus' words. The Samaritans said to the woman, "We no longer believe just because of what you said; now we have heard for ourselves, and we know that this man really is the Savior of the world."

For the Samaritans, becoming a Jesus follower involved believing that Jesus is the Savior of the world.

And, by the way, he's also interested in being the Savior of gay people.

If you want to be perfect, go, sell your possessions and give to the poor, and you will have treasure in heaven. Then come, follow me.

Matthew 19:21

On one occasion a rich young ruler came to Jesus and asked him, "Teacher, what good thing must I do to get eternal life?" Jesus responded by saying that he should keep the commandments. The man then responded by asking which commandments. Jesus talked about murder, adultery, stealing, false testimony, honoring your father and mother, and loving your neighbor. The man responded that he had kept all of those commandments. Then he asked, "What do I still lack?" Jesus said, "If you want to be perfect, go, sell your possessions and give to the poor, and you will have treasure in heaven. Then come, follow me."

I was playing golf a number of years ago with a wealthy businessman from our community. He was telling me that having wealth is a huge challenge. "Everybody asks you for money," he said. "I could spend all of my time just listening to people who need money. And while all the causes are good, I just can't give to them all. It's also hard to know who really is your friend. Are these people friends *because* of what I can do for them, or are they friends *regardless* of what I do for them?"

This conversation went back and forth for quite some time. As we stood on the green of the seventeenth hole, he got ready to putt a long putt. Just before he hit the ball, I said, "Well, you could do the Jesus thing."

"What's that?"

"Sell everything you have, give it to the poor, and follow Jesus!"

He looked at me, shocked. I don't know if he was shocked because I spoke in the middle of his putt or by what I said. But he was shocked.

This is what Jesus said to the rich young ruler. Keeping the commands was not enough. Obeying the law was not enough. For this young man, it was necessary to sell everything he had and give the money away. Then he could follow Jesus. Apparently he had an issue with greed. The story continues, "When the young man heard this, he went away sad, because he had great wealth."

Wealth is an obstacle to following Jesus. Jesus went on to say, "I tell you the truth, it is hard for a rich man to enter the kingdom of heaven."

So what does it mean to follow Jesus?

1. It means I'm willing to leave everything behind and come to him.

2. It means I'm willing to walk in his dust to follow behind him.

3. It means I'm willing to attach myself to him to be like him.

4. It means I'm born from above by the Spirit, which is a mystery.

5. It means I believe that Jesus is the Savior of the world as well as my own personal savior.

6. It means I'm willing to sell everything to follow him.

Sometimes when I preach, I offer a prayer at the end of the service for those who want to become followers of Jesus. The prayer goes like this: "Lord, I acknowledge to you that I am a sinner. Please forgive me. I believe that Jesus died and rose again for me. Come into my life, Lord Jesus. I accept you as my savior. It is my desire to follow you for the rest of my life."

It's a simple prayer. And I still believe it. But what does this prayer have to do with all of the people who ended up following Jesus in the Gospels? Following Jesus is the total commitment of our lives and our futures to him. This is what it means to follow Jesus. It's more than keeping rules and regulations. It's more than going to church and being baptized. It's more than reading the Bible and praying. Rather, it's the commitment of our life (mind, body, eyes, hands, feet, heart, and everything) to him.

Living Like a Jew

Today, December 19, is my second-to-last Shabbat of the year.

Early in the year I went to the synagogue to talk with Rabbi David about Shabbat. He has been helpful in guiding me through this journey and as a result has invited me to speak to his congregation about my experiences. He hopes it will stir them to become more serious about their Judaism.

One of the first things I talked with him about were the regulations for Shabbat. "How do you prepare for and observe Shabbat?" I asked.

He smiled. "Actually, my wife does most of the preparation."

So I thought there's not much difference between a Jew and a Gentile—both of our wives do most of the work!

"First," he said, "I make sure that all of the work for the next day is done ahead of time. Then, before the sun goes down, I turn on the oven, turn on the hotplate and the hot-water urn. I turn on lights that will be necessary—for example, the one in the bathroom. We're not allowed to turn switches on and off during

Shabbat. I then unscrew the refrigerator light so it will not come on when the door is opened. We eat the Shabbat meal together and afterward we read or play kids' games. I try to go to bed early. We get up in the morning, eat breakfast, and walk to the synagogue. I usually get home by 1:00 p.m. Sometimes I take a nap after lunch. Sometimes I play games with the kids. Sometimes I read the newspaper. Sometimes I go for a bike ride. But when I ride the bike I have to be careful. If I ride the bike on a soft trail and leave a trail mark, that would be a violation of Shabbat. So I generally ride on hard pavement."

"So you actually spend most of Shabbat sleeping," I said.

"Exactly!" he said with a smile.

There is one other text relating to the Sabbath that I find interesting:

> If you keep your feet from breaking the Sabbath
>> and from doing as you please on my holy day,
> if you call the Sabbath a delight
>> and the LORD's holy day honorable,
> and if you honor it by not going your own way
>> and not doing as you please or speaking idle words,
> then you will find your joy in the LORD,
>> and I will cause you to ride on the heights of the land
>> and to feast on the inheritance of your father Jacob.
>
> **Isaiah 58:13–14**

We are to call the Sabbath "a delight." I'm not sure I ever considered the Sabbath "a delight" before. I've been so consumed with making sure that I don't work, don't create, don't turn on lights, and so on, that I really haven't considered it "a delight." But nearly everything I have read about the Sabbath, as well as everything Jews who practice it consistently have told me, convinces me that it is certainly something to be enjoyed. It is a delight.

We exchanged gifts tonight because my oldest son and his

family always go to Georgia for Christmas. We ate together, laughed together, drank together, and had a great time. It was a delightful evening. But it was a violation of the Sabbath. So I'm ending my year the way I lived it all along, by not fully obeying the Sabbath. But not celebrating Christmas with my eldest son and his family would have been foolish.

It is hard to express exactly what I've learned this year in trying to live like Jesus, but one thing I've learned is that living like a Jew is a pain in the neck! Keeping the Sabbath—hard to do in this culture. Eating kosher—requires constant vigilance. Wearing tassels —a nuisance. Observing the feasts and festivals—makes having a job and doing it well difficult to do. Very little in Western culture is sympathetic toward living like a Jew. I have come away with a deep respect for conservative and Orthodox Jews. They do all of the above in a more consistent and serious way than I have done. It is not easy to do. And as a follower of Jesus I'm most grateful that I'm not required to do these things.

Christmas Day

This morning I logged on to the *Grand Rapids Press* online edition. I wanted to read the article for myself. And I was really pleased. I appreciated the fact that the writer prefaced my vote for Senator Obama by saying that I disagreed with him on the issue of abortion. I also appreciated the fact that the writer prefaced my comments about drinking beer with the fact that I had always been a teetotaler. The photographs, however, looked awful. The beard made me look like a crazy man. Maybe even a Jesus freak!

January

The New Year

It's the first of January. For the first time in over a year I am free of my obligation to live like Jesus. I call a photographer friend and ask if he would take some photographs of me with my long beard. We meet at his studio and he shoots a series of photos.

I leave the studio and go see the woman who cuts my hair. I ask her to trim back my beard so that it's no more than an eighth of an inch long. As I sit there watching her in the mirror, I'm amazed at how long it is. When I walked in to have it cut, the wind was blowing outside, and it was blowing my beard as well. When I walked out the wind was still blowing—but my beard wasn't.

I felt naked. I missed the beard.

Last week I was speaking with a friend who asked me about my year of trying to live like Jesus. I explained how difficult it was to keep kosher. I told him that all through the month of December I kept thinking about all the things I would eat when the year was over. "I love bacon. Just the smell of cooking bacon is wonderful. I'm looking forward to having bacon for the first time. I love shrimp. When I first came to the United States I'd never eaten shrimp. Some of the wealthy people in our church would take us out to eat at the Holiday Inn every Sunday. They ordered shrimp cocktails. I looked forward to the Holiday Inn on Sundays and eating shrimp cocktails. So now that my year is over, I plan to eat shrimp."

My friend said nothing at the time, but on New Year's Eve, he came by the house and gave me a whole bunch of shrimp wrapped in bacon!

The next evening we invited our family over for dinner. We cooked the shrimp and ate them. I savored every bite. Normally I eat quickly but that night I ate slow. I wanted to enjoy every single bite. It was unbelievable to be able to eat something that I could not eat for the past year. And before the meal we had a cheese spread. Eating milk products and meat together was absolutely wonderful.

For the next several weeks I ate something nonkosher every day. I ate my chicken burritos with cheese and sour cream. I ate sausage. I ate crab. It was as if I'd been confined for a year and was finally let loose. And did I ever get loose! After a couple of weeks of overeating, I started to realize that I actually missed eating kosher! Eating kosher forced me to think about what I ate. Now that I was free, I didn't pay any attention.

Maybe I'll go back to eating kosher for short periods of time. Then again, maybe I won't!

Word of My Year Gets Around

The article about my year of living like Jesus was uploaded to a religious news service and appeared in newspapers all over the country. It was also picked up by the online edition of *USA Today*. The people at the weekend edition of *Good Morning America* saw the article in *USA Today*, called me, and asked if I'd come to New York and appear on the show Sunday morning. I agreed to do it. So my youngest son and I flew to New York on Saturday afternoon and appeared on the show early the next day.

It had been a long time since I was involved with the national media. When I worked for Jerry Falwell I appeared in *Time* magazine and the *New Yorker*. I appeared on the *Phil Donahue Show* as well as all sorts of local talk shows. I loved every minute of it.

Usually I was the lone voice defending spiritual and moral

values. Usually the host and the audience were against me. I was always prepared really well and would jump into the middle of every argument defending moral values. Almost all of the talk shows were confrontational. Them against me. But as I sat there on the set of *Good Morning America*, waiting for the interview, I realized that this was not going to be confrontational.

There was nothing to argue about.

There was nothing to defend.

I was there to tell my story of following Jesus.

The interview lasted four and a half minutes. I was told by the producer that this was a very long segment for television. But it went by really fast. I had no idea what the host would ask, so I just responded and went with the flow. Of course, the fact that I'd voted for Senator Obama was probably the deciding factor in having me on the show in the first place. I was fully aware of that. At the end of the segment, the host asked me how I'd like my experience to impact other people. I simply said that I hoped people, whether religious or not, would pick up the Bible and read it. If even one person did that, then my year was a success.

At the beginning of the year I never dreamed I'd be on *Good Morning America*, in *USA Today*, and in newspapers all over the country. All I wanted to do was spend twelve months getting serious about the teachings of Jesus. And now, at the end of the year, I felt I was only beginning to understand Jesus' teachings and live them out. There is so much I still want to do.

I spent some time recently reading the responses to the article on the *Grand Rapids Press* and *USA Today* websites. There were hundreds of them. Most of them were critical. After a while I had to quit reading them because they were starting to get to me, which made me feel very un-Jesus-like.

> How could he vote for Obama when Obama is into murdering babies?

He should have kept his vote for Obama secret.

All that reading of the Gospels did him absolutely no good.

I will never listen to him preach again.

He completely missed the mark.

How in the world could you vote for Obama and be a follower of Jesus?

Some people were mystified, but most were flat-out angry. Even though the article clearly stated that I disagreed with Obama on abortion, that didn't seem to matter. I even stated on *Good Morning America* that I was not saying everybody should have voted for Obama, nor was I saying that Jesus would've voted for him. But in spite of that, I created a huge controversy. And that controversy was with "religious" people, not secular people.

Not those outside the Church.

Not those who deny the Bible.

But "Christian" people.

My oldest son reminded me, "Remember that the people who were most disturbed by Jesus' teaching were the religious leaders. The religious establishment opposed him. If you're going to follow Jesus, can you expect anything less?"

What concerns me most was that these religious people completely ignored everything else I had to say. They were upset that I'd voted for Obama, even though I also said that I had little faith in politicians of either party. Still, that didn't seem to matter. It seemed as if all these people cared about was that I'd voted for a Democrat. Part of me wanted to say, "Get a life!" But that would not be a very Jesus thing to do—even though it's January now and I'm not obliged to live like Jesus!

Well, actually, I am.

In addition to those who were upset with my vote for Obama, some people at Cornerstone were puzzled by my drinking beer.

Even though I did not have to sign the lifestyle statement, as I've mentioned before, a number of people were concerned that, as vice president for spiritual formation, I'd been inconsistent by violating the policy.

And you know, they're right. I should have either signed the statement or refused the opportunity to serve at the university. I'm not sure what I would have done had I been asked to make that choice. Part of me thinks that I would have signed it and lived by it. But the other part of me thinks that I would have walked away, since signing that statement would have prohibited me from being an authentic follower of Jesus.

But I was not asked to sign it. I did not sign it. So I felt free to ignore it.

In response to the concerns at Cornerstone University, I wrote a short email that was published on their website. The president also wrote in response to the controversy. I regret any problems that I may have caused the university, but I do not regret anything I did or said during this last year. I intend to keep having a beer at the bar, and I intend to be at cocktail parties, and I intend to continue to hang out with people who are outside the kingdom.

Back in Florida, I was standing in line at a restaurant. A friend came up to me, leaned over, and whispered in my ear, "Do not cast your pearls before swine."

This is from the Bible, of course. I've read that text many times. In fact, it is an important text in my own personal life. When I worked for Jerry Falwell, I often spoke to the media when he was not able to. On one occasion I was on the *Phil Donahue Show*—at that time the most popular show on television. I was defending the Boy Scouts, who were barring an Eagle Scout from continued participation because he was an atheist. When Mr. Donahue announced that I worked for Jerry Falwell, the crowd booed. I loved it. I enjoyed everything about the show.

On my way back from the show, I was in Charlotte, North Carolina, waiting for the plane back to Lynchburg. One of the Bible teachers at Liberty was on the same flight.

"Where have you been?" he asked.

"I've been on the *Phil Donahue Show*. It was a wonderful opportunity to represent moral values," I said.

"You're casting your pearls before swine," he said. "You're a pastor and a Bible teacher, and you're wasting your time doing all these media things. You ought to focus on teaching the Bible. Everything else is just casting your pearls before swine."

At first I thought he was a complete idiot. But the more I thought about it, the more I realized he was right. So over the next year my wife and I began to pray about the possibility of leaving Jerry Falwell and becoming a pastor in the local church.

So when the man in Florida whispered in my ear, "Do not cast your pearls before swine," I immediately thought of my experience at the Charlotte airport.

Then he leaned over again and whispered, "Do not give the dogs what is sacred."

By this time I was confused. I had no clue what he was talking about. After a few moments of awkward silence he leaned over again and whispered, "I'm talking about your vote for Obama. Your vote was the same as casting your pearls before swine and giving what is sacred to dogs."

I really didn't know what to say. I think he was simply saying, "You wasted your vote!"

What Have I Learned?

Over the past year I've learned how difficult it is to follow Jesus' teachings. Some people probably think that my year of trying to live like Jesus was simply a bizarre idea. Maybe. But for me it was the next step in my journey of trying to follow Jesus more closely. It is a journey that began years ago in Northern Ireland. It brought me to the United States and to Bob Jones University, where I earned a BA and an MA. I'm deeply appreciative of the education I received there and for the solid foundation it gave me for ministry. That journey then took me to Lynchburg, Virginia, where I worked for Jerry Falwell at Liberty University. After my father, Jerry Falwell had more influence on my life than any other human being. He was the kindest, most generous person I've ever met. It took me to Grand Rapids, Michigan, where I served for eighteen and a half years as senior pastor of Calvary Church. I enjoyed my time there. Those years are clearly the highlight of my public ministry.

I found Jesus in all of those places! They all contributed to my ongoing desire to know and follow Jesus better.

I also realize that no church, no denomination, and no theological system has the inside track on truth. I grew up in a fundamentalist environment where we believed we were right and everybody else was wrong. Nothing could be further from the truth. This last year I grew in my appreciation for the Roman Catholic faith. I was moved by praying the rosary and praying through the Stations of the Cross. The emphasis on the sufferings of Christ has helped me. This last year I also grew in my appreciation for the Orthodox Church. I was deeply moved every time I prayed the Orthodox prayer rope. The emphasis of the Orthodox Church on the incarnation and its implications encouraged me. This last year I grew in my appreciation for Cornerstone University. That institution too is on a journey of becoming more like Jesus. But none of the above groups, including the church I served for eighteen and a half years, has the inside track on truth. We can all learn from each other.

I'm reminded of the disciple John who came to Jesus and said, "Teacher, we saw a man driving out demons in your name and we told him to stop, because he was not one of us." Jesus replied, "Do not stop him. No one who does a miracle in my name can in the next moment say anything bad about me, for whoever is not against us is for us" (Mark 9:38–40).

This last year I learned that anybody who is for Jesus is a friend of mine. Bob Jones Sr., the founder of the University that bears his name and the place where I attended college, once said, "If a hound dog comes through town barking for Jesus, I'm on the hound dog's side."

Me too!

I'm also reminded of what Father Dan (an Orthodox priest) often said to me. "Remember, truth is not an idea or concept. It's a person. And that person is Jesus Christ!" Thank you, Father Dan. It has been my passion this past year to pursue truth in the person of Jesus. I have read and reread the Jesus story all year. I have paid attention to his birth, his baptism, his temptation, his teachings, his parables, his miracles, his suffering, his death, and his resurrection.

So what's the bottom line with Jesus?

Jesus Was More than a Rabbi

Jesus was a rabbi and a good one. He was a brilliant teacher. But he was so much more. On one occasion he asked his disciples, "Who do people say the Son of Man is?" They answered, "Some say John the Baptist; others say Elijah; and still others, Jeremiah or one of the prophets." Then Jesus said, "But what about you?... Who do you say I am?" This was—and still is—the ultimate question. It's not about what others think of Jesus that matters. It's what I think of Jesus that matters. Peter responded, "You are the Christ, the Son of the living God" (Matthew 16:13–16).

Peter was declaring that Jesus was the Christ, the "anointed one," which is the Greek term for the Hebrew idea of "the Messiah." Peter was declaring that Jesus was the Messiah, the one prophesied in the Hebrew Scriptures. He also said that Jesus was "the Son of the living God," a direct reference to the fact that Jesus is God.

So Jesus is more than just a rabbi. He's the Messiah, and he's the Son of God.

Throughout this year as I prayed the rosary, I repeated the Apostles' Creed, part of which says, "... and in Jesus Christ, his only Son, who was conceived by the Holy Spirit and born of the Virgin Mary." This is who the real Jesus is!

Jesus Is the Great Liberator

In the story of Jesus' birth, an angel appeared to Joseph, who was engaged to be married to Mary. Since Mary was already pregnant, Joseph decided to quietly offer her a bill of divorce. He didn't want to embarrass her. But the angel appeared to him and told him that the one conceived in Mary's womb was conceived by the Holy Spirit: "She will give birth to a son, and you are to give him the name Jesus, because he will save his people from their sins" (Matthew 1:21). The name *Jesus* means "savior, deliverer, or liberator." What does he save people from? What does he deliver people from? What kind of a liberator is he? The answers are found in the words of the angel: "He will save his people from their sins."

At the end of his earthly life, Jesus celebrated Passover with his disciples. During the meal he took bread, broke it, and said, "This is my body which is broken for you." He then took wine, blessed it, and said, "This is my blood of the covenant, which is poured out for many for the forgiveness of sins" (Matthew 26:28). It is true that Jesus taught many wonderful ideas. It is true that he told many stories that have helped people understand truth. It is true that he performed miracles. But the real reason he came was to offer himself as a sacrifice for sins so that we could be forgiven and restored to God. How is this possible? John, in his gospel, writes, "Yet to all who received him, to those who believed in his name, he gave the right to become children of God—children born not of natural descent, nor of human decision or a husband's will, but born of God" (John 1:12–13). It is by believing in who Jesus is and what he did on the cross and receiving him (turning your life over to him) that we become part of the family of God.

Jesus Is More than the Way to Heaven

Jesus himself said that he was the way, the truth, and the life. Most people interpret this to mean that he is the way to heaven, which I believe as well. But he is much more than that. He is the way of living as well. He is the way we order our lives. He is the way we act and react to others. And this year I found out that following the way of Jesus is a difficult—nearly impossible—task. He wants us to live like him, act like him, talk like him, pray like him, and think like him. The idea that Jesus is "the way" doesn't mean "the way to heaven" so much as it means "how we live in the here and now." Heaven is only a side benefit.

Limitations

> In the beginning was the Word, and the Word was with God, and the Word was God. He was with God in the beginning.
>
> Through him all things were made; without him nothing was made that has been made. In him was life, and that life was the light of men. The light shines in the darkness, but the darkness has not understood it.
>
> **John 1:1–5**

The apostle John begins his gospel with a prologue in which he compares Jesus to the Word. He states that the Word was with God, the Word was God, and all creation was made by him (referring to Jesus). Later in the prologue he states that the Word (Jesus) became flesh and lived among us. This must have been an unbelievable step for Jesus. Jesus is fully God. Jesus was involved in the creation of the world. Yet this one, who was God, became a human being. The creator of the world became one of the creatures in the world. He limited himself within the boundaries of human flesh. And he did so willingly. Later in the epistles, the apostle Paul writes that Jesus "emptied himself." He gave up all of the privileges of deity and limited himself to the confines of human flesh. I have often wondered, was this frustrating for Jesus?

While I have spent a year living like Jesus, my ALS has progressed. I can no longer lift my right arm above my shoulder. The fine motor skills in my fingers have deteriorated. I now get cramps in my legs. From time to time, I feel the frustrations of a body that is deteriorating. I can no longer do the things I used to do. I cannot pick up my latest grandchild. I cannot button my shirts. Sometimes I have difficulty even zipping up my pants. I have difficulty tying my shoes. And sometimes I get really mad. Not very Jesus-like.

Nowhere in the Gospels does Jesus ever seem to get frustrated with the limitations of his human body. But I sympathize with him. I'm simply dealing with muscles that no longer work, while he had to deal with the reality that as God, he had confined himself to the limitations of the human body. In no way do my limitations compare to his.

But I feel a similar struggle. One of the many good things about this year has been that when I get up every morning, I focus on reading the Gospels and trying to live like Jesus instead of focusing on my latest muscle that doesn't work. Focusing on Jesus and his teachings keeps me from unduly focusing on my own disease and deterioration.

A Talk with Pastor Jim

Pastor Jim succeeded me as the pastor at Calvary Church. He began attending the church when he was in high school. Then he went to the University of Michigan, where he majored in engineering. He lived in a coed dorm because he felt that's where he could have the greatest witness for Christ. After graduating, he took a job in Dallas, and while working there full-time, he began taking courses at Dallas Theological Seminary, which led to a struggle between staying in business or going to seminary.

We talked on many occasions as he faced that decision. Finally he quit his job and went to Dallas Theological Seminary full-time. After graduation, he and his wife came back and worked on our church staff for a year. I had an arrangement with the church that anyone who had completed seminary could work full-time at the church for one year to get some experience in the real world.

After finishing his year at the church, he was accepted at Oxford University in England for a doctorate in New Testament studies. When he was home one summer, I had a long talk with him about my own future and Calvary Church.

"My doctors have all told me that the best thing I can do is step aside as pastor," I said. "They've told me that the stress of preaching, leading, doing funerals and weddings, overseeing the staff, and dealing with crises is very bad for me. They feel it might speed up the disease."

Jim listened carefully. "But what if it's God's will that you pour your life into the church and, as a result, your life is shortened?" he said. "Are you willing to do God's will and not your doctors'? Are you willing to shorten your life to do what God wants you to do?"

No one else had asked me that question. Nearly everyone I talked to had encouraged me to step down—but not Jim. He has a way of asking the toughest questions and forcing you back to the issue "What does God want?"

For that reason, I decided to talk to Jim at the beginning of my one-year commitment to live like Jesus. I wanted his advice.

"I'm sure you've noticed I'm growing my beard. I'm trying to be like Jesus. Throughout this year I've made a commitment to read through the Gospels every week, keep the Sabbath, eat kosher, observe the feasts and festivals."

Jim listened carefully. Then, in typical Jim fashion, he began asking the tough questions, like "Are you going to walk everywhere?"

"Probably not. But you raise a good question."

"Are you going to sell everything you have and give it away?"

"How in the world do you do that?"

"Maybe you need to talk with the lawyer and temporarily turn all your possessions over to your wife. And are you going to fast and pray for forty days in the wilderness?"

"I'm definitely not going to fast for forty days in the wilderness. Given the fact that I have this disease and that I'm supposed to eat as much as possible, fasting for an extended period is not a good idea. But I do plan to fast for at least a day and go out into the wilderness."

"Are you going to pray all night and then choose twelve disciples?"

"Dude, I'm not Jesus. I'm not building a church. So I don't think I'll be choosing twelve people to walk around with me."

"Are you going to follow Jesus in his pain and suffering?"

I looked at him.

"Don't just do the easy things," he said. "Growing your beard, keeping the Sabbath, eating kosher, and going to the synagogue are easy. Do the hard things!"

"I hear you. Don't do the easy stuff—do the hard stuff."

Then he said, "Remember the time you had a 'kiddie' pool up on the platform, and you talked about total commitment?"

"Of course I remember. It was one of those mornings that everybody remembered who was there."

"You said before that Sunday that you were going to take your shoes and socks off and splash around in a kiddie pool. But I told you you needed to jump all the way into the pool from the platform."

"Yeah, I told you that if I did that it would ruin my suit and shoes."

"But you did it! *That* is what you should do with the teachings of Jesus. At the end of the year, you should feel that following Jesus is a *very* difficult and painful thing to do."

And he was right.

Notes

January

1. Don Colbert, *The What Would Jesus Eat Cookbook* (Nashville: Nelson, 2002), xv.
2. Louis Jacobs, *The Book of Jewish Practice* (West Orange, N.J.: Behrman House, 1989), 71.
3. Ibid.

February

1. Jacobs, *Book of Jewish Practice*, 70.

March

1. Rabbi Hayim H. Donin, *To Pray as a Jew: A Guide to the Prayer Book and the Synagogue Service* (New York: Basic Books, 1980), 5.
2. Ibid., 7.
3. Ibid., 7.
4. Joseph Telushkin, *Biblical Literacy* (New York: William Morrow, 1997), 480.

April

1. *The Way of the Pilgrim*, trans. Helen Bacovcin (New York: Image, 1985), 3.
2. Ibid., 12.
3. Ibid., 15.
4. Shoshana Silberman, *A Family Haggadah* (Kar-Ben, 1997), 20.
5. Ibid., 44.
6. Ibid.

October

1. Michael Strassfeld, *The Jewish Holidays: A Guide and Commentary* (New York: HarperCollins, 1985), 95–96.
2. Ibid., 103.
3. Ibid., 101.
4. Rabbi Jules Harlow, ed., *Mahzor for Rosh Hashanah and Yom Kippur: A*

Prayer Book for the Days of Awe (New York: The Rabbinical Assembly, 1972), 12.

5. Strassfeld, *Jewish Holidays*, 112.

6. Ibid., 113.

7. Ibid., 353.

8. Ibid., 325.

9. Maimonides, quoted in Strassfeld, *Jewish Holidays*, 427.

10. Strassfeld, *Jewish Holidays*, 121.

11. Maimonides, quoted in Strassfeld, *Jewish Holidays*, 329.

12. Ibid., 557.

13. Adapted from Strassfeld, *Jewish Holidays*, 117.

14. Maimonides, quoted in Strassfeld, *Jewish Holidays*, 721.

15. Ibid., 731.

November

1. Rabbi Sosson Scherman, *The Chumash: The Torah: Haftaros and Five Megillos with a Commentary Anthologized from the Rabbinic Writings* (Brooklyn: Mesorah Publications, Ltd., 1993), 423.

Bibliography

Brianchaninov, Bishop Ignatius. *On the Prayer of Jesus: The Classic Guide to the Practice of Unceasing Prayer as Found in* The Way of a Pilgrim. Boston: New Seeds Books, 2006.

Davis, Rabbi Menachem, ed. *Siddur for Weekdays with an Interlinear Translation*. Brooklyn: Mesorah Publications, Ltd., 2002.

Doerr, Nan Lewis and Virginia Stem Owens. *Praying with Beads: Daily Prayers for the Christian Year*. Grand Rapids: Eerdmans, 2007.

Donin, Rabbi Hayim Halevy. *To Pray as a Jew: A Guide to the Prayer Book and the Synagogue Service*. New York: Basic Books: A member of Perseus Books Group, 1980.

Harlow, Rabbi Jules, ed. *Mahzor for Rosh Hashanah and Yom Kippur: A Prayer Book for the Days of Awe*. New York: The Rabbinical Assembly, 1972.

Heschel, Abraham. *The Sabbath: Its Meaning for Modern Man*. New York: Farrar, Straus and Giroux, 1951.

The Rosary with Luminous Mysteries: Scripture Meditations and Prayers from the Liturgy. Baltimore: Barton-Cotton, Inc., 2003.

Satterfield, Very Rev. Msgr. Carroll E., STD. Baltimore: Barton-Cotton, Inc. 1980.

Scherman, Rabbi Nosson. *The Chumash: The Torah: Haftaros and Five Megillos with a Commentary Anthologized from the Rabbinic Writings*. Brooklyn: Mesorah Publications, Ltd., 1993.

Silberman, Shoshana. *A Family Haggadah II*. Minneapolis: Kar-Ben Publishing, Inc., 1997.

Strassfeld, Michael. *The Jewish Holidays: A Guide and Commentary*. New York: HarperCollins, 1985.

The Way of the Cross: Stations of the Cross. Composed by Saint Alphonse Ligouri. Italy: Gerffert-Hirten, 2004.

Prayers and Promises When Facing a Life-Threatening Illness

30 Short Morning and Evening Reflections

Ed Dobson

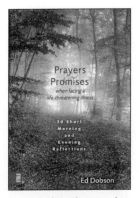

Having a life-threatening illness is a constant reminder that today is precious. *Prayers and Promises When Facing a Life-Threatening Illness* offers encouragement and hope to those who suffer and those who love and care for them. Written by a fellow pilgrim on his own journey with Lou Gehrig's disease, this powerful and inspiring devotional guide offers thirty short reflections to nurture your faith and boost your strength.

Each reflection is a small dose of spiritual truth to start or complete your day. Morning selections include a brief prayer and reflection. Evening readings are based on God's promises to encourage and enlighten you. Some of the prayers and promises include:

- God, remind me that there is more to life than this disease.
- God, give me strength to believe that you can heal me.
- God, give me something to laugh about.
- God, help me to leave a legacy for my family.
- God, I don't feel like praying.

After completing the thirty-day cycle, Dr. Dobson encourages you to repeat it again and again for continued spiritual nourishment that is needed during this time.

Hardcover, Jacketed: 978-0-310-27427-8
Audio CD, Unabridged: 978-0-310-27611-1

Pick up a copy today at your favorite bookstore!

ZONDERVAN®
.com

Share Your Thoughts

With the Author: Your comments will be forwarded to the author when you send them to *zauthor@zondervan.com*.

With Zondervan: Submit your review of this book by writing to *zreview@zondervan.com*.

Free Online Resources at
www.zondervan.com

Zondervan AuthorTracker: Be notified whenever your favorite authors publish new books, go on tour, or post an update about what's happening in their lives.

Daily Bible Verses and Devotions: Enrich your life with daily Bible verses or devotions that help you start every morning focused on God.

Free Email Publications: Sign up for newsletters on fiction, Christian living, church ministry, parenting, and more.

Zondervan Bible Search: Find and compare Bible passages in a variety of translations at www.zondervanbiblesearch.com.

Other Benefits: Register yourself to receive online benefits like coupons and special offers, or to participate in research.